The Vintage Car Guide

**Compiled by
Cecil Clutton, Paul Bird,
Anthony Harding**

**Doubleday & Company Inc
Garden City New York**

ISBN 0-385-12576-3
LCCN 76-14573

Printed in Great Britain

Acknowledgment

The Authors and the Publishers are greatly indebted to the following for the loan of photographs and for their permission to reproduce them in this book:

P. M. Adorian, p. 44; Alfa Romeo, Milan, p. 12 upper, 14; *Autocar*, p. 27, 45, 48 upper, 75, 76, 83 lower, 89 upper, 91 lower, 94, 108 lower, 142, 158 upper and lower, 179, 212 upper, 224; Alvis Ltd., p. 15 upper; Pierre Badré, p. 80 lower, 167 centre; Bentley Drivers' Club Ltd., 41; Charles L. Betts, Jr., p. 87; British Leyland Motor Corporation, p. 28, 29, 133, 150 top and bottom, 155 centre, 176, 177 upper; Citroën Cars Ltd., p. 65 upper and lower; Daimler Co. Ltd., p. 72, 73 lower; Daimler-Benz A.G., p. 145, 146 upper and lower; John Ellis, p. 187 lower; Fiat (England) Ltd., p. 95, 96, 97 upper and lower; Ford Motor Co. Ltd., p. 99 upper and lower, 135 upper and lower; Paul Frère, p. 33 upper; Derek Fulluck, p. 12 lower; the late Col. Clive Gallop, p. 110; G. N. Georgano, p. 126 upper, 165; Geoffrey Goddard, p. 170, 217; Guy Griffiths, p. 52; C. W. P. Hampton, 51, 112, 122 upper, 180; Dr. G. E. Hicks, p. 195; F. W. Hutton-Stott, p. 32, 126; D. B. Jocelyn, p. 18; H. E. Kingsman, p. 177 lower; Lancia, Turin, p. 128 lower; Lt. Col. L. S. Michael, O.B.E., p. 125 upper; *Motor*, p. 81 upper, 198 lower; National Motor Museum, p. 8, 11, 16, 17, 19 upper and lower, 20, 23, 24 upper and lower, 25, 26, 34, 35 upper, 37, 38, 40, 46, 47, 48 lower, 49, 54, 56, 57, 59, 60, 62, 63, 66, 69, 70, 71, 73 upper, 78, 80 upper, 81 lower, 84, 85, 86, 87 upper, 88, 91 upper left and right, 92, 93 upper and lower, 95 upper, 100, 101, 102, 105 upper and lower, 106, 107, 109 lower, 113, 114, 116 lower, 117, 118, 119, 120 upper, 123 upper, 125 lower, 127, 128 upper, 129, 131 upper and lower, 134, 138, 139 right, 140 upper, 141, 143, 147, 148, 152, 153, 155 bottom, 156, 157, 159, 161, 162 lower, 164 upper, 166, 169 upper and lower, 172, 173 upper, 174, 175, 178, 185, 186 lower, 187 upper, 189, 190 upper and lower, 191, 192, 193, 194, 196 upper and lower, 199, 200, 203, 204, 205 lower, 206, 207, 208, 209, 210, 211 upper and lower, 215, 218, 219 upper and lower, 220, 221, 223; George A. Oliver, D.A., p. 22; Renault Ltd., 173, lower; Rolls-Royce Ltd., p. 181, 182; Rover Co. Ltd., p. 183, 184; Michael Sedgwick, p. 155 top; Steyr-Daimler-Puch A.G., p. 30 upper; Studio 3, p. 39 lower; United States Information Service, p. 116 upper; Vauxhall Motors Ltd., p. 214; Bruce Whitehouse, p. 33 lower; Jonathan Wood, p. 36.

The remainder of the illustrations are taken from the Authors' and the Publisher's Collections.

Contents

Introduction to the Second Edition

This book started life in 1959 with the sesquipedalian title of *The Vintage Motor Car Pocketbook* but despite this handicap it sold in very large numbers and has long been out of print.

Despite the exhaustive research and the spate of literary matter which has been lavished upon every aspect of Veteran and Vintage motoring since 1959, it seems that nothing has replaced the 'VMCPB', and the publishers have therefore felt justified in giving it a new lease of life.

In this edition, most of the pictures are different from those in the first edition, but the subject matter seems to have stood the test of time pretty well and has not been altered very much.

The object of the exercise was to provide in compact shape and size as much information as possible about as many Vintage cars as possible. It gives pictures and specifications of most important models, and a good many unimportant ones as well. There are also short notes about the majority of makes, either on grounds of their interest, popularity, rarity, or sometimes just because they are so funny.

In giving short specifications it has been remarkably difficult to decide where to stop. Generally, it is the first appearance of a model which is quoted; but many models were current through most or all of the vintage decade, changing gradually throughout its run. In such cases, the size of the book makes it impossible to give the specification year by year and the first year seemed the most sensible to quote. The really frightening multifariousness of some manufacturers also precludes a complete list. For example, in 1928 Daimlers listed no less than twenty-one quite separate models.

*   *   *

It is impossible to plunge into a study of vintage motor-cars (or anything else for that matter) without understanding what went before.

With a few important exceptions, manufacturers of the veteran era (up to 1904) were concerned with making the motor-car work, *somehow*. In the so-called Edwardian decade (1905–15) they were concerned in making it work *well*, and in this they succeeded thoroughly—at a price. But if you wanted luxury you could not expect a lot of performance, and vice versa; if you wanted a cheap motor-car you got, on the whole, something fairly nasty.

The vintage decade (1920–30) was one of consolidation. The luxury car became faster; the fast car became more luxurious and the cheap car became very much better than its predecessor. As a whole, the vintage car was the product of cheap skilled labour, and the world depression of 1929 effectively killed it. The transition from skilled labour to mass production was not a very happy one, and accounted, in large measure, for the deplorable standards of design and manufacture during the 1930s. Nowadays, the technique of mass-production has been thoroughly mastered. Nearly all cars are good and some are very good indeed; but the individuality in design and the craftsmanship in execution have gone.

The more one studies vintage motor-cars the more apparent does it become that the period 1919–24 was one of outstanding interest and importance, yet most of the vintage cars in use today belong to the second half of the decade and are of nothing like comparable interest. The absorption of 1914–18 air-craft practice into car design produced many designs of great interest, although it usually became quickly apparent that they were not compatible with commercial production at an economic price.

Surviving examples of this advance-guard, mostly with overhead camshafts —Hispano-Suiza (outstandingly); Bugatti, Bentley, Lanchester, and Napier, are now rare prizes indeed. In 1920, too, there were still many designs which were to all intents and purposes Edwardian. Rolls-Royce and Vauxhall, for example, have most of the appeal of true Edwardians—refinement, flexibility, simplicity, and comfort. There were also the beginnings of the fairly simple, robust and efficient designs which make up the bulk of surviving vintage machinery. The 12/50 Alvis, and the many manifestations of the Anzani engine are the outstanding examples.

All these types have their beginnings in Edwardian motoring. Rolls-Royce, of course, set the standard for luxury and refinement. Such makes as Vauxhall, Talbot, and Sunbeam showed how real power could be got out of straight-forward side-valve engines. Bugatti, Porsche (then with Austro-Daimler), and Henry (and his imitators) pointed the way to modern high efficiency. Finally, Ford showed that a cheap car could be a good car as well, and the bull-nosed Morris was just in time to be an Edwardian.

Even four-wheel braking was well-established by 1914, when it was first used in racing; and all Isotta Fraschinis have had a brake on each wheel since 1910.

The one battle which the vintage car fought unsuccessfully was against increasing weight, both sprung and unsprung, and in the end it was this, almost as much as economic conditions, which sounded its death-knell. It was to be a very long time before this battle was won, although the seeds of victory were sowed as early as 1934, by B.M.W.

It is all this interweaving of influences which makes the study and driving of vintage cars so fascinating and enjoyable. It is the aim of this book to provide as much information about the subject as can be compressed into a volume of reasonable size.

C.C.

A.B.C. England

The All British Company went into production very soon after the 1918 Armistice. The ingenious Mr Granville Bradshaw designed their horizontally opposed, air-cooled, twin-cylinder engine which powered a handsome and effective light car and, suitably scaled down, a very famous motor-cycle. The latter, with its four-speed, car-type gearbox and leaf-sprung front and back wheels, was years ahead of its time, and directly inspired the German B.M.W. motor-cycle which is still an advanced design.

The 'square' car engine of 1200 cc (91·5 × 91·5 mm) had steel cylinders and produced the then remarkable output of 30 bhp at the then high speed of 3400 rpm, representing 25 bhp per litre at a time when most manufacturers were content with half as much. Its Achilles heel was the overhead valve gear of which the pushrods were liberally scattered across the countryside; otherwise it was a very good and long-lived engine.

Also unusual in light cars of that time was a gearbox with four speeds, although the vertically disposed gate was difficult to operate. With a chassis weight of only 8 cwt, and light, polished aluminium body, the performance was really brisk and well upwards of 60 mph was ensured.

In 1925 came the Supersports model with bore increased to 96·1 and credited with upwards of 40 bhp and some 70 mph; but soon after this the car went out of production. The day of air-cooled twins was over, not to be revived until the funny bubble-cars of the late 1950s.

In 1920, by way of variety, the company offered a radial-engined car with cone brakes.

Year: 1920
Maker's HP: 12
R.A.C. Rating: 10·37 hp
Number of Cylinders: 2
Bore and Stroke: 91·5 × 91·5 mm
Engine Capacity: 1·2 litres

Valves: overhead. Air Cooled
Wheelbase: 8′ 6″
Forward Speeds: 4
Final Drive Ratio: 4 to 1
Tyres: 710 × 90

Year: 1925	*Engine Capacity:* 1·3 litres
Model: Supersports	*Valves:* overhead
Maker's H.P.: 12/40	*Wheelbase:* 8′ 6″
R.A.C. Rating: 11·6 hp	*Forward Speeds:* 4
Number of Cylinders: 2	*Final Drive Ratio:* 4·5 to 1
Bore and stroke: 96·1 × 91·5 mm	*Tyres:* 710 × 90

A.C. England

The Auto-Carrier Company was founded in 1904 and produced a weird commercial light three-wheeled van which was nevertheless successful. It later appeared in passenger-carrying form as the A.C. Sociable when it did quite well in trials.

Four-wheelers were experimented with in 1912–14 but did not go into production until after 1918 when the A.C. rapidly made a pre-eminent name for itself among the early vintage light cars.

The first model had the 1½-litre, side-valve Anzani proprietary engine, which was later used by so many other makers, notably Frazer Nash. The very first models had a bore of only 65 mm but this was soon increased to the usual Anzani 69 mm. In 1919 came the prototype 6-cylinder which saw 44 years of continuous production and finally gave 110 bhp. It is universally thought of as a 2-litre, and it is very little known that it was also offered in 1½-litre form with a bore of 56 mm. This advanced engine had wet steel liners in an aluminium block, single overhead camshaft and four main bearings. Originally producing 40 bhp, in the 1960s models this output was more than doubled with unimpaired reliability and flexibility.

above The 1½-litre, 4-cylinder Anzani-engined A.C. was perhaps the best of the early Vintage light cars
left The A.B.C. 12/40 Supersports model, with bodywork by Compton & Hermon of Hersham, Surrey, cost £275 in 1925

Both models were handicapped by a very light, three-speed gearbox attached to the back axle, having inevitably ill-assorted (and by now usually very noisy) ratios. The transmission brake was worn behind the back axle—logically enough, even if it did not work very well.

A special 4-cylinder A.C. was the first 1½-litre car to cover 100 miles in an hour; in 1925 a 6-cylinder broke the 24-hour record at 82·58 mph and, in 1926, won the Monte Carlo Rally. Also in this year was produced the 3-carburettor, 6-cylinder Montlhéry model capable of 85 mph. The 4-cylinder model went out of production in 1927–28 but the 6-cylinder continued until 1963.

Year: 1919
Maker's HP: 12
R.A.C. Ratings: 11·9 hp
Number of Cylinders: 4
Bore and Stroke: 69 × 100 mm
Engine Capacity: 1·5 litres

Valves: side
Wheelbase: 8′ 10″
Forward Speeds: 3
Final Drive Ratio: 4·5 to 1
Tyres: 700 × 80

Year: 1920
Maker's HP: 16
R.A.C. Rating: 15·7 hp
Number of Cylinders: 6
Bore and Stroke: 65 × 100 mm
Engine Capacity: 2 litres

Valves: overhead
Wheelbase: 9′ 2½″
Forward Speeds: 3
Final Drive Ratio: 4·5 to 1
Tyres: 26 × 3

Year: 1926
Model: Montlhéry
Maker's HP: 16/66. As above but tyre size 27 × 4·4

left 1927 'Montlhéry': the model name celebrates the 1926 24-hour record at that track by a similar 6-cylinder 2-litre car

right The Type G.3 Albert, produced in 1922–3, had a spacious aluminium body

Albert   England

The Albert motor-car was yet another product of the car concessionaire who turned to manufacture after the war. This one was produced by Adam Grimaldi & Co. of Portland Street, and first appeared in 1920 as a substantially built 11 hp light car. The engine was a proprietary Dorman overhead-valve which pulled either an open 4-seater or a rather handsome 2-seater coupé body. Their distinguishing feature, however, was that they belonged to that select band who copied the Rolls-Royce radiator.

In 1922 Albert were taken over by Gwynne Pumps of Chiswick who continued to market the 11 hp Albert and also introduced a 14 hp ohv Gwynne-Albert. This new lease of life was short as those models did not reappear in 1924. There are, however, known to be at least three of the 11 hp Alberts and one 14 hp Gwynne-Albert model surviving today.

Year: 1920
Maker's HP: 12
R.A.C. Rating: 11·9 hp
Number of Cylinders: 4
Bore and Stroke: 68 × 103 mm
Engine Capacity: 1·5 litres

Valves: overhead
Wheelbase: 9′ 6″
Forward Speeds: 4
Final Drive Ratio: 4·6 to 1
Tyres: 760 × 90

Year: 1922
Maker's HP: 14
R.A.C. Rating: 13·9 hp
Number of Cylinders: 4
Bore and Stroke: 75 × 110 mm
Engine Capacity: 1·9 litres

Valves: overhead
Wheelbase: 9′ 6″
Forward Speeds: 4
Final Drive Ratio: 4·5 to 1
Tyres: 30 × 3½

Alfa Romeo   Italy

In 1906 Alexandre Darracq decided to introduce his cars to Italy and started a factory in Naples for assembly of components sent from France. A sales and service department was opened in Milan to market the finished product. The models marketed were the 8 hp single and 10 hp twin cylinder models, but due to lack of adequate brakes they were not a success. In 1909 the Company sold their interest to an Italian concern who renamed the Company 'Anonima Lombarda Fabbrica Automobili', and modified the current Darracq designs to suit the Italian market. In 1911 Nicola Romeo obtained a controlling interest in the firm and after the war the Company emerged under his directorship as 'Alfa-S.P.A.' shortly changing to 'Alfa Romeo'.

In 1922 the type RL was introduced, followed in 1924 by the RM. The RL appeared as a 3-litre, 6-cylinder touring car known as the 21/70, with overhead valves operated by pushrods, wet sump lubrication and was distinguished by its flat radiator. The lesser known type RM was similar but was a 4-cylinder 2-litre. However, the best known early vintage Alfa is the RLSS, 22/90, or

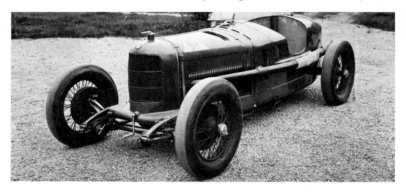

sports version of the 21/70. This car had two Solex carburettors, dry sump lubrication and a smaller 'V' radiator. Although the gear ratios proved to be unsuitable for English roads the 22/90 was as good a performer as most English '3-litres'. Two cars raced successfully at Brooklands, and on the Continent 22/90's also performed creditably in the Targa Florio and in Italian road races.

In 1926, following the overwhelming Grand Prix success of their famous P.2, 8-cylinder, 2 ohc racing cars, the Company produced a new 1½-litre touring car with a 6-cylinder single overhead camshaft engine, capable of revving to 6000 rpm. This was quickly followed by the 1½-litre twin ohc model and in 1929 the supercharged version appeared, and was an immediate racing success. The enlarged 1¾-litre version was even more successful and won every race for which the factory entered it in 1929. The production model, known as the 17/95, developed 95 bhp and with the handsome open two-seater Zagato coachwork, it was quite one of the most desirable vintage and post-vintage sports cars.

Year: 1922   *Valves:* side
Maker's HP: 20/30   *Wheelbase:* 9' 6"
R.A.C. Rating: 25·8 hp   *Forward Speeds:* 4
Number of Cylinders: 4   *Final Drive Ratio:*
Bore and Stroke: 102 × 130 mm   *Tyres:* 820 × 120
Engine Capacity: 4·3 litres

Year: 1924   *Valves:* overhead
Maker's HP: 15/20   *Wheelbase:* 9' 8"
R.A.C. rating: 13·9 hp   *Forward Speeds:* 4
Number of Cylinders: 4   *Final Drive Ratio:* 5·1
Bore and Stroke: 75 × 110 mm   *Tyres:* 765 × 165
Engine Capacity: 1·9 litres

---

top left The P2 Grand Prix car came out in 1924 and won its first-ever race—at Cremona—and the French and Italian GPs in the same year

left 1927 22/90 RLSS 4-seater, with Peter Hull, Secretary of the Vintage Sports-Car Club, at the wheel

Year: 1925
Model: RL
Maker's HP: 21/70
R.A.C. Rating: 20·9 hp
Number of Cylinders: 6
Bore and Stroke: 75 × 110 mm
Engine Capacity: 2·9 litres
Valves: overhead
Wheelbase: 11' 4½"
Forward Speeds: 4
Final Drive Ratio: 4·1 to 1
Tyres: 820 × 120

Year: 1926
Maker's HP: 12/50
R.A.C. Rating: 14·3 hp
Number of Cylinders: 6
Bore and Stroke: 62 × 82 mm
Engine Capacity: 1·5 litres

Valves: overhead
Wheelbase: 9' 6½"
Forward Speeds: 4
Final Drive Ratio: 4 to 1
Tyres: 29 × 5

Year: 1927
Model: RLSS
Maker's HP: 22/90
R.A.C. Rating: 21·5 hp
Number of Cylinders: 6
Bore and Stroke: 76 × 110 mm

Engine Capacity: 3 litres
Valves: overhead
Wheelbase: 10' 4"
Forward Speeds: 4
Final Drive Ratio: 3·75 to 1
Tyres: 820 × 120

Year: 1929/30
Model: 6C
Maker's HP: 17/95
R.A.C. Rating: 15·7 hp
Number of Cylinders: 6
Bore and Stroke: 65 × 88 mm

Engine Capacity: 1·75 litres
(supercharged)
Valves: overhead
Wheelbase: 9' 0"
Forward Speeds: 4
Final Drive Ratio: 4 to 1
Tyres: 27 × 4·75

The 1930 6C-1750 Super Sport was designed by Vittorio Jano, and the bodywork is by Zagato

Alvis   England

Few names of the vintage decade are more respected than Alvis.

The Company was founded in 1919 and went into production with the side-valve 10/30, 1½-litre, which did in fact develop 30 bhp and was good for 60 mph or more. Next, the 65 × 110 engine was enlarged to 68 × 110, as the 12/40 and in 1923–24 it appeared as the 12/50 with pushrod operated overhead valves, and the bore finally enlarged to 69 mm.

The 12/50 was durable, simple, economical, usefully fast, and handsome, and few vintage cars enjoyed—and enjoy—a better reputation or survive in greater numbers in active use. Their considerable weight, to which they partly owe their durability, robbed them of any very startling acceleration, but the engines had a capacity for sustained revs: which was quite unusual in the early twenties.

The 69×110 engine had a capacity of 1645 cc, so for $1\frac{1}{2}$-litre competition purposes there was a 68×103 mm.

The model continued in production until 1932 when it was supplanted by the 12/60 and finally by the dreadfully heavy 'Firefly'.

In 1928 came the almost equally good and successful 6-cylinder 'Silver Eagle' which, in 3-carburettor form, was capable of 85 mph.

below 1920 10/30 model. The hare radiator mascot was worn by Alvis cars between 1920 and 1929–30
bottom 1924 12/50 Model S.A. 'ducks-back' 2-seater sports car with dickey seat

Alvis was also a pioneer of front-wheel drive although it had been experimented with since the beginning of the century. Although potential winners, the front-drive cars were seldom very lucky, yet so great was the makers' confidence in them that for about a year they almost dropped all other models; a policy which brought them to the brink of insolvency. The 4-cylinder F.W.D. car had what amounted to a 12/50 engine turned back to front, and with an overhead camshaft. It was first made in racing form in 1925, followed by what was intended to be a Grand Prix 8-cylinder, overhead camshaft, 1½-litre, in 1926. They were not, however, put on the market until 1928, in 4-cylinder form, and in 8-cylinder form in 1929–30. Survivors are now very rare, but the 12/50 and 'Silver Eagle' continue to give stalwart service, whether with open tourer or saloon coachwork, or in 1½-litre form with the handsome 'Ducks-back' and 'Beetle-back' 2-seater bodies.

Year: 1920
Maker's HP: 10/30
R.A.C. Rating: 10·5 hp
Number of Cylinders: 4
Bore and Stroke: 65 × 110 mm
Engine Capacity: 1·5 litres

Valves: side
Wheelbase: 9' 2"
Forward Speeds: 4
Final Drive Ratio: 4 to 1
Tyres: 760 × 90

Year: 1924
Model: S.A.
Maker's HP: 12/50
R.A.C. Rating: 11·4 hp
Number of Cylinders: 4
Bore and Stroke: 68 × 103 or
69 × 110 mm

Engine Capacity: 1·5 or 1·7 litres
Valves: overhead
Wheelbase: 9' 0½"
Forward Speeds: 4
Final Drive Ratio: 4·33 to 1
Tyres: 28 × 3½

Year: 1925
Model: S.C. As Model S.A. but
Wheelbase 9' 4½", and *Tyres*
29 × 4·95

Year: 1926
Model: T.F. as Model S.C. but
Bore and Stroke only 68 × 103 mm
and *Final Drive Ratio:* 4·77 to 1

1930 'Silver Eagle' 'Atlantic' saloon

Year: 1928	*Engine Capacity:* 1·9 litres
Model: T.A.	*Valves:* overhead
Maker's HP: 14/75	*Wheelbase:* 9′ 4½″
R.A.C. Rating: 14·75 hp	*Forward Speeds:* 4
Number of Cylinders: 6	*Final Drive Ratio:* 5·22 to 1
Bore and Stroke: 63 × 100 mm	*Tyres:* 29 × 4·75

Year: 1929	*Engine Capacity:* 2·2 litres
Model: T.A. as for 1928 but	*Wheelbase:* 9′ 10½″
Bore and Stroke 67·5 × 100 mm	*Tyres:* 30 × 5·25

Year: 1930	*Engine Capacity:* 1·5 litres
Model: F.A. (front wheel drive	*Valves:* overhead
supercharged)	*Wheelbase:* 10′ 0″
Maker's HP: 8/15	*Forward Speeds:* 4
R.A.C. Rating: 15 hp	*Final Drive Ratio:* 5 to 1
Number of Cylinders: 8	*Tyres:* 29 × 4·75
Bore and Stroke: 55 × 78·5 mm	

Front-wheel-drive 'works' team cars for the 1928 *Vingt-quatres Heures du Mans*. Drivers were (left) S. C. H. Davis/Urquhart Dykes and (right) Maurice Harvey/Harold Purdy, who came home 9th and 6th overall respectively

Amilcar   France

The Amilcar was first sold in 1922, as a very light car: almost a cycle-car. But although these earliest models probably weighed only half a ton they had none of the wire-and-bobbin character of the true cycle-car and were very practicable little cars, offering outstanding value for money and useful performance.

An increase from 900 to 1100 cc produced the type C.G.S. or 'Grand Sport', and when endowed with further mechanical refinements such as pressure lubrication the C.G.S. or 'Surbaisse' became a really formidable machine. Its exiguously rakish, doorless French body had staggered seats, pointed tail and usually fixed, cycle-type mudguards. In this form it claimed 35 bhp at 4500 rpm and still weighed less than 12 cwt.

In the meantime, a twin ohc, 6-cylinder, 1100 cc supercharged model had been prepared for voiturette racing and was sold to special order from 1926. However, they do not seem to have been generally marketed until 1928. Providing over 100 mph and staggering value for money, they had great competition success in this country.

The last vintage models were a refined straight-eight two litre and another of 66 mm bore and 2·3 litre capacity, and one is thought to survive in this country.

Cheap and lively, the 1925 C.G.S. Grand Sport was one of the best-selling of the contemporary small French sports cars

Year: 1922
Maker's HP: 8
R.A.C. Rating: 7·5 hp
Number of Cylinders: 4
Bore and Stroke: 55 × 95 mm
Engine Capacity: 0·9 litre

Valves: side
Wheelbase: 7′ 8″
Forward Speeds: 3
Final Drive Ratio: 4·28 to 1
Tyres: 700 × 80

Year: 1928
Models: C.G.S. and C.G.S.S.
Maker's HP and *R.A.C. Rating:* 8·9 hp
Number of Cylinders: 4
Bore and Stroke: 60 × 95 mm

Engine Capacity: 1·1 litres
Valves: side
Wheelbase: 7′ 7¾″
Forward Speeds: 3
Final Drive Ratio: 4·5 to 1
Tyres: 27 × 4

Year: 1928
Model: Special Sports
Maker's HP: 11
R.A.C. Rating: 11·6 hp
Number of Cylinders: 6
Bore and Stroke: 55·9 × 74 mm
Engine Capacity: 1·1 litres (super-charged)
Valves: overhead
Wheelbase: 7' 0"
Forward Speeds: 4
Final Drive Ratio: 4·5 to 1
Tyres: 27 × 4·4

Year: 1930
Maker's HP: 20
R.A.C. Rating: 19·6 hp
Number of Cylinders: 8
Bore and Stroke: 63 × 80 mm
Engine Capacity: 2 litres
Valves: overhead
Wheelbase: 10' 0"
Forward Speeds: 4
Final Drive Ratio: 4·75 to 1
Tyres: 29 × 4·95

top A 1926 twin ohc 6-cylinder C.6 competing in the 1937 500 Miles Race at Brooklands
above 1930 8-cylinder 20 hp C.8, which was capable of nearly 80 mph in spite of weighing 27 cwt

Angus Sanderson   England

Of the Durham firm of Sir William Angus, Sanderson & Co. we read, in a press report of 1921: 'It was intended that there should be a mass production of this car that it might be placed on the market at a reasonable price. The mass production is yet to come but the price is not high.'

In an equally laconic statement of 1928 we read merely that 'this car is not being manufactured'.

Year: 1920   *R.A.C. Rating:* 14·3 hp
Maker's HP: 14   *Number of Cylinders:* 4

Bore and Stroke: 76 × 127 mm
Engine Capacity: 2·3 litres
Valves: side
Wheelbase: 10′ 0″

Forward Speeds: 3
Final Drive Ratio: 4·2 to 1
Tyres: 815 × 105

1922 14·3 hp tourer. Very much assembled from bought-out components, the 4-cylinder engine was built by Tylor, who also included lavatory cisterns among their wares

Ansaldo Italy

Like so many Italian vintage cars, the Ansaldo hovered between being a sports and a touring car. Its overhead camshaft and slightly inclined valves gave useful performance and stamina, but a wide-ratio three-speed gearbox and low back axle ratio largely stultified this promise. Despite this it had some sprint successes in England in the 1923–25 seasons. Only late in its career did the 6-cylinder model acquire a more useful four-speed gearbox. It is quite remarkable how uniformly inept were Italian gearboxes of the early twenties.

1925 4CS 2-litre, 4-cylinder. Ansaldo cars were made by a subsidiary of the large and old-established Italian engineering firm of Societa Anonima Italiana Giovanni Ansaldo of Turin, from 1920 to 1931

Year: 1923	*Engine Capacity:* 1·8 litres
Model: 4A	*Valves:* overhead
Maker's HP: 12	*Wheelbase:* 9′ 1″
R.A.C. Rating: 12·1 hp	*Forward Speeds:* 3
Number of Cylinders: 4	*Final Drive Ratio:* 4·6 to 1
Bore and Stroke: 70 × 120 mm	*Tyres:* 765 × 105

Year: 1923	*Engine Capacity:* 2 litres
Model: 6A	*Valves:* overhead
Maker's HP: 16	*Wheelbase:* 9′ 10″
R.A.C. Rating: 15·7 hp	*Forward Speeds:* 3
Number of Cylinders: 6	*Final Drive Ratio:* 4·5 to 1
Bore and Stroke: 65 × 100 mm	*Tyres:* 765 × 105

Year: 1930	*Valves:* overhead
Model: 22	*Wheelbase:* 10′ 10″
R.A.C. Rating: 27·9 hp	*Forward Speeds:* 4
Number of Cylinders: 8	*Final Drive Ratio:*
Bore and Stroke: 75 × 110 mm	*Tyres:* 30 × 6·5
Engine Capacity: 3·5 litres	

Argyll Scotland

The Glasgow firm of Argyll were early pioneers of front-wheel braking, and the single-sleeve valve (as opposed to the Knight double-sleeve employed by Daimlers) which performed its dual function by means of an exotic corkscrew motion. It was, in fact, a quite good if undistinguished car.

The Argyll Company seldom entered in competitive events, so that when their Scottish rivals, the Arrol-Johnston, won the 1905 T.T. race, they were stung to comment that 'having a bit of common sense the company do not waste their time and money on building racing machines which prove nothing one way or the other'.

In 1913 a Captain Kelsey attempted to motor from Capetown to Cairo in an Argyll, but after suffering from various mechanical difficulties the expedition finally came to an untimely end in Central Africa when its leader had a fatal encounter with a leopard.

In a press report of 1921 appeared the following somewhat enigmatic commentary: 'This car is apparently built by a firm reconstructed from the original Argyll Company, which many years ago constructed vast works near Glasgow, after several successful seasons with the Argyll car. Owing to reasons entirely unconnected with the design and quality of the car, the Company failed and reconstruction became necessary.'

Year: 1920
Model: A
Maker's HP: 15/30
R.A.C. Rating: 15·9 hp
Number of Cylinders: 4
Bore and Stroke: 80 × 130 mm
Engine Capacity: 2·6 litres
Valves: sleeve
Wheelbase: 10' 0"
Forward Speeds: 4
Final Drive Ratio: 4·3 to 1
Tyres: 880 × 120

1920 15·9 hp single sleeve-valve
Model A tourer

Year: 1930
Maker's HP: 18/50
R.A.C. Rating: 17·9 hp
Number of Cylinders: 6
Bore and Stroke: 69·5 × 105 mm
Engine Capacity: 3·2 litres

Valves: sleeve
Wheelbase: 10' 1"
Forward Speeds: 3
Final Drive Ratio: 4·45 to 1
Tyres: 31 × 5·25

Ariès   France

The name of Ariès is closely associated with the 24-hour races at Le Mans where the firm competed consistently in the 1100 cc class, although with no outstanding success. In 1927 they entered a 3-litre model, which was leading at the end of 23 hours when it was pushed so hard by a 3-litre Bentley that the camshaft drive sheared and the Bentley went through to win. It is perhaps ironical that when a 3-litre Bentley is sufficiently hard pressed, the cross-shaft drive of the camshaft gear is often the first component to fail.

The 1927 Le Mans-type Ariès was marketed in the following year and had some competition success.

In Edwardian days the Ariès was also a distinguished *marque* and was a pioneer of the V4 and V6 in production form.

Year: 1925
Maker's HP: 8/10
R.A.C. Rating: 8·9 hp
Number of Cylinders: 4
Bore and Stroke: 60 × 96 mm
Engine Capacity: 1·1 litres

Valves:
Wheelbase:
Forward Speeds: 3 or 4
Final Drive Ratio:
Tyres: 815 × 115

Year: 1925	*Valves:* overhead
Maker's HP: 15/20	*Wheelbase:* 10′ 5″
R.A.C. Rating: 17·9 hp	*Forward Speeds:* 3 or 4
Number of Cylinders: 4	*Final Drive Ratio:*
Bore and Stroke: 85 × 140 mm	*Tyres:* 880 × 120
Engine Capacity: 3·2 litres	

Year: 1928	*Valves:* overhead
Type: 3-litre	*Wheelbase:*
R.A.C. Rating: 16·7 hp	*Forward Speeds:* 4
Number of Cylinders: 4	*Final Drive Ratio:*
Bore and Stroke: 82 × 140 mm	*Tyres:* 880 × 120
Engine Capacity: 2·9 litres	

Le Mans, 1927: the 3-litre of Chassagne/Laly which led the race for seventeen hours, only to retire ninety minutes from the end

Armstrong Siddeley — England

The various companies in which the name 'Siddeley' has appeared are confusingly numerous, ranging from the 'Siddeley Autocar Co.', 'Wolseley-Siddeley Cars', 'Siddeley-Deasy Motor Car Co. Ltd.', and finally to 'Armstrong Siddeley Motors'.

Coming on the market very early after 1918 the 30 hp Armstrong Siddeley made a considerable impression. With its massive pointed radiator and sphinx mascot, solid disc wheels, and big razor-edge saloon coachwork it gave an appearance of almost architectural massiveness in an age when most cars still looked rather spindly. The equally massive ohv, 5-litre engine claimed a modest 60 bhp.

Later came the 18 hp six, which was also ahead of its time in appearance, and coupled smooth running with quite useful performance.

Compared with these, the 14 hp 4-cylinder with its flat-fronted radiator and negligible performance was an undistinguished sort of machine. Nevertheless, several have survived.

Year: 1919
Maker's HP: 30
R.A.C. Rating: 29·5 hp
Number of Cylinders: 6
Bore and Stroke: 88·9 × 133·4 mm
Engine Capacity: 5 litres
Valves: overhead
Wheelbase: 11′ 3″
Forward Speeds: 3
Final Drive Ratio: 3·7 to 1
Tyres: 820 × 135

1924 30 hp saloon with division. Although it was originally intended for the owner-driver, it was usually driven by chauffeurs

Year: 1922
Maker's HP: 18
R.A.C. Rating: 17·9 hp
Number of Cylinders: 6
Bore and Stroke: 69·5 × 104·8 mm
Engine Capacity: 2·4 litres
Valves: overhead
Wheelbase: 10′ 0″
Forward Speeds: 3
Final Drive Ratio: 4·7 to 1
Tyres: 815 × 105

Year: 1924
Maker's HP: 14
R.A.C. Rating: 14·4 hp
Number of Cylinders: 4
Bore and Stroke: 76 × 102 mm
Engine Capacity: 1·9 litres
Valves: overhead
Wheelbase: 9′ 3″
Forward Speeds: 3
Final Drive Ratio: 4·7 to 1
Tyres: 760 × 90

1924 18 hp with 'All-Weather' bodywork by Offord. Chassis price: £480

Arrol-Johnston

Scotland

In the early years of the century the Arrol-Johnston Company 'dog-cart' continued to be marketed with a rear engine of massive appearance and mysterious shape, and enormous wooden cartwheels with solid tyres. It would not have been out of place in 1895, but apparently its archaic design continued to appeal to the conservative Scot long after the turn of the century. Possibly it was a convenient layout for carrying dead stags.

However, in 1905 the Company suddenly developed sporting proclivities, and although their machine was largely devoid of merit it proceeded to win the 1905 T.T. race ahead of a Rolls-Royce, to the considerable chagrin of the latter company. Again in 1911 the Arrol-Johnston team was the only team to finish intact in the *Coupe de l'Auto*.

In the early vintage era, however, the Company relapsed into designs of uncompromising stolidity, the 2·4-litre engine claiming only 22 bhp, which was very low, even by current standards, when 12 or 13 bhp per litre was a usual minimum.

The 1919 'Victory Model' was used to carry the Prince of Wales on a tour of the West country, but after a succession of mechanical failures it was abandoned in Yeovil.

Year: 1920	*Engine Capacity:* 2·4 litres
Model: A	*Valves:* side
Maker's HP and R.A.C. Rating: 15·9 hp	*Wheelbase:* 10' 0"
	Forward Speeds: 4
Number of Cylinders: 4	*Final Drive Ratio:* 4 to 1
Bore and Stroke: 80 × 120 mm	*Tyres:* 815 × 105

1919 2651 cc, ohv 'Victory' model. The price was £600 for the chassis, or £700 complete

Year: 1924
Model: 'Empire E'
Maker's HP and R.A.C. Rating:
20 hp
Number of Cylinders: 4
Bore and Stroke: 89·75 × 130 mm

Engine Capacity: 3·3 litres
Valves: side
Wheelbase: 10' 0"
Forward Speeds: 4
Final Drive Ratio: 4·25 to 1
Tyres: 820 × 120

Aston Martin England

It has been stated by a reliable authority that if the successive sponsors of Aston Martin (prior to the recent David Brown era) had given £70 to every-one who thought of buying an Aston Martin, to dissuade them from doing so, the company would have been better off than was in fact the case.

Despite this mournful calculation—or perhaps as a result of it—there has seldom been a bad Aston Martin. They have enjoyed some success in racing and, mostly, a first-class reputation.

Lionel Martin put a special Coventry Simplex engine into a small Isotta Fraschini chassis before 1914 and this was the basis of the early production models. The name Aston Martin is a combination of Aston Clinton, the famous hill-climb of early vintage days, and Lionel Martin. After 1918 Bamford and Martin formed a company for manufacture, and 1921–23 was spent in experiment, including considerable racing success. There was the Coventry Simplex side-valve engine intended for production, and two, twin ohc, 4-cylinder, 16 valve, 1½-litre engines, were also made. Eventually the company went into production with the side-valve car in 1922. In the course of three years, about sixty in all were constructed. They were in every way excellent

1923 side-valve, with aluminium 'engine-turned' bodywork by Compton & Hermon

cars with refinement, good road-holding, good brakes, good lines, and respectable performance from the 35 bhp, 1½-litre, side-valve engine. They were also extremely expensive.

In 1926 the Company was taken over by Renwick & Bertelli who brought out an equally excellent machine with a single, chain-driven ohc, 8 valve, 1½-litre engine. Acceleration suffered from its somewhat excessive weight. Although this model ran on well into the thirties, less than twenty cars had been made by 1930.

Thus the high vintage reputation of this make rests upon much less than 100 cars, of which very few indeed have survived.

Year: 1922	*Valves:* side
Maker's HP and R.A.C. Rating:	*Wheelbase:* 8' 7½"
11 hp	*Forward Speeds:* 4
Number of Cylinders: 4	*Final Drive Ratio:* 3·73 to 1
Bore and Stroke: 66·5 × 107 mm	*Tyres:* 710 × 90
Engine Capacity: 1·5 litres	

Year: 1926	*Valves:* overhead
Maker's HP: 11	*Wheelbase:* 8' 0"
R.A.C. Rating: 10·4 hp	*Forward Speeds:* 4
Number of Cylinders: 4	*Final Drive Ratio:* 3·5 or 4·1 to 1
Bore and Stroke: 65 × 112 mm	*Tyres:* 710 × 90 or 29 × 4·4
Engine Capacity: 1·5 litres	

1930 Irish Grand Prix: S. C. H. Davis' 1½-litre 'International' hard pressed by Alfa Romeo

Austin England

Herbert Austin started his long designing career with the Wolseley Company before setting up on his own, which he did inconspicuously during the Edwardian era, with cars which were medium in every way.

The heavy '20', with a monobloc engine, was continued as the first post-war model and carried enormous and hideous bodies in a leisurely, uncomplaining sort of way which endeared it greatly to hire companies in provincial towns. Nevertheless, in the optimistic style of the early twenties, one was raced at Brooklands and lapped persistently at 85 mph, while a single-seater managed a lap at nearly 95 mph—it is difficult to imagine how and why.

Of greater fame, and great merit, was the 'heavy 12/4' introduced in 1922 which survived in basic form, as a taxi, into the post-1945 years. Its heavy, well-made bodies had leather seats of the highest quality and comfort; the engine was smooth, flexible and sluggish; and infinitely reliable; the gearbox slow and unconquerably unpredictable. The steering was good; the brakes—were never a strong point on any vintage Austin.

But the model which really brought fame to Herbert Austin was the 'Seven', also introduced in 1922. Apart from such pioneer efforts as the Edwardian 'Bébé' Peugeot, and the later Peugeot 'Quadrilette', to which the Austin design appears to be somewhat indebted, Austin was the first to make a real, 4-cylinder car available to the marginal motorist. The first specimens developed only $10\frac{1}{2}$ bhp but could manage 60 mpg when driven carefully. The original 55×75 mm bore and stroke were soon increased to 56×76 mm, and the crankshaft was supported by two ball bearings. They had electric lighting and starting as standard (apart from a very few prototypes) and front-wheel brakes, even if of more than usually inefficient design. The 'Seven' continued in production until 1938 by which time it could show 17 bhp, and became the basis of innumerable specials and even racers. In 1930 an Austin 'Seven' won the 500-mile race at Brooklands at 83·42 mph. In all, well over a quarter of a million Austin 'Sevens' gave immense pleasure to many people who would otherwise have had to go by train.

Sound and solid: the 1661 cc 'Twelve' was introduced in 1922—good, hard-wearing material at £550

Year: 1919
Maker's HP: 20
R.A.C. Rating: 22·4 hp
Number of Cylinders: 4
Bore and Stroke: 95 × 127 mm
Engine Capacity: 3·6 litres
Valves: side
Wheelbase: 10′ 9″
Forward Speeds: 4
Final Drive Ratio: 3·93 to 1
Tyres: 820 × 120

1924 7 hp 'Chummy' tourer, with
Herbert Austin at the wheel

Year: 1922
Maker's HP: 7
R.A.C. Rating: 7·2 hp
Number of Cylinders: 4
Bore and Stroke: 55 × 75 mm
Engine Capacity: 0·7 litre

Valves: side
Wheelbase: 6′ 3″
Forward Speeds: 3
Final Drive Ratio: 5·4 to 1
Tyres: 26 × 3·6

Year: 1922
Maker's HP: 12
R.A.C. Rating: 12·8 hp
Number of Cylinders: 4
Bore and Stroke: 72 × 102 mm
Engine Capacity: 1·7 litres

Valves: side
Wheelbase: 9′ 4″
Forward Speeds: 4
Final Drive Ratio: 5·1 to 1
Tyres: 765 × 105

Year: 1928
Maker's HP: 16
R.A.C. Rating: 15·9 hp
Number of Cylinders: 6
Bore and Stroke: 65·5 × 111 mm
Engine Capacity: 2·5 litres

Valves: side
Wheelbase: 9′ 4″
Forward Speeds: 4
Final Drive Ratio: 5·1 to 1
Tyres: 31 × 4·75

Austro-Daimler   Austria

Austro-Daimler had as their designer Dr Ferdinand Porsche, possibly the greatest, and certainly the most versatile designer in the whole of automobile history. He is the outstanding exception to the rule that one man only produces one basic design in his lifetime, for Porsche produced at least five—the Edwardian, 'Prince Henry' competition Austro-Daimler; the vintage Austro-Daimler (an entirely dissimilar design); the big vintage and just post-vintage Mercedes (not his best effort); the Auto-Union racing cars; and finally the Volkswagen 'Beetle'.

The Edwardian 'Prince Henry' cars were completely outstanding, with overhead camshaft and inclined valves in a 5¾-litre, 4-cylinder engine; but the company entered the vintage era with some sound, if fairly staid side-valve models. It was not until about 1927 that they got the Porsche-designed, sporting Model ADM into production. With its refined but efficient overhead camshaft engine, superb steering and powerful brakes, this was one of the outstanding vintage motor-cars. A team of them won the Team Prize in the 1928 T.T., and in 1930 an Austro-Daimler made fastest time of the day at Shelsley Walsh in 42·8 seconds.

In 1930 came the even more splendid 8-cylinder 'Alpine' model, with a tubular backbone chassis.

Very few Austro-Daimlers survive in Britain, though fortunately among the survivors is an Edwardian 'Prince Henry'. The striking, oval-shaped radiator gives them an appearance which is quite in keeping with their performance.

Year: 1920
Maker's HP: 20/30
R.A.C. Rating: 20·1 hp
Number of Cylinders: 4
Bore and Stroke: 90 × 140 mm
Engine Capacity: 3·6 litres

Valves: side
Wheelbase: 10' 2"
Forward Speeds: 4
Final Drive Ratio: 3·2:1
Tyres: 820 × 120

Year: 1922
Maker's HP: 17/60
R.A.C. Rating: 26·9 hp
Number of Cylinders: 6
Bore and Stroke: 85 × 130 mm
Engine Capacity: 4·5 litres

Valves: overhead
Wheelbase: 11' 4"
Forward Speeds: 4
Final Drive Ratio: 3·78 to 1
Tyres: 895 × 135

Year: 1927
Model: A.D.M.
Maker's HP: 19/100
R.A.C. Rating: 21·6 hp
Number of Cylinders: 6
Bore and Stroke: 76 × 110 mm

Engine Capacity: 3 litres
Valves: overhead
Wheelbase: 9' 0¼" or 11' 5"
Forward Speeds: 4
Final Drive Ratio: 4·58 to 1
Tyres: 820 × 120

Year: 1930
Model: A.D.R. 'Alpine'
Maker's HP: 32/100
RAC Rating: 31·8 hp
Number of Cylinders: 8
Bore and Stroke: 80 × 115 mm

Engine Capacity: 4·6 litres
Valves: overhead
Wheelbase: 12' 2½"
Forward Speeds: 4
Final Drive Ratio: 4 to 1
Tyres: 6·5 × 20

1927 Type A.D.M. 3-litre Sport. Designed by the great Dr. Ferdinand Porsche, these cars had 100 bhp available and a maximum of over 100 mph. They took the team prize in the 1928 Ulster Tourist Trophy

A.V.   England

The A.V. monocar deserves special mention because in an age of highly improbable cycle-cars, it stands out by its exuberant optimism. This it inherited from its parent the Edwardian Carden.

Made by Ward & Avey Ltd. (whence the phonetic 'A.V.') it was strictly a single-seater and carried a V-twin air-cooled, J.A.P. engine immediately behind (and at times uncomfortably close to) the driver. This was started by pulling a chain which worked on a spring-and-rachet extension of the flywheel. The drive was by two-speed epicyclic gearbox and final chain. There was, of course, no reverse. Steering was by the then popular wire-and-bobbin and the front of the machine ended in a sharp point, which may have had its tactical uses as the brakes were not noticeably effective.

With its narrow track, motor-cycle tyres, powerful engine, and all up weight of 6 cwt the A.V. was capable of speeds far ahead of its limits of control; albeit, at any rate one hero drove 'The Streamlined Monocar' at Brooklands at 75 mph.

Crude and popular, the 1921 rear-engined monocar with plywood body was succeeded by versions with two seats in tandem, and then in the usual side-by-side position.

Year: 1919　　　　　　　　　　　*Engine Capacity:* 0·9 litre
Maker's HP: 8　　　　　　　　　*Valves:* side
R.A.C. Rating: 8·96 hp　　　　　*Wheelbase:* 7′ 0″
Number of Cylinders: 2　　　　　*Forward Speeds:* 2
Bore and Stroke: 85 × 85 mm　　*Final Drive Ratio:* Optional
(alternative bore: 76)　　　　　　*Tyres:* 26 × 2¼

Ballot

France

The Ballot firm started by making proprietary engines and taxicabs. Presumably they also made handsome profits during 1914–18, as immediately afterwards the Company entered the field of international racing in a very big way. The Swiss Henry, who had designed the epoch-making racing Peugeots of 1912–14, joined Ernest Ballot in building a team of 5-litre Ballots for the 1919 Indianapolis race. With its 8-cylinder-in-line engine and two overhead camshafts, this car set the standard for racing design over the whole inter-wars period. In 1921 followed a 3-litre Grand Prix car on similar lines, but time and again Ballots just failed to secure a richly deserved success. They did, however, win the Italian Grand Prix in 1921.

In 1922 they retired from racing, but marketed a 2-litre, 4-cylinder car closely following the racing designs. These had two overhead camshafts, four valves per cylinder and ball main bearings. Claiming 75 bhp, these cars were a lower-built, sleeker edition of the better known later vintage Ballots and must have been immensely effective. They were certainly the first production cars to have twin overhead camshafts. Probably only 100 were made

One of the 1919 Indianapolis cars when it was owned by the well-known
Vintage enthusiast Anthony Heal

between 1922 and 1925, and it is believed that one survives.

Shortly after this sports model came the 2LT, with the same bore and stroke, plain bearings, and a single overhead camshaft. In 1925 this developed into the more famous 2LTS which was basically the same engine with inclined valves. It claimed, and probably developed, 60 hp, as it would drag an immense saloon body along at nearly 80 mph and cruise at over 60 mph, coupled with commendable refinement, excellent steering and powerful, servo-operated brakes.

In 1927 came two overhead camshaft 8-cylinder models, but they did not enjoy the reliability nor high reputation of the 2LTS.

In 1931 the Company was taken over by Hispano-Suiza.

above Grand Prix de Tourisme, San Sebastian, 1925: Pierre Decrose in the 1924 production-type 2LS he shared with René Debuck. The exhaust system has been modified
below Drophead-coupé coachwork by Figoni on the 1926/27 2LTS

Year: 1922
Model: '2 cam, sports'
R.A.C. Rating: 12·1 hp
Number of Cylinders: 4
Bore and Stroke: 69·9 × 130 mm
Engine Capacity: 2 litres

Valves: overhead
Wheelbase: 9' 2"
Forward Speeds: 4
Final Drive Ratio: 3·75 to 1
Tyres: 815 × 105

Year: 1925
Model: 2LTS
Maker's HP: 13/60
R.A.C. Rating: 12·1 hp
Number of Cylinders: 4
Bore and Stroke: 69·9 × 130 mm
Engine Capacity: 2 litres

Valves: overhead
Wheelbase: 10' 2"
Forward Speeds: 4
Final Drive Ratio: 4·7 to 1
Tyres: 31 × 5·25
(Note: the 1922 2LT had practically the same specification)

Year: 1927
Model: '8-in-line'
Maker's HP: 20
R.A.C. Rating: 19·6 hp
Number of Cylinders: 8
Bore and Stroke: 63 × 105 mm

Engine Capacity: 2·6 litres
Valves: overhead
Wheelbase: 10' 11"
Forward Speeds: 4
Final Drive Ratio: 4·7 to 1
Tyres: 30 × 5·75

Year: 1929
Model: 'RH2'
Maker's HP: 22/80
R.A.C. Rating: 21·6 hp
Number of Cylinders: 8
Bore and Stroke: 66 × 105 mm

Engine Capacity: 2·9 litres
Valves: overhead
Wheelbase: 10' 11"
Forward Speeds: 4
Final Drive Ratio: 5 to 1
Tyres: 32 × 6

1929 RH2 straight-eight. For 1930, the bore was enlarged to 68 mm, thus giving the RH3 model a capacity of 3,050 cc. It survived until 1932

Bayliss-Thomas   England

An undistinguished light car which nevertheless rose slightly above its fellows by some success in events such as the Lands End Trial. It also had quite good lines and a rather Rolls-Royce style of radiator. Several are still running, including the rare Supersports model.

Year: 1923
Maker's HP: 9/19
R.A.C. Rating: 8·9 hp
Number of Cylinders: 4
Bore and Stroke: 66 × 109·5 mm
Engine Capacity: 1·5 litres
Valves: side
Wheelbase: 8′ 3″
Forward Speeds: 3
Final Drive Ratio: 4·5 to 1
Tyres: 700 × 80

Year: 1924
Maker's HP: 10/20
R.A.C. Rating: 9·8 hp
Number of Cylinders: 4
Bore and Stroke: 63 × 100 mm
Engine Capacity: 1·3 litres

Valves: overhead
Wheelbase: 8′ 3″
Forward Speeds: 3
Final Drive Ratio: 4·5 to 1
Tyres: 700 × 80
(Also Supersports model)

Bean   England

The origin of the Bean can be traced back to 1826 when the firm of A. Harper Sons & Bean Ltd. produced drop-forgings, castings and stampings. This grounding perhaps accounted for the sturdy and durable qualities found in most Bean models. One of them successfully completed the arduous trans-Australian crossing. In 1919 the 11·9 hp model was produced with a 4-cylinder side-valve engine—typical of the specification of early vintage light cars. In 1929 came the equally tough 'Hadfield' model with some sporting pretensions.

top right 1923 9/19 Bayliss-Thomas tourer, made by the Excelsior Motor Company of Birmingham, who are better known for their bicycles and motor-cycles

right 1925 14 hp Bean motors past a 1929 Morris 'Cowley' in an M.C.C. trial

Year: 1919
Maker's HP and R.A.C. Rating:
11·9 hp
Number of Cylinders: 4
Bore and Stroke: 69 × 120 mm
Engine Capacity: 1·8 litres

Valves: side
Wheelbase: 8' 6"
Forward Speeds: 3 or 4
Final Drive Ratio: 4·5 or 4 to 1
Tyres: 30 × 3·5

Year: 1924
Maker's HP and R.A.C. Rating:
14·0 hp
Number of Cylinders: 4
Bore and Stroke: 75 × 135 mm
Engine Capacity: 2·4 litres

Valves: side
Wheelbase: 9' 6"
Forward Speeds: 4
Final Drive Ratio: 4·5 to 1
Tyres: 31 × 4

Year: 1929
Model: 'Hadfield Sports'
Maker's HP: 14/70
R.A.C. Rating: 13·96 hp
Number of Cylinders: 4
Bore and Stroke: 75 × 130 mm

Engine Capacity: 2·3 litres
Valves: side
Wheelbase: 10' 0"
Forward Speeds: 4
Final Drive Ratio: 4·4 to 1
Tyres: 31 × 5·25

above From 1927 the cars were known as Hadfield-Beans: 1929 14/70
sports-tourer
opposite 1924 14/70 2-litre Beardmore 'Supersports' 3-seater. The leading
works driver was Cyril Paul

Beardmore   Scotland

During the 1914 war this versatile Scottish company built battleships, cruisers,
destroyers, submarines, tanks, guns, shells, aero engines, aeroplanes and
airships.

Afterwards it produced an excellent sports car combining good lines with good performance and a quite advanced specification.

The 'Supersports' model usually carried a three-seater, polished aluminium body, and the slightly pointed radiator was also of most distinguished design. The overhead camshaft engine claimed 70 bhp which may have been somewhat on the high side, as the guaranteed maximum speed was only 70 mph.

The Beardmore did well in speed hill-climbs, its outstanding success being fastest-time-of-day at Shelsley Walsh in 1924, with the then highly creditable time of 50·5 seconds.

In addition to the two models listed below there was a little known 4-cylinder, 4-litre model.

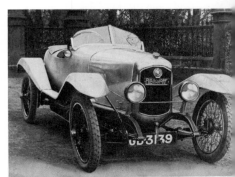

Year: 1922
Maker's HP: 11
R.A.C. Rating: 11·5 hp
Number of Cylinders: 4
Bore and Stroke: 68 × 114 mm
Engine Capacity: 1·6 litres
Valves: overhead
Wheelbase: 8′ 11″
Forward Speeds: 4
Final Drive Ratio: 4·5 or 4·15 to 1
Tyres: 760 × 90

Year: 1924
Model: 'Supersports'
Maker's HP: 14/70
R.A.C. Rating: 13·5 hp
Number of Cylinders: 4
Bore and Stroke: 74 × 114 mm

Engine Capacity: 2 litres
Valves: overhead
Wheelbase: 8′ 4″
Forward Speeds: 4
Final Drive Ratio: 4·15 to 1
Tyres: 30 × 3½

Belsize   England

In 1897 amongst the British firms making motor-cars were Marshall & Co., who became Belsize in 1902. The first wheel-steered cars were very Panhard in appearance but had pneumatic tyres. Early Edwardian models were of 40 hp but in 1911 a 10/12 hp model was standardized.

In 1920 a 20 hp 4-cylinder appeared, but in 1922 came the model for which Belsize is best known—type BB. Designed by Granville Bradshaw it had a 90 degree twin-cylinder, oil-cooled engine of such smoothness that between 18 and 36 mph it was impossible to tell whether the car had two or four cylinders. It attained a top speed of 42 mph with a petrol consumption of 40 mpg. The motoring periodicals spoke extremely favourably of it, their only adverse comments being 'that the method of checking the oil is tiresome and dirty' and 'the car is not easy to start as an air strangler is lacking'.

The 'BB' was succeeded in 1924 by an ohv 4-cylinder, and a 'light 6' also appeared in this year—an example of which survives and has proved to be completely indestructible. The Company ceased manufacture in 1926.

Year: 1920	*Valves:* side
Maker's HP: 15	*Wheelbase:* 9′ 8″ or 10′ 4″
R.A.C. Rating: 20·08 hp	*Forward Speeds:* 4
Number of Cylinders: 4	*Final Drive Ratio:* 3·5 to 1
Bore and Stroke: 90 × 110 mm	*Tyres:* 815 × 105
Engine Capacity: 2·5 litres	

Year: 1922	*Engine Capacity:* 1·2 litres
Model: 'BB'	*Valves:* side
Maker's HP: 9	*Wheelbase:* 8′ 3″
R.A.C. Rating: 8·9 hp	*Forward Speeds:* 3
Number of Cylinders: 2	*Final Drive Ratio:* 4·2 to 1
Bore and Stroke: 85 × 114 mm	*Tyres:* 700 × 80

Year: 1924	*Valves:* overhead
Maker's HP: 10/20	*Wheelbase:* 8′ 3″
R.A.C. Rating: 8·9 hp	*Forward Speeds:* 3
Number of Cylinders: 4	*Final Drive Ratio:* 4·2 to 1
Bore and Stroke: 60 × 100 mm	*Tyres:* 700 × 80
Engine Capacity: 1·2 litres	

Year: 1924	*Valves:* overhead
Maker's HP: 14/30	*Wheelbase:* 10′ 0″
R.A.C. Rating: 13·4 hp	*Forward Speeds:* 4
Number of Cylinders: 6	*Final Drive Ratio:* 4·72 to 1
Bore and Stroke: 60 × 100 mm	*Tyres:* 765 × 105
Engine Capacity: 1·9 litres	

1923 'BB' three-seater coupé. Granville Bradshaw was also the designer of the air-cooled flat-twin A.B.C. (q.v.)

Bentley

Until the 1950s successes of Jaguar cars, the vintage Bentleys could certainly claim to have the pre-eminent reputation as British sports cars. This was not achieved so much by outstanding speed capabilities as stamina, and W. O. Bentley would never countenance a degree of tuning which might prejudice reliability. When the blown 4½-litre was introduced it was despite Mr Bentley's firm opposition. The immense factor of safety in the original design is shown by the tremendous performance now extracted from the 3- and 4½-litre engines, of which the 4½-litres must be giving nearly twice their original power output. There has, however, been a corresponding loss of reliability.

The design common to all models was a fixed-head cylinder block containing four, slightly inclined valves per cylinder, operated by a single overhead camshaft. Six different gearboxes were listed, giving variously graduated ratios from fairly wide to very close, according to the requirements of the model in question.

Although first offered for sale in 1921, very few were made in the first year

top 1924 3-litre, with Vanden Plas bodywork, in a rally at Bournemouth
above 1929 4½-litre: Bentley Driver's Club Concours winner, 1961, restored by Richard C. Wheatley

or two and indeed, throughout the company's ten years of life, the long list of racing successes only took place against a background of recurrent financial crises.

The 3-litre model always had a cone clutch, but the sporting and touring editions may be distinguished by the radiator badges, which are described later. In 1925 the engine was partly redesigned, and later models may be recognized by the integral sump, as opposed to the earlier models, in which the base-chamber was quite separate from the crank chamber proper. The power output of the 3-litre engine rose gradually from 65 to 92 bhp. The last was made in 1927.

In 1928 came the $4\frac{1}{2}$-litre, 4-cylinder, aiming to give a little more performance with greatly improved flexibility, and only 110 bhp was claimed. In standard form the $4\frac{1}{2}$-litre was capable of a little over 90 mph. The earlier models had cone clutches but the last series had a heavy plate clutch. In 1930 a supercharged edition became available, capable of some 105 mph, with a quite dreadful fuel consumption, its merit in the light of subsequent history being the immensely strong, balanced crankshaft which is the foundation of the present very fast Bentleys.

The 6-cylinder, $6\frac{1}{2}$-litre model arrived in 1925, at first intended entirely as a luxury car; but in 1929 it was developed into the 'Speed Six', which was probably the best car the Company ever made. Just in time for the vintage era came the 8-litre, a chassis capable of carrying luxurious saloon coachwork at 100 mph, but in later times, even this proved itself capable of taking World Records and travelling at 140 mph.

Just post-vintage came the totally undistinguished and quite un-Bentley-like 4-litre. Almost immediately after its introduction the Company went into liquidation and was acquired by Rolls-Royce. (See also 'Napier'.)

The whole epic story of the Company is told in *'W.O.' The Autobiography of W. O. Bentley*. (Published by Hutchinson.)

Before proceeding to the specifications, the exceptional importance of this

1929 Speed Six: the $6\frac{1}{2}$-litre car which won the Le Mans race of that year driven by Woolf Barnato/Tim Birkin, seen taking Mulsanne

make merits setting out the colour of the enamel filling in the radiator badges, by which, to a large extent, the different models may be recognized.

3-litre long chassis and all cars up to 1924	Blue
3-litre short chassis speed models from 1924	Red
3-litre 100 mph chassis (radiator narrower at bottom than top) mostly	Green
4½-litre (including supercharged)	Black
6½-litre Standard Six (radiator same shape as 100 mph, 3-litre)	Blue
6½-litre Speed Six—to choice, but normally	Green
4- and 8-litre	Blue

Year: 1921
Model: 3-litre
Maker's HP and R.A.C. Rating:
15·9 hp
Number of Cylinders: 4
Bore and Stroke: 80 × 149 mm

Engine Capacity: 3 litres
Valves: overhead
Wheelbase: 9′ 8½″
Forward Speeds: 4
Final Drive Ratio: 3·53 to 1
Tyres: 820 × 120

Year: 1925
Model: Standard Six
Maker's HP and R.A.C. Rating:
37·2 hp
Number of Cylinders: 6
Bore and Stroke: 100 × 140 mm

Engine Capacity: 6·5 litres
Valves: overhead
Wheelbase: 12′ 0″
Forward Speeds: 4
Final Drive Ratio: 3·8 or 4·23 to 1
Tyres: 33 × 6·75

Year: 1926
Model: 3-litre Speed model.
Particulars as for 3-litre above but
Wheelbase 9′ 9½″

Final Drive Ratio: 3·78 or 4·23 to 1
The 100 mph model had *Wheelbase*
9′ 0″ and *Final Drive Ratio* 3·53 to 1.
All had *Tyres* 820 × 120

1930 8-litre with Weymann panelled saloon bodywork by Freestone & Webb. The engine produced 200/225 bhp depending on the compression ratio, and the chassis weight was 37 cwt

Year: 1928
Model: 4½-litre
Maker's HP and R.A.C. Rating: 24·8 hp
Number of Cylinders: 4
Bore and Stroke: 100 × 140 mm

Engine Capacity: 4·4 litres
Valves: overhead
Wheelbase: 10' 10½"
Forward Speeds: 4
Final Drive Ratio: 3·53 to 1
Tyres: 21 × 5·25

Year: 1929
Model: 'Speed Six'
Maker's HP and R.A.C. Rating: 37·2 hp
Number of Cylinders: 6
Bore and Stroke: 100 × 140 mm

Engine Capacity: 6·5 litres
Valves: overhead
Wheelbase: 11' 8½"
Forward Speeds: 4
Final Drive Ratio: 3·53 or 3·8 to 1
Tyres: 33 × 6

Year: 1930
Model: 4½-litre Supercharged. Details all as for 4½-litre but

Final Drive Ratio optional 3·3 or 3·53 to 1

Year: 1930
Model: 8-litre
Maker's HP and R.A.C. Rating: 44·9 hp
Number of Cylinders: 6
Bore and Stroke: 110 × 140 mm

Engine Capacity: 8 litres
Valves: overhead
Wheelbase: 12' or 13'
Forward Speeds: 4
Final Drive Ratio: 3·53 or 3·8 to 1
Tyres: 33 × 6·75

Benz

Germany

Whatever claims may be put forward for the invention of the motor-car there can be no doubt at all that Karl Benz was the first person to manufacture and sell it on a commercial footing. As early as 1888 he had fifty men working for him making motor-cars.

Benz's idea of a motor-car was essentially that of a horseless carriage, and he persisted in this notion long after other people were making recognizable motor-cars. He thus nearly brought his firm to ruin and it was only saved in 1903 by bringing in a completely new designer. Even ten years after that, Benz could still be seen driving about placidly in one of his horseless carriages.

Nevertheless, some very effective Benz cars were produced during the Edwardian era, including a powerfully teutonic affair for the motor-car trials of the period, its successes including outright wins in the Herkomer Trophy of 1907 and the Prince Henry contest of 1908. There is a wealth of conflicting evidence as to the Company's post-war models, but there seems to be some measure of agreement about the two quoted below. In 1925 Benz and Mercedes amalgamated as the Daimler-Benz Company, and their combined products were known as Mercedes-Benz.

The largest model in the early Vintage range was the 7-litre 27/70 PS. The caption to this 'works' picture refers to it as a 'Benz-Runabout' which sounds a little skittish for a 100 × 150 mm 6-cylinder . . .

Year: 1922
Maker's HP: 8/20
R.A.C. Rating: 13·9 hp
Number of Cylinders: 4
Bore and Stroke: 74 × 120 mm
Engine Capacity: 2 litres

Valves: side
Wheelbase: 9′ 4¼″
Forward Speeds: 4
Final Drive Ratio: 4·5 to 1
Tyres: 815 × 105

Year: 1922
Maker's HP: 27/70
R.A.C. Rating: 37·2 hp
Number of Cylinders: 6
Bore and Stroke: 100 × 150 mm
Engine Capacity: 7 litres

Valves: side
Wheelbase: 11′ 11¾″
Forward Speeds: 4
Final Drive Ratio: 3·125 to 1
Tyres: 935 × 135

Berliet   France

The Berliet was one of the numerous French touring cars of medium-quality finish and extremely sturdy construction. Even into the 'sixties they might still be seen in agricultural districts of France, going about their now menial tasks in that state of utter neglect of which only the French are capable. It was nevertheless a machine of quite distinguished appearance in its day, with a well-proportioned, almost flat-topped radiator.

Berliets ran in the first 24-hour race at Le Mans in 1923, but they did not reappear there subsequently. Two also raced at Brooklands, one of which, from the peculiar noise it made, was called 'Whistling Rufus'.

Year: 1920
Maker's HP: 15/20
R.A.C. Rating: 20·1 hp
Number of Cylinders: 4
Bore and Stroke: 90 × 130 mm
Engine Capacity: 3·3 litres
Valves: side
Wheelbase: 10' 3"
Forward Speeds: 3
Final Drive Ratio: 4·2 to 1
Tyres: 820 × 120

1922 15·9 hp 12CV. Marius Berliet's Lyons works was better known for its locomotives than its cars, thus the latter incorporated a railway motif in their radiator badges

Year: 1922
Maker's HP: 12/15
R.A.C. Rating: 15·9 hp
Number of Cylinders: 4
Bore and Stroke: 80 × 130 mm
Engine Capacity: 2·6 litres
Valves: side
Wheelbase: 10' 3¼"
Forward Speeds: 3
Final Drive Ratio: 4·2 to 1
Tyres: 765 × 105

Year: 1922
Maker's HP: 25
R.A.C. Rating: 24·8 hp
Number of Cylinders: 4
Bore and Stroke: 100 × 140 mm
Engine Capacity: 4·4 litres
Valves: side
Wheelbase: 11' 2"
Forward Speeds: 4
Final Drive Ratio: 3·6 to 1
Tyres: 895 × 150

Year: 1928
Model: V.I.H.
Maker's HP: 14/40
R.A.C. Rating: 14·4 hp
Number of Cylinders: 6
Bore and Stroke: 62 × 100 mm
Engine Capacity: 1·8 litres
Valves: side
Wheelbase: 10' 0"
Forward Speeds: 4
Final Drive Ratio: 5·2 to 1
Tyres: 740 × 140

Beverley-Barnes   England

The Beverley-Barnes was a praiseworthy attempt by its makers, Messrs. Lanaerts & Dolphens, general engineers, to produce a machine combining comfort, above-average performances, and very fine mechanical finish. The show chassis was certainly a thing of beauty, but there is a great dearth of contemporary reports from which it might be judged how far they reached their high ideals. Despite a price which was modest in relationship to the undoubtedly high finish, the public do not seem to have responded to the venture with any marked enthusiasm.

All models had eight cylinders in line, but in addition to the two fairly well-known ones listed below, there was also a very rare 5-litre, known as the type A2, 30/90 which, despite an output of 90 bhp at only 2700 rpm, was stated to have a maximum of only '65–75 mph at normal revs'—but possibly this may refer to the recommended cruising speed.

The 1930, 3-litre model had two overhead camshafts driven by a train of gears, which may have been rather noisy in operation. There was an almost perfectly spaced, close-ratio, 4-speed gearbox. A sports edition was also available with twin Cozette carburettors and a supercharger.

As late as 1930 a largely new model was introduced in which it is noticeable that the train of gears driving the camshafts had been replaced by a silent chain. A supercharger was fitted as standard.

Year: 1924
Maker's HP: 24/80
R.A.C. Rating: 27·8 hp
Number of Cylinders: 8
Bore and Stroke: 75 × 112 mm
Engine Capacity: 4 litres

Valves: overhead
Wheelbase: 12′ 6″
Forward Speeds: 3
Final Drive Ratio: several to choice
between 3·8 and 5 to 1
Tyres: 820 × 120

Year: 1930
Maker's HP: 22/90
R.A.C. Rating: 21·6 hp
Number of Cylinders: 8
Bore and Stroke: 66 × 108 mm
Engine Capacity: 3 litres

Valves: overhead (supercharger
optional)
Wheelbase: 9′ 8″
Forward Speeds: 4
Final Drive Ratio: 3·9 to 1
Tyres: 31 × 6

1924 24/80 saloon with division. The cars, of which no more than a dozen or so can have been made, came from the Beverley works at Barnes, SW London

Bianchi   Italy

The Bianchi was one of those numerous Italian vintage cars whose general layout is almost indistinguishable by modern British observers. The Company had been making cars since 1900 and continued in production until 1939.

Year: 1921
Model: 15
Maker's HP: 12/20
R.A.C. Rating: 12·1 hp
Number of Cylinders: 4
Bore and Stroke: 70 × 110 mm
Engine Capacity: 1·7 litres
Valves: side
Wheelbase: 9′ 4″
Forward Speeds: 4
Final Drive Ratio: 4·7 to 1
Tyres: 765 × 105

1921 12/20, from SA Automobile e Velocipedi Eduardo Bianchi of Milan

Year: 1922
Model: B.3
Maker's HP: 20/30
R.A.C. Rating: 22·3 hp
Number of Cylinders: 4
Bore and Stroke: 95 × 130 mm
Engine Capacity: 3·7 litres
Valves: side
Wheelbase: 10′ 3″
Forward Speeds: 4
Final Drive Ratio: 3·7 to 1
Tyres: 820 × 120

Year: 1928
Model: Sports
Maker's HP: 15/60
R.A.C. Rating: 15 hp
Number of Cylinders: 4
Bore and Stroke: 78 × 120 mm
Engine Capacity: 2·3 litres
Valves: overhead
Wheelbase: 10′ 4″
Forward Speeds: 4
Final Drive Ratio: 4·6 to 1
Tyres: 31 × 5·25

Bignan   France

Before the 1914 war M. Jacques Bignan manufactured proprietary engines. In 1920 he modified one of these engines—a 'T' head 1500 cc 4-cylinder—to compete in the 1920 *G.P. des Voiturettes* at Le Mans, the four-wheel-braked chassis being designed by M. de la Fournaise. The cars produced about 28 hp and gained 2nd and 3rd places to the winning Bugatti. In 1921 a 3-litre 4-cylinder car was designed, its engine being of a very advanced specification with 16 valves driven by a single overhead camshaft. This car proved itself by winning the tortuous *G.P. de la Corse*.

In 1922 came the design that was the most significant in the life of the Bignan car. It was a 2-litre 75 × 112 mm engine with desmodromic valve operation, and developed 70 bhp at 5000 rpm—an unusually high engine speed for the period. Only two of these cars were produced, one winning the 2-litre class of the 24-hour race at Spa. An overhead camshaft, 16-valve, 2-litre was produced in 1923. It is interesting that although only 4500 rpm were realized 75 bhp were produced from this engine. This car proved fast and thoroughly reliable and obtained 2nd and 4th places (dead-heating with the Bentley) at the first Le Mans 24-hour race. For this model Bignan used servo-assisted front-wheel brakes and a single transmission brake at the back. A 6-cylinder, 3-litre was made in 1924, producing about 125 bhp; it combined outstanding speed and unreliability. From this point Bignan began to decline and in 1927 the firm became bankrupt. Only one example of this *marque* is still known to exist.

The 1925 11CV 2-litre car could be had with 8 valves in 'Normal' or 'Sport' versions or with 16 in competition guise

Year: 1921
Maker's HP: 17/50
R.A.C. Rating: 17·9 hp
Number of Cylinders: 4
Bore and Stroke: 85 × 130 mm
Engine Capacity: 2·9 litres
Valves: side
Wheelbase: 10′ 6″
Forward Speeds: 4
Final Drive Ratio: 4·5 to 1
Tyres: 835 × 135

Year: 1923
Type: 2-litre
Maker's HP: 12/30
R.A.C. Rating: 13·9 hp
Number of Cylinders: 4
Bore and Stroke: 75 × 112 mm
Engine Capacity: 2 litres
Valves: overhead
Wheelbase: 10′ 0″
Forward Speeds: 4
Final Drive Ratio: 4·5 to 1
Tyres: 820 × 120

Blériot-Whippet

England

This voiturette was made by the Air Navigation Company, which was founded by Louis Blériot, the famous aeronaut and first pilot to fly across the English Channel, in a monoplane of his own construction.

The 'Whippet' had a Blackburn V-twin air-cooled engine giving a useful 14 bhp. Transmission was by a variable gear giving a range from 4·1 to 10·4 to 1. Otherwise it differed little from its contemporaries.

1920 'Whippets' about to be unleashed . . .

Year: 1920
Maker's HP: 8
R.A.C. Rating: 8·9 hp
Number of Cylinders: 2
Bore and Stroke: 85 × 88 mm
Engine Capacity: 1 litre
Valves: side
Wheelbase: 6' 9"
Forward Speeds: variable
Final Drive Ratio: 4·1 to 1
Tyres: 700 × 80

B.N.C.

France

One is happy to be able to report that the B.N.C. was made by Messrs Bollack, Netter et Cie. It lived up to this excellent start in life by being a most effective little car, typical of the French sporting tradition.

The Company started life with a rather uninteresting little side valve, but really came into its own with the 'Monza' and 'Montlhéry', as listed below, while to complete the three M's there was a 'Miramas', which was a long-chassis edition of the 'Monza'. The 'Montlhéry' had a Cozette supercharger as standard equipment.

Circuit de Galtières, 1928. The 'Monza' and 'Montlhéry' models, introduced in 1928, were preceded by the 1927 'Type Course', the first B.N.C. to have the distinctive backward-sloping radiator

Year: 1924
Maker's HP and R.A.C. Rating:
8 hp
Number of Cylinders: 4
Bore and Stroke: 57 × 95 mm
Engine Capacity: 1 litre

Valves: side
Wheelbase: 8′ 2″
Forward Speeds: 3
Final Drive Ratio: 4 to 1
Tyres: 700 × 80

Year: 1928
Model: 'Monza'
Maker's HP: 8/10
R.A.C. Rating: 8·9 hp
Number of Cylinders: 4
Bore and Stroke: 60 × 97 mm

Engine Capacity: 1·1 litres
Valves: overhead
Wheelbase: 7′ 10″
Forward Speeds: 3
Final Drive Ratio: 3·8 to 1
Tyres: 27 × 4

Year: 1928
Model: 'Montlhéry'
Maker's HP: 8/10
R.A.C. Rating: 9·2 hp
Number of Cylinders: 4
Bore and Stroke: 61 × 94 mm
Engine Capacity: 1·1 litres
(supercharged)

Valves: overhead
Wheelbase: 7′ 10″
Forward Speeds: 4
Final Drive Ratio: 4 to 1
Tyres: 27 × 4

Bond   England

Although the Bond is frequently mentioned, in fact very few were made, and a supercharged model was listed of which at any rate one was made.

The make started as early as 1922 with a long-stroke, 2-litre engine, but it is with the extremely sporting and handsome 1927–28 two-seater, with Meadows pushrod engine, that the name of Bond is usually associated. This is also the model that was to have been supercharged.

1927 1½-litre with bodywork by Jarvis of Wimbledon. F. W. Bond & Co. built cars at Brighouse, Yorkshire, from 1922–1928

Year: 1922
Maker's HP: 14/40
R.A.C. Rating: 13·9 hp
Number of Cylinders: 4
Bore and Stroke: 75 × 120 mm
Engine Capacity: 2 litres

Valves: overhead
Wheelbase: 9' 10½"
Forward Speeds: 4
Final Drive Ratio: 4·5 to 1
Tyres: 815 × 105

Year: 1928
Maker's HP: 12/50
R.A.C. Rating: 11·9 hp
Number of Cylinders: 4
Bore and Stroke: 69 × 100 mm
Engine Capacity: 1·5 litres

Valves: overhead
Wheelbase: 8' 9"
Forward Speeds: 4
Final Drive Ratio: 3·9 or 4·3 to 1
Tyres: 27 × 4·4. (Model 'S.1' also available supercharged)

Bugatti
France

Ettore Bugatti was Italian by birth; German by nationalization; and French by domicile. He thus early provided for the air of mystery and complication that quite unjustifiably enshrouds all his subsequent doings—they were all so strictly straightforward that people simply cannot believe it.

To begin with, he made but one design, which lasted for the whole thirty years of his manufacturing life. Many components of 1909 were current in 1939, and the handling of a 1909 and 1939 Bugatti are instantly recognizable as the same thing.

Bugatti studied as a sculptor and this undoubtedly accounts for the architectural appearance of his engines. He was also devoted to horses, and made his radiators in the shape of a horse-shoe. His cars had to have all the instant response and verve of a thoroughbred horse. It is these two qualities that stamp all his work. Not everyone can appreciate it, which is a matter of congratulation for those who are able to do so.

Bugatti may have had a hand in designing the Isotta Fraschini for the 1908

Type 41 —'La Royale': Ettore Bugatti's personal coupé-de-ville

Ernest Friderich who won the voiturette race for the 1921 Italian Grand Prix at Brescia. Subsequent short-chassis Type 13 cars were known as 'Brescia' models

Coupe des Voiturettes and two of these cars survive in Australia. There is certainly a strong similarity between it and his own first production Bugatti, the type 13 of 1909–10. This was in all ways a very expensive miniature luxury car, and was entirely revolutionary at a time when a small car was also, almost as a matter of course, cheap and nasty.

The fundamental Bugatti design consisted of a fixed-head, overhead camshaft engine; multi-plate clutch; final drive by open propeller shaft and torque arm; semi-elliptic springs in front and (except in the very earliest cars) reversed quarter-elliptic at the back.

At different periods the single overhead camshaft operated two, three or four valves per cylinder, but in the vintage era, three was the popular number. There were two inlet and one exhaust, all set vertically. The two small inlet valves helped the remarkable flexibility for which all the models so provided are notable.

The 1909 type 13, originally with 8 valves, continued as the type 13 (16 valve), also known as the 'Brescia' until 1925, with its longer wheelbase variants, the types 22 and 23.

Bugatti turned to 3 valves per cylinder in the 1912 Type 'Garros', and his first entirely new vintage model was the 1923, type 30, straight 8, 2-litre. Like the type 13, this had plain big-end and ball main bearings, and despite its pioneer importance it was not Bugatti's most successful model. Thereafter, his engines had either all roller, or all plain bearings. The important plain-bearing, vintage models are the types 37, 40, 41, 44, 46 and 49. The important roller-bearing types are the 35, 39 and 43.

After 1930 Bugatti went over to two overhead camshafts and two valves per cylinder, with the types 50, 51, 55, 57 and 59. Of the single cam models, only the 46 remained current until 1939.

Of the touring types, the '37' and '40' are 4-cylinders, the '37' for racing and the '40' for touring. The '44' is, virtually, two type 40's, and is an extremely

51

practicable, 85 mph touring car. The '49' is a slightly enlarged edition of it. The '41' is the fabulous, 12¾-litre 'Royale' of which only six were made, but the '46', which is a 5·3-litre scaled-down edition of it, is more common and is an extremely regal town carriage with a 5–90 mph top gear performance.

The various sub-types of '35' were Bugatti's most successful Grand Prix car, the '39' being a 1½-litre edition of it and the '43' its supercharged sporting version, capable of about 112 mph in road trim.

Year: 1910–25. Type 13 (and 22 and 23 with longer wheelbase)
Maker's HP: 10/12
R.A.C. Rating: 11·4 hp
Number of Cylinders: 4
Bore and Stroke: 68 × 100 mm
Engine Capacity: 1·5 litres

Valves: overhead
Wheelbase: 6' 5" (type 23: 7' 11")
Forward Speeds: 4
Final Drive Ratio: various, but usually 3·43 to 1
Tyres: 710 × 90

Year: 1923. Type 30.
Maker's HP and R.A.C. Rating: 17·8 hp
Number of Cylinders: 8
Bore and Stroke: 60 × 88 mm
Engine Capacity: 2 litres

Valves: overhead
Wheelbase: 9' 0"
Forward Speeds: 4
Final Drive Ratio: 4·15 or 4·5 to 1
Tyres: 765 × 105

Year: 1924. Type 35 Grand Prix
Maker's HP and R.A.C. Rating: 17·8 hp
Number of Cylinders: 8
Bore and Stroke: 60 × 88 mm
Engine Capacity: 2 litres
Valves: overhead
Wheelbase: 7' 10½"
Forward Speeds: 4
Final Drive Ratio: to choice

Tyres: 710 × 90 or 29 × 5 (35A is Modified G.P. 35C is supercharged. 35T is 2·3-litre unsupercharged (60 × 100 mm) and 35B is 2·3-litre supercharged. Type 39 is 1½-litre (60 × 66 mm) and 39A 1½-litre supercharged. Type 43 (year 1927) is practically identical with 35B but was equipped and sold for road use)

Year: 1926. Type 40
Maker's HP and R.A.C. Rating:
11·9 hp
Number of Cylinders: 4
Bore and Stroke: 69 × 100 mm
Engine Capacity: 1·5 litres
Valves: overhead

Wheelbase: 8′ 11″
Forward Speeds: 4
Final Drive Ratio: 4·5 or 4·66 to 1
Tyres: 27 × 4·4. (The type 37 is
generally similar but *Wheelbase*
7′ 10½″ and *Final Drive Ratio* to
choice)

Year: 1927. Type 44 tourer
Maker's HP and R.A.C. Rating:
23·6 hp
Number of Cylinders: 8
Bore and Stroke: 69 × 100 mm
Engine Capacity: 3 litres
Valves: overhead

Wheelbase: 10′ 3″
Forward Speeds: 4
Final Drive Ratio: 4·17 to 1
Tyres: 29 × 5
(The type 49 is very similar, 3·3
litres, 72 × 100 mm; introduced in
1930)

Year: 1929. Type 46 tourer.
Maker's HP and R.A.C. Rating:
32·6 hp
Number of Cylinders: 8
Bore and Stroke: 81 × 130 mm
Engine Capacity: 5·3 litres

Valves: overhead
Wheelbase: 11′ 6″
Forward Speeds: 3
Final Drive Ratio: 3·91 to 1
Tyres: 32 × 6

above 1928 Type 44 four-seater with an Italian-built touring body to the order
of Count Catelan
left 1930 Type 35B Grand Prix car. The Type 35 came out in 1924, was
supercharged in 1926 and succeeded by the twin ohc Type 51 in 1931

Buick   America

It was in 1901 that D. Buick, a plumber who had made money by making
bathtubs, first conceived the Buick car. After an uneasy start in which he
became bankrupt in his first year of production, the firm settled down to

building a dull but reliable 2-cylinder car. By 1907 the inevitable 4-cylinder cars were being produced, these cars attaining considerable popularity for their durability and ruggedness.

Much the same may be said of their vintage products which, however, differed from the great majority of their American brethren in having over-head valves.

left 1927 20/60 Buick 'Light Six'. The range of 6-cylinder models was introduced in 1925

right 1928 Model 341. Cadillac pioneered the synchromesh gearbox on their 1929 cars

Year: 1922
Maker's HP: 18
R.A.C. Rating: 18·2 hp
Number of Cylinders: 4
Bore and Stroke: $3\frac{3}{8}'' \times 4\frac{3}{4}''$
Engine Capacity: 2·8 litres

Valves: overhead
Wheelbase: 9′ 1″
Forward Speeds: 3
Final Drive Ratio: 4·6 to 1
Tyres: 31 × 4

Year: 1922
Maker's HP: 27
R.A.C. Rating: 27·3 hp
Number of Cylinders: 6
Bore and Stroke: $3\frac{3}{8}'' \times 4\frac{3}{4}''$
Engine Capacity: 4·2 litres

Valves: overhead
Wheelbase: 9′ 10″
Forward Speeds: 3
Final Drive Ratio: 4·4 to 1
Tyres: 35 × 4

Year: 1927
Maker's HP: 20/60
R.A.C. Rating: 23·4 hp
Number of Cylinders: 6
Bore and Stroke: $3\frac{3}{8}'' \times 4\frac{3}{4}''$
Engine Capacity: 3·5 litres

Valves: overhead
Wheelbase: 9′ 6½″
Forward Speeds: 3
Final Drive Ratio: 5·1 to 1
Tyres: 31 × 5·25

Cadillac

America

Cadillac is one of the oldest-established American makes, dating from 1903.

In 1908 the firm won the Dewar Trophy for a 'standardization test' in which three cars were dismantled, the pieces shuffled, and re-assembled, after which the cars were driven round Brooklands for 500 miles. The Dewar Trophy was won a second time for pioneering the electric starter.

But Cadillac's most important pioneering venture was the V-8 engine. As a layout, the V-8 was nothing new, but the V-8 Cadillac, when produced in 1915, was the first to be made in quantity and sold at a competitive price.

Although having a side-valve, fixed-head engine, accessibility was good,

since not only were there caps over the valves, but also over the pistons which could be removed for decarbonizing.

The engine was not only extremely smooth and flexible, but quite powerful for an Edwardian American, running up to 2300 rpm.

Consistent with the general high standard of the machine, the roller-bearing back axle was fitted with a spiral bevel crown-wheel and pinion which was claimed to have 'the efficiency of bevel gearing with the quietude of a worm'.

The Cadillac offered a wide range of optional equipment including an engine-driven tyre pump and electric starter and lighting.

A design so advanced in 1915 was able to carry the Cadillac through the vintage decade with little alteration, but in 1929 a shorter-stroke, larger-capacity model was introduced.

In 1903 a single-cylinder Cadillac competed successfully in the 1000 mile trial of that year, driven by Mr F. S. Bennett, the British Cadillac concessionaire. In 1953, the same Cadillac, then aged fifty, and Mr Bennett, aged eighty, re-enacted the complete 1903 trial, with equal success; a very remarkable achievement.

Year: 1915

Maker's HP and R.A.C. Rating:
31·25 hp

Number of Cylinders: 8

Bore and Stroke: $3\frac{1}{8}'' \times 5\frac{1}{8}''$

Engine Capacity: 5·2 litres

Valves: side

Wheelbase: 10′ 5″ or 11′ 0″

Forward Speeds: 3

Final Drive Ratio: 4·43 to 1

Tyres: 895 × 135

Year: 1929
Model: 341
Maker's HP and R.A.C. Rating:
35·1 hp
Number of Cylinders: 8
Bore and Stroke: $3\frac{5}{16}'' \times 4\frac{15}{16}''$

Engine Capacity: 5·6 litres
Valves: side
Wheelbase: 10′ 0″ or 11′ 8″
Forward Speeds: 3
Final Drive Ratio: 4·75 to 1
Tyres: 32 × 6·75

Calcott

England

The late Edwardian Calcott was an extremely advanced little machine, whose engine produced a quite unreasonable amount of power. In vintage form, the emphasis was more on refinement and it was, in fact, a very pleasant little car. Should one be encountered it may easily be recognized by a radiator not unlike the contemporary Standard. In 1926 came a rather undistinguished 6-cylinder which did not achieve any pronounced success.

1922 11·9 hp. The Company survived only until 1926 when it was taken over by Singer

Year: 1918
Maker's HP and R.A.C. Rating:
10·5 hp
Number of Cylinders: 4
Bore and Stroke: 65 × 110 mm
Engine Capacity: 1·5 litres

Valves: side
Wheelbase: 7′ 9″
Forward Speeds: 3
Final Drive Ratio: 4 to 1
Tyres: 700 × 80

Year: 1920
Maker's HP and R.A.C. Rating:
11·9 hp
Number of Cylinders: 4
Bore and Stroke: 69 × 110 mm
Engine Capacity: 1·6 litres

Valves: side
Wheelbase: 8′ 6″
Forward Speeds: 3
Final Drive Ratio: 4 to 1
Tyres: 710 × 90

Year: 1926
Maker's HP: 16/50
R.A.C. Rating: 19·3 hp
Number of Cylinders: 6
Bore and Stroke: 72 × 105 mm
Engine Capacity: 2·5 litres

Valves: side
Wheelbase: 10' 0"
Forward Speeds: 4
Final Drive Ratio: 4·5 to 1
Tyres: 29 × 4·95

Calthorpe England

Calthorpe's had a long sporting history before 1914 when they were regular supporters of the *Coupe de l'Auto* races. The cars, with a sharply pointed V radiator, looked quite formidable, but they never achieved any great success.

In vintage form they went on the market in 1918 with a small touring car of no outstanding merit, but it could also be had in sporting form when it became highly effective. It had a three-bearing crankshaft, drilled connecting rods, light aluminium pistons and a wet, multi-plate clutch. In this form it would pull well over 3000 rpm in top gear and achieve about 60 mph.

Another model was the 'Minor', a two-seater coupé, which many people considered to be the most desirable vintage light car.

In the middle twenties, like so many other makes, Calthorpe produced a rather uninteresting 6-cylinder, of which not much was heard. The Company survived until 1931.

A 'Sporting Four', with bull-nose Morris (left), near Broadway in 1920. The aluminium bodies of the two- and four-seater sporting models were built by Mulliner, then a subsidiary company

Year: 1918	*Valves:* side
Maker's HP: 10	*Wheelbase:* 8' 3"
R.A.C. Rating: 10·4 hp	*Forward Speeds:* 3
Number of Cylinders: 4	*Final Drive Ratio:* 4·33 to 1
Bore and Stroke: 65 × 95 mm	*Tyres:* 650 × 65
Engine Capacity: 1·2 litres	

Year: 1923	*Valves:* side
Maker's HP: 12/20	*Wheelbase:* 9' 0"
R.A.C. Rating: 11·9 hp	*Forward Speeds:* 4
Number of Cylinders: 4	*Final Drive Ratio:* 4·875 to 1
Bore and Stroke: 69 × 100 mm	*Tyres:* 760 × 90
Engine Capacity: 1·5 litres	

Year: 1925	*Valves:* overhead
Maker's HP: 15/45	*Wheelbase:* 9' 0"
R.A.C. Rating: 15·7 hp	*Forward Speeds:* 3
Number of Cylinders: 6	*Final Drive Ratio:* 4·3 to 1
Bore and Stroke: 65 × 100 mm	*Tyres:* 765 × 105
Engine Capacity: 2·1 litres	

Ceirano Italy

The Ceirano was sold in England as the Newton-Ceirano and fitted with Newton, piston-type shock absorbers. The radiator was very like a Lancia 'Lambda'.

above 1925 Tipo N150, which looked rather like the Lancia 'Lambda' (q.v.). Its side-valve, 1½-litre, 4-cylinder engine produced 30 bhp. The N150S version had overhead valves. (*See* Newton-Ceirano, page 160)
right 1922 18/24 landaulette. The large Vintage Charrons were uninspiring cars, though the Company did manage to survive until 1930

It was yet another Italian car which had all the makings of a sports car, but failed, because of the customary, disastrously widely spaced gear ratios.

In its first vintage form, however, it was not sporting at all, with a conventional 2·3-litre side-valve engine. In 1925 came the more purposeful 1½-litre, pushrod ohv engine, with a claimed 40 bhp at 3500 rpm. There was a dry, multi-plate clutch and an unusual feature was that all controls, including the steering box, were mounted on a cradle fixed to the engine. The front springs passed through the axle.

Accuracy of all the controls was perhaps the outstanding quality of the Ceirano. It was a typical example of fine Italian engineering.

Signor Ceirano was previously chief designer to the S.C.A.T. Company in whose car the Englishman, Cyril Snipe, won the 1912 Targa Florio race.

Year: 1920	*Valves:* side
Maker's HP: 15/20	*Wheelbase:* 9′ 6″
R.A.C. Rating: 13·9 hp	*Forward Speeds:* 4
Number of Cylinders: 4	*Final Drive Ratio:* 4 to 1
Bore and Stroke: 75 × 130 mm	*Tyres:* 765 × 105
Engine Capacity: 2·3 litres	

Year: 1925	*Engine Capacity:* 1·4 litres
Model: S.150	*Valves:* overhead
Maker's HP: 14	*Wheelbase:* 8′ 9″
R.A.C. Rating: 10·4 hp	*Forward Speeds:* 4
Number of Cylinders: 4	*Final Drive Ratio:* 4·5 to 1
Bore and Stroke: 65 × 110 mm	*Tyres:* 765 × 105

Charron   France

The Edwardian Charron was a fairly high-class tourer with a dashboard radiator, very much like a Renault. Its maker was famous in early racing days when he was in partnership with MM. Girardot & Voigt to make C.G.V.

racing cars including a straight eight in 1903.

Like so many others, the vintage Charron was remarkably like its Edwardian predecessor, and again following the pattern of such firms, in 1925 came the death gasp in the form of a 2½-litre 6-cylinder side-valve.

Year: 1920	*Valves:* side
Maker's HP: 18/24	*Wheelbase:* 11′ 2″
R.A.C. Rating: 17·9 hp	*Forward Speeds:* 4
Number of Cylinders: 4	*Final Drive Ratio:* 4 to 1
Bore and Stroke: 85 × 150 mm	*Tyres:* 880 × 120
Engine Capacity: 3·4 litres	

Year: 1923	*Engine Capacity:* 1·1 litres
Model: R.C.	*Valves:* side
Maker's HP: 8	*Wheelbase:* 7′ 6″
R.A.C. Rating: 8·3 hp	*Forward Speeds:* 3
Number of Cylinders: 4	*Final Drive Ratio:* 4·5 to 1
Bore and Stroke: 58 × 100 mm	*Tyres:* 710 × 90

Year: 1925	*Valves:* side
Maker's HP and R.A.C. Rating:	*Wheelbase:* 10′ 6″
18·2 hp	*Forward Speeds:* 4
Number of Cylinders: 6	*Final Drive Ratio:* 4·1 to 1
Bore and Stroke: 70 × 120 mm	*Tyres:* 860 × 160
Engine Capacity: 2·7 litres	

Charron-Laycock   England

Although having connections with the French company, the Charron-Laycock was a British concern, manufactured by the latter-day makers of the Laycock de Normanville overdrive gear now absorbed by B.L.M.C.

It was a car of refinement and good workmanship in which perhaps the most unusual feature was the camshaft drive consisting of helical gear-wheels made of compressed paper, and pressure lubricated.

Year: 1920	*Valves:* side
Maker's HP: 10	*Wheelbase:* 8' 2"
R.A.C. Rating: 10·4 hp	*Forward Speeds:* 3
Number of Cylinders: 4	*Final Drive Ratio:* 4·5 to 1
Bore and Stroke: 65 × 110 mm	*Tyres:* 710 × 90
Engine Capacity: 1·4 litres	

Chenard-Walcker   France

This make has to its credit a series of most distinguished designs, all as French as you please.

The first Chenard-Walcker was made in 1901, but the first vintage model was a 3-litre side-valve, whose most unusual feature was the back axle, described by a contemporary as being '. . . of special design. Two separate axles are fitted, the rear one carrying the weight of the car and that in front transmitting the power to gear wheels at each end, these wheels engaging with the toothed interior of drums bolted to the road wheels"—it sounds to have been a noisy arrangement. It was, however, sound theory, having the effect of a de Dion axle.

In 1923 Chenard-Walcker won the first 24-hour race held at Le Mans and for 1924 they entered a 4-litre straight eight with twin overhead camshafts which, however, was not successful in the race. In 1925 they ran a team of streamlined, beetle-shaped, 1100 cc cars which won their class and had a most

left 10 hp Charron-Laycock in the 1922 Scottish Six Day Trial. W. S. Laycock Ltd. of Sheffield were manufacturers of railway equipment
below The victorious Chenard-Walcker team of 3-litre cars at Le Mans in 1923. 1st: Lagache/Leonard, No. 9; 2nd: R. Bachmann/Dauvergne, No. 11; 7th: F. Bachmann/Glaszmann

successful subsequent racing history.

In 1925 the two best-known Chenard-Walcker models appeared, both with extremely tough, single ohc engines, with the unusual characteristic of brakeless back axles. There were normal drums on the front wheels, but braking to the back wheels was effected solely by a transmission brake. They performed effectively in a thumping sort of way which seemed in keeping with the ponderous-looking oval-shaped radiator.

Year: 1920
Maker's HP: 15/25
R.A.C. Rating: 15·9 hp
Number of Cylinders: 4
Bore and Stroke: 80 × 150 mm
Engine Capacity: 3 litres

Valves: side
Wheelbase: 10′ 6″
Forward Speeds: 4
Final Drive Ratio: 4·1 to 1
Tyres: 880 × 120

Year: 1924
Maker's HP: 10/15
R.A.C. Rating: 11·9 hp
Number of Cylinders: 4
Bore and Stroke: 69 × 100 mm
Engine Capacity: 1·5 litres

Valves: overhead
Wheelbase: 7′ 11″
Forward Speeds: 3
Final Drive Ratio:
Tyres: 710 × 90

Year: 1924
Maker's HP and R.A.C. Rating:
23·8 hp
Number of Cylinders: 8
Bore and Stroke: 69·5 × 130 mm
Engine Capacity: 4 litres

Valves: overhead
Wheelbase: 12′ 2″
Forward Speeds: 4
Final Drive Ratio:
Tyres: 935 × 135

Year: 1925
Model: 2-litre
Maker's HP: 12/25
R.A.C. Rating: 11·95 hp
Number of Cylinders: 4
Bore and Stroke: 69·5 × 130 mm

Engine Capacity: 1·9 litres
Valves: overhead
Wheelbase: 10′ 0″
Forward Speeds: 4
Final Drive Ratio: 4·5 to 1
Tyres: 820 × 120

Year: 1925	*Engine Capacity:* 3 litres
Model: 3-litre	*Valves:* overhead
Maker's HP: 15/30	*Wheelbase:* 10′ 2″
R.A.C. Rating: 15·7 hp	*Forward Speeds:* 4
Number of Cylinders: 4	*Final Drive Ratio:* 4·5 to 1
Bore and Stroke: 79·5 × 150 mm	*Tyres:* 895 × 135

Chevrolet America

The brothers Louis and Arthur Chevrolet both joined the Buick racing team in 1909. Arthur, however, was also appointed to the post of chauffeur to William C. Durant, the founder of General Motors. By 1911 Louis Chevrolet was producing his own car, a 6-cylinder touring car; still under Durant sponsorship. This was available as both a 'classic' (heavy coachwork) and a 'light six'. In 1916 a new 4-cylinder 21·7 hp known as the '490' was produced in touring form and at once became the most popular of all pre-1918 Chevrolets.

The post-war Chevrolet achieved considerable popularity on account of its cheapness and economy, and with only 2·7 litres it was a small car by American standards.

Year: 1920
Maker's HP: 21·7
R.A.C. Rating: 21·7 hp
Number of Cylinders: 4
Bore and Stroke: $3\frac{11}{16}″ \times 4″$
Engine Capacity: 2·7 litres
Valves: overhead
Wheelbase: 8′ 6″
Forward Speeds: 3
Final Drive Ratio: 4·6 to 1
Tyres: 30 × 3½

1920 '490'. This type number indicates the price in dollars when the model was introduced in 1916

Chrysler America

It is not generally known that the Chrysler was directly developed in 1923 from the Maxwell car of the Edwardian era. The Maxwell achieved considerable success in the Glidden tours of later Edwardian days with the 24 hp 4-cylinder model. A car was also entered for the 1907 Vanderbilt Cup race, with an 8-cylinder engine and two radiators—one at each end of the engine.

left Saloon bodywork on the 1925 2-litre Chenard-Walcker chassis

The Chrysler of the vintage period followed the general trend of American cars with ash-spoked wheels, a large slow revving engine and top gear flexibility. Probably the most famous model was the machine which was creditably placed in the Le Mans 24-hour race in 1928. This model produced about 75 bhp at 3200 rpm from its 6-cylinder engine. The carburettor was a Stromberg and four-wheel hydraulically operated brakes were fitted.

In production form the Model '70' was one of the toughest and most effective of vintage Americans. In the mid-thirties they could be picked up for 30s; at which they were undeniably good value for money.

1928 'Imperial 80'. Although it was not 'America's Most Powerful Car' as its advertisements claimed, it was still good for speeds up to about 90 mph

Year: 1925	*Valves:* side
Maker's HP: 22	*Wheelbase:* 9' 4¾"
R.A.C. Rating: 21·6 hp	*Forward Speeds:* 3
Number of Cylinders: 6	*Final Drive Ratio:* 4·6 to 1
Bore and Stroke: 3" × 4½"	*Tyres:* 30 × 5·77
Engine Capacity: 3 litres	

Year: 1930	*Engine Capacity:* 3·6 litres
Model: 70 N.P.	*Valves:* side
Maker's HP: 23·5	*Wheelbase:* 9' 8"
R.A.C. Rating: 23·5 hp	*Forward Speeds:* 3
Number of Cylinders: 6	*Final Drive Ratio:* 4·1 to 1
Bore and Stroke: 79·4 × 120·7 mm	*Tyres:* 5·5 × 18

Citroën   France

The vintage Citroën was a pure hack that went about its nameless duties with all the uncomplaining philosophy of a donkey and frequently as brutally misused.

Just at the end of the vintage era the Company aspired to slightly higher things with a sound but undistinguished 6-cylinder, 2½-litre, but it was not until 1934 that they produced their front-wheel-driven model which proved to be one of the classic designs of motoring history, and dominated the French roads for twenty years, succeeded by the equally successful D-S and their modern derivatives.

Year: 1919
Maker's HP: 10
R.A.C. Rating: 10·4 hp
Number of Cylinders: 4
Bore and Stroke: 65 × 100 mm
Engine Capacity: 1·3 litres
Valves: side
Wheelbase: 9′ 6″
Forward Speeds: 3
Final Drive Ratio: 4·45 to 1
Tyres: 710 × 90

1919 Type A 10 hp at 7,950 francs or £500 to choice. 10,000 were made in 1921

Year: 1922
Maker's HP and R.A.C. Rating: 7·5 hp
Number of Cylinders: 4
Bore and Stroke: 55 × 90 mm
Engine Capacity: 0·9 litre
Valves: side
Wheelbase: 7′ 4½″
Forward Speeds: 3
Final Drive Ratio: 4·8 to 1
Tyres: 650 × 65

Year: 1922
Maker's HP and R.A.C. Rating: 11·4 hp
Number of Cylinders: 4
Bore and Stroke: 68 × 100 mm
Engine Capacity: 1·4 litres
Valves: side
Wheelbase: 9′ 6″
Forward Speeds: 3
Final Drive Ratio: 4·45 to 1
Tyres: 710 × 90

1922 5CV 7·5 hp 'Cloverleaf'. In 1925 Noel Westwood drove one round the outside edge of Australia (more or less!)

Year: 1929
Model: 2½-litre
R.A.C. Rating: 19·3 hp
Number of Cylinders: 6
Bore and Stroke: 72 × 100 mm
Engine Capacity: 2·4 litres

Valves: side
Wheelbase: 9′ 8″
Forward Speeds: 3
Final Drive Ratio: 4·77 to 1
Tyres:

Clement-Talbot   See Talbot.   England

Clyno   England

Although the design of the Clyno was undistinguished it is not generally
known that it pioneered among small cars two important features—namely,
four-wheel brakes and large section tyres.

Having supplied the British Army during the war with twin-cylinder
motor-cycle combinations, Clyno produced its first car in 1922 with a Coventry
Simplex side-valve engine. This model was the basis of Clyno's effort throughout the vintage period and proved reliable, comparing favourably with the
contemporary Morris 'Cowley'. The sheer weight of the Morris organization
however eventually put it out of production.

In the last year of its life there was a 9 hp model which to the layman is
practically indistinguishable from its mysterious contemporary the Cluley.
As the Authors confess themselves to be amongst those unable to make this
fine distinction, the Cluley is not separately dealt with in this book.

Year: 1922
Maker's HP: 11
R.A.C. Rating: 10·8 hp
Number of Cylinders: 4
Bore and Stroke: 66 × 100 mm
Engine Capacity: 1·4 litres

Valves: side
Wheelbase: 8′ 6″
Forward Speeds: 3
Final Drive Ratio: 4·2 to 1
Tyres: 710 × 85

Year: 1928
Maker's HP: 9
R.A.C. Rating: 8·3 hp
Number of Cylinders: 4
Bore and Stroke: 58 × 90 mm
Engine Capacity: 1 litre

Valves: side
Wheelbase: 7' 3"
Forward Speeds: 3
Final Drive Ratio: 5·5 to 1
Tyres: 27 × 4

Cord

America

The Cord is one of the most outstanding cars to have come from America. It was by far the largest front-wheel-driven car to get into serious production, and although its transmission arrangements were not without drawbacks (notably a tendency to crack and eventually abandon its front wheels) they were on the whole successful.

The only model made in vintage years was the 'L.29' produced between 1929 and 1932. The engine was an eight-cylinder side-valve 'Lycoming' unit of 4934 cc turned back to front, with a three-speed gearbox placed between it and the differential. The front suspension was reminiscent of the Miller racing car and based on the de Dion principle, the front axle was located by double elliptic springs and the front brakes were inboard.

There seems to be no doubt that the 'L.29' was the handsomest model of the Dusenberg-Cord-Auburn range but its performance was more questionable. The top speed was not more than 75–80 mph and the excessively long engine made for bad weight distribution. It is said however that the 'L.29' inspired André Citroën to his Traction Avant of 1933.

above 1930 Model L.29. The first Cord was designed by Carl van Ranst who had been associated with Miller's fwd racing cars, and it was manufactured at the Auburn works at Auburn, Indiana, where E. L. Cord was in charge
left 1926 10·8 hp Clyno. Front-wheel brakes became standard (instead of an 'optional extra' that year). Its price was identical with that of its great rival, the Morris 'Cowley', at £135 as a chassis and £162.10s. with tourer body

It is by the later model '810', with coffin-shaped bonnet, that Cord is remembered. Available with or without supercharger and with suction-electrically operated gearbox it could quickly reach speeds in excess of 100 mph.

Year: 1929	*Valves:* side
Maker's HP and R.A.C. Rating: 33·8 hp	*Wheelbase:* 10' or 11' 5"
	Forward Speeds: 3
Number of Cylinders: 8	*Final Drive Ratio:* 4·076 (or lower
Bore and Stroke: 82·5 × 114 mm	to choice) to 1
Engine Capacity: 4·9 litres	*Tyres:* 30 × 6·5

Cottin-Desgouttes   France

Cottin-Desgouttes made an extremely fine 10½-litre, chain-driven Edwardian which was not far off the Grand Prix class, and one survives in this country. For the vintage market they were less adventurous, but certainly qualified as sports cars, with a pushrod operated overhead-valve engine, and gained some success in the early Paris–Nice trials.

In 1926 the same engine appeared in the all-independently sprung *sans secousse* model.

In 1927 came the inevitable 6-cylinder, side-valve and ohv models (albeit larger than usual) which seems to have signed the death-warrant of so many makes at this time, including Cottin-Desgouttes.

'Harmony of outline in a 1922 model' to quote the contemporary *Autocar*: 4-cylinder, 3·2-litre tourer with 4-speed gearbox and cantilever rear springs

Year: 1924	*Valves:* overhead
Maker's HP: 12	*Wheelbase:* 10' 3"
R.A.C. Rating: 15·9 hp	*Forward Speeds:* 4
Number of Cylinders: 4	*Final Drive Ratio:* 3 to 1
Bore and Stroke: 80 × 130 mm	*Tyres:* 820 × 120
Engine Capacity: 2·6 litres	

Year: 1929
Model: 20 CV-SS
Maker's HP: 20
R.A.C. Rating: 26·9 hp
Number of Cylinders: 6
Bore and Stroke: 82 × 112 mm

Engine Capacity: 3·5 litres
Valves: overhead
Wheelbase: 11' 0"
Forward Speeds: 4
Final Drive Ratio: 4·75 to 1
Tyres: 33 × 6

Crossley   England

Crossley was a name to conjure with in the early vintage years, and having regard to this it is remarkable that so few have survived.

Before the war they had a very effective 'Shelsley' model, a 2½-litre side-valve, which had also run in the T.T. race; but, misguidedly this was not resumed after the hostilities, and Crossleys faced the brave new world with their 25/30, which went back to 1908, and had done valiant war service with the Royal Flying Corps. This model continued until 1926, and in the firm's commercial vehicles it went on for another ten years.

It was, however, fairly early supplemented by a somewhat smaller side-valve, 4-cylinder, still of extremely conservative power output of which a very small number still survives. It was a pleasant touring car still predominantly Edwardian in character, but from the maintenance standpoint it was designed for the owner-driver. In 1923 it was made the basis of the 20/70, with a power increase of nearly 50 per cent and again sometimes referred to as a 'Shelsley' model.

The final vintage effort was a 2-litre, ohv 6-cylinder model whose excellent engine was later used in the 16/80 Lagonda.

Crossley also had one or two curious little side-ventures, one of which was sponsoring the almost sub-utility American Willys-Overland. Another was building the remarkable Burney Streamlined Car which used a Crossley engine. Yet another was an attempt to build 'Brescia' Bugattis in this country; but the effort was too much for them.

1920 25/30 tourer. Proved as a staff car and as an ambulance among other applications, the 25/30 found favour with the Royal Family after the war, and was regularly used by King George V and the Prince of Wales

Year: 1919
Maker's HP: 25/30
R.A.C. Rating: 25·6 hp
Number of Cylinders: 4
Bore and Stroke: 4" × 5½"
Engine Capacity: 4·5 litres
Valves: side
Wheelbase: 11' 3"
Forward Speeds: 4
Final Drive Ratio: 4 to 1
Tyres: 920 × 120

In 1926 the old 25/30 was replaced by the new 18/50, seen here transporting the Duke of York (later King George VI), during an official visit to Portsmouth

Year: 1920
Maker's HP and R.A.C. Rating: 19·6 hp
Number of Cylinders: 4
Bore and Stroke: 90 × 150 mm
Engine Capacity: 3·7 litres
Valves: side
Wheelbase: 10' 4¼"
Forward Speeds: 4
Final Drive Ratio: 3·57 to 1
Tyres: 820 × 120

Year: 1923
Model: 20/70
All as 19·6 hp above but Final Drive Ratio: 3·33 to 1

Year: 1923
Maker's HP: 14
R.A.C. Rating: 15·6 hp
Number of Cylinders: 4
Bore and Stroke: 80 × 120 mm
Engine Capacity: 2·4 litres
Valves: side
Wheelbase: 9' 4⅜"
Forward Speeds: 3
Final Drive Ratio: 4 to 1
Tyres: 760 × 90

Year: 1926
Model: Sports
Maker's HP: 18/50
R.A.C. Rating: 17·7 hp
Number of Cylinders: 6
Bore and Stroke: 69 × 120 mm
Engine Capacity: 2·7 litres
Valves: overhead
Wheelbase: 10' 5"
Forward Speeds: 4
Final Drive Ratio: 4·5 to 1
Tyres: 820 × 120

Crown Magnetic   America

This was one of the brave attempts at electric transmission coupled, in this instance, with a very large petrol engine.

There seems to have been some silly idea that the thing was complicated, which the manufacturers hastened to dispel in the following explanatory memorandum:

'This system comprises two dynamo-electric machines, located between the prime mover and the drive-shaft of the vehicle, the first having its field mounted upon the crankshaft of the gas engine in the place of the usual flywheel and having its armature fixedly attached to the drive shaft, and a second dynamo-electric machine having its armature also fixedly attached to the drive-shaft and its field attached to the chassis frame of the vehicle and consequently stationary with respect to this armature. This relation of the machines must

The prototype car on test in 1921. It employed Entz electric transmission, to which Crown had acquired the rights. It was also used in the British Ensign car *q.v.*

be firmly grasped in order to arrive at a proper understanding of the system and much confusion results from neglecting the fact that both elements of the first machine are movable and that the current generated in this machine is therefore a function of the difference in speed of two moving elements, one connected to the gas engine prime mover and the other to the vehicle drive-shaft. It will be evident from consideration of this point that an increase in speed of the driveshaft, so that the ratio of the speed of the prime mover to the speed of the drive-shaft approaches unity, will cause a decrease in the amount of current generated in the first machine.' *See?*

Year: 1920
Maker's HP: 30
R.A.C. Rating: 38·5 hp
Number of Cylinders: 6
Bore and Stroke: 102 × 140 mm
Engine Capacity: 6·8 litres

Valves: overhead
Wheelbase: 11′ 10″
Forward Speeds: variable
Final Drive Ratio: (if any?)
Tyres: 895 × 135

Daimler   England

The English Daimler Company was founded in 1896 and re-formed in 1904.

In 1908 it pinned its faith in the Knight engine, with its two sleeve-valves per cylinder. It thus created a fashion which profoundly affected the European motor industry for the next twenty years.

That the sleeve-valve engine is remarkably silent in operation is true. It is also true that at high speeds it is singularly prone to seizure, which some other makers sought to avoid by excessive lubrication. Daimlers avoided the issue by making sure that their engines did not attain high speeds. Even so, however, the larger engines were far from silent at much over 1000 rpm, while if not warmed up very carefully the sleeve valves were prone to break away from the lugs by which they were driven. Owing to the immense amount of built-in friction, Knight engines were also very difficult to turn when cold.

Despite all these disadvantages, and the manifest superiority of the Rolls-Royce, both as to silence and performance, the Daimler prospered, doubtless greatly assisted by Royal patronage, and they persisted in sleeve valves throughout the vintage era. They also adhered resolutely to worm-drive for the back axle.

During this time they showed a startling degree of vacillation and in 1927 alone for example no less than twenty-two models were listed, varying from the pathetically underpowered 12 hp to the fabulous V-12. The following specifications can therefore do no more than point out the more important and basic models of the decade.

The handsome and originally functional finned radiator has been ingeniously retained under B.L.M.C. management.

Year: 1919
Maker's HP: 30
R.A.C. Rating: 30·1 hp
Number of Cylinders: 6
Bore and Stroke: 90 × 130 mm
Engine Capacity: 5 litres

Valves: sleeve
Wheelbase: 10' 8¼" or 11' 9½"
Forward Speeds: 4
Final Drive Ratio:
Tyres: 895 × 135

Year: 1919	*Valves:* sleeve
Maker's HP and R.A.C. Rating:	*Wheelbase:* 12' 2"
45 hp	*Forward Speeds:* 4
Number of Cylinders: 6	*Final Drive Ratio:*
Bore and Stroke: 110 × 130 mm	*Tyres:* 895 × 150
Engine Capacity: 7·5 litres	

Year: 1922	*Valves:* sleeve
Maker's HP: 20	*Wheelbase:* 11' 0"
R.A.C. Rating: 20·8 hp	*Forward Speeds:* 4
Number of Cylinders: 4	*Final Drive Ratio:*
Bore and Stroke: 90 × 130 mm	*Tyres:* 880 × 120
Engine Capacity: 3·3 litres	

Year: 1923	*Valves:* sleeve
Maker's HP: 12	*Wheelbase:* 9' 9$\frac{3}{8}$"
R.A.C. Rating: 12·9 hp	*Forward Speeds:* 4
Number of Cylinders: 6	*Final Drive Ratio:* 6·17 to 1
Bore and Stroke: 59 × 94 mm	*Tyres:* 765 × 105
Engine Capacity: 1·5 litres	

above 1928 35/120 hp short-chassis tourer
left 1920 30 hp. The earlier 6-cylinder Daimlers tended to a sluggish
performance brought about by a combination of feeble engine output for its
capacity and heavy, formal coachwork
below Royal Carriages in Buckingham Palace Mews, 1924

Year: 1927
Maker's HP: 50
R.A.C. Rating: 49·4 hp
Number of Cylinders: 12
Bore and Stroke: 81·5 × 114 mm
Engine Capacity: 7·2 litres

Valves: sleeve
Wheelbase: 12' 11½" or 13' 7"
Forward Speeds: 4
Final Drive Ratio: 4·38 to 1
Tyres: 37 × 7·3

Year: 1930
Maker's HP: 30
R.A.C. Rating: 31·4 hp
Number of Cylinders: 12
Bore and Stroke: 65 × 94 mm
Engine Capacity: 3·7 litres

Valves: sleeve
Wheelbase: 12' 1½"
Forward Speeds: 4
Final Drive Ratio: 5 to 1
Tyres: 32 × 6

Darracq   France

What with Darracq, Talbot-Darracq, Clement-Talbot, and two lots of Talbot, one pronounced in French and one in English; and not to mention Talbots (in French) suddenly turning up as Sunbeams (in English) it is all a very confusing business.

Plain Darracq goes back to 1897 and had early racing successes in the *voiture légère* and *voiturette* classes where they finally managed to cram an engine of nearly 6-litres capacity into a machine weighing only 13 cwt. In the production range, the 1904, 4-cylinder 'Flying Fifteen' was one of the outstanding cars of its time, and in the 1950's, one of them put up averages across Europe of which no modern car need feel ashamed.

In 1906 a V-8, 200 hp Darracq achieved 112 mph and in 1907 and 1908 Darracqs competed with fair success in the T.T. races. In 1912–13 the Company had a mild attack of sleeve valves from which, however, they recovered quite quickly.

In the early vintage period a V-8 seems to have been the only model which appeared impartially as Darracq and Talbot-Darracq but in 1929–30 they were again in mutual production.

These strongly built, fast touring cars achieved deserved popularity, the 12/32 having a considerable following in this country.

Year: 1920
Maker's HP: 20
R.A.C. Rating: 27·8 hp
Number of Cylinders: 8
Bore and Stroke: 75 × 130 mm
Engine Capacity: 4·6 litres

Valves: side
Wheelbase: 11' 6"
Forward Speeds: 4
Final Drive Ratio: 3·85 to 1
Tyres: 835 × 135

1920 V-8. This model was known as the Type A, and its 4·6-litre engine developed 60 bhp

Year: 1927	*Engine Capacity:* 1·7 litres
Model: DD	*Valves:* overhead
Maker's HP: 12/40	*Wheelbase:* 10' 3"
R.A.C. Rating: 11·9 hp	*Forward Speeds:* 4
Number of Cylinders: 4	*Final Drive Ratio:* 5·1 to 1
Bore and Stroke: 69·5 × 110 mm	*Tyres:* 765 × 105

Year: 1929	*Engine Capacity:* 2 litres
Model: M.67	*Valves:* overhead
Maker's HP: 16	*Wheelbase:* 10' 7"
R.A.C. Rating: 16·7 hp	*Forward Speeds:* 4
Number of Cylinders: 6	*Final Drive Ratio:* 5·7 to 1
Bore and Stroke: 67 × 94·5 mm	*Tyres:* 32 × 6

Year: 1930	*Engine Capacity:* 3·8 litres
Model: H.78	*Valves:* overhead
Maker's HP: 30	*Wheelbase:* 10' 11½" or 11' 11"
R.A.C. Rating: 30·1 hp	*Forward Speeds:* 4
Number of Cylinders: 8	*Final Drive Ratio:* 4·82 to 1
Bore and Stroke: 78 × 100 mm	*Tyres:* 32 × 6

De Dion Bouton   France

The de Dion Bouton Company goes back to 1882 when the Comte de Dion was producing a variety of steam vehicles ranging from a bicycle in 1880 to a 30 hp, 20-seat omnibus in 1895.

At the end of the century the Count entered into partnership with M. Bouton who had designed the extremely efficient 3½ hp single-cylinder petrol engine. This was so successful that 2,000 cars had been made by 1902, during which year the 3½ hp had evolved into the 8 hp, type K, and by 1907 4-cylinder models were being made. The de Dion back axle had been abandoned to await its revival in Grand Prix circles in 1937.

In 1909 de Dion Bouton made the first production 8-cylinder car. This model was available in a variety of sizes ranging from 25 hp to 50 hp.

After the war the V-8 was retained in company with the 12/14 and 18/20 models. They were all extremely distinguished cars with 'V'-shaped radiators, and some had wire wheels, being available with almost every known type of coachwork. In 1923 the V-8's were discontinued and two overhead-valve models introduced—the 12/28 and 15/43. They were available with four-wheel brakes, but had low compression ratios limiting the performance to no more than average.

In 1924 the directors sought to draw attention to the 12/28 by racing an example in 2-seater form at Brooklands, engaging Dr Benjafield to drive it. This venture was unsuccessful as at 2300 rpm the exhaust valves burnt out, the best lap speed attained being at 73·2 mph.

At this point the Company began to sink into obscurity mainly due to competition from Talbot and Bentley, and finally succumbed at the end of the vintage period.

Year: 1920	*Valves:* side
Maker's HP: 12/14	*Wheelbase:* 9' 6"
R.A.C. Rating: 12·1 hp	*Forward Speeds:* 4
Number of Cylinders: 4	*Final Drive Ratio:* 4·1 to 1
Bore and Stroke: 70 × 120 mm	*Tyres:* 760 × 90
Engine Capacity: 1·8 litres	

Year: 1920	*Valves:* side
Maker's HP: 18/20	*Wheelbase:* 10' 6"
R.A.C. Rating: 20·2 hp	*Forward Speeds:* 4
Number of Cylinders: 8	*Final Drive Ratio:*
Bore and Stroke: 65 × 100 mm	*Tyres:* 815 × 105
Engine Capacity: 2·6 litres	

1922 IE-type 12/14, 1·8-litre, 4-cylinder tourer. One of the great *marques* of the Veteran and Edwardian periods, De Dion Bouton declined rapidly in the 1920s because of their refusal to up-date their designs. The Company finally succumbed in 1932

Year: 1920
Maker's HP: 25
R.A.C. Rating: 24·3 hp
Number of Cylinders: 8
Bore and Stroke: 70 × 120 mm
Engine Capacity: 3·6 litres

Valves: side
Wheelbase: 11' 2"
Forward Speeds: 4
Final Drive Ratio:
Tyres: 880 × 120

Year: 1924
Maker's HP: 22/60
R.A.C. Rating: 22·4 hp
Number of Cylinders: 4
Bore and Stroke: 95 × 140 mm
Engine Capacity: 4 litres

Valves: overhead
Wheelbase: 11' 9"
Forward Speeds: 4
Final Drive Ratio: 4·4 to 1
Tyres: 895 × 135

Year: 1924
Maker's HP: 15/43
R.A.C. Rating: 15 hp
Number of Cylinders: 4
Bore and Stroke: 78 × 130 mm
Engine Capacity: 2·5 litres

Valves: overhead
Wheelbase: 11' 2½"
Forward Speeds: 4
Final Drive Ratio: 4·2 to 1
Tyres: 805 × 105

Year: 1924
Maker's HP: 12/28
R.A.C. Rating: 12·1 hp
Number of Cylinders: 4
Bore and Stroke: 70 × 120 mm
Engine Capacity: 1·8 litres

Valves: overhead
Wheelbase: 10' 2"
Forward Speeds: 4
Final Drive Ratio: 4·4 to 1
Tyres: 765 × 105

Deemster

England

The Wilkinson Touring Motor Cycle Company, an offshoot of the Wilkinson Sword & Tool Making Company, made a light car called the Wilkinson in 1912. In 1914 they sold the manufacturing rights to the Ogston Motor Company of Acton who produced the car under the name of 'Deemster', its

1923 12 hp model taking part in the Vintage Sports Car Club 21st Anniversary Rally at Goodwood, 1955

trade mark being a smug-looking black-cat. Although production ceased in 1924 the company marketed a smart small car with shallow-V radiator and also a rakish sports model. Later, Anzani engines were used and a tuned model ran at Brooklands and in the 1921 200-mile race.

A solitary Anzani-engined model is known to exist.

Year: 1923	*Valves:* side
Maker's HP: 12	*Wheelbase:* 8′ 0″ or 9′ 3″
R.A.C. Rating: 11·9 hp	*Forward Speeds:* 3
Number of Cylinders: 4	*Final Drive Ratio:* 4·5 to 1
Bore and Stroke: 69 × 100 mm	*Tyres:* 710 × 90
Engine Capacity: 1·5 litres	

Delage   France

Delage started with a single-cylinder model in 1906 and in 1909 came a very beautiful 11 hp car with monobloc 4-cylinder engine. M. Delage had also produced some interesting machines for the *Coupe de l'Auto* and Grand Prix races. These were uniformly bedevilled by his unusual ideas about valves and their operation.

V-12 2-litre Grand Prix cars at the 1926 Targa Florio. Albert Divo is in No. 12, with Count Masetti, who was killed in the race, behind the tail

After 1918 Delage was one of the earliest makers to standardize four-wheel brakes and as these were available in conjunction with a soundly designed chassis, and engine of great refinement and considerable power output, the vintage Delage was a very desirable property. Undoubtedly the most famous and popular models were those with the 4-cylinder, pushrod ohv, 2·1-litre engine. These originated with the 72 × 130 mm, side-valve engine of 1921 which was later decreased to 75 × 120 mm and in 1924 acquired overhead-valves, as the model DI. The DIS, with larger valves, followed in 1925, and the DISS in

1926; but in 1927 the DISS was abandoned again in favour of the DIS, with a closer-ratio gearbox.

Like so many French cars of this age and size, the various manifestations of DI (there was really very little to choose between them as to performance) were somewhat sluggish in acceleration but made up for this by a remarkably high maximum and cruising speed, and excellent steering and road holding. The only really weak point of the DI models was the plate clutch, which was inclined to slip.

The 6-litre GL model, introduced in 1924, had a single overhead camshaft, but in 'Grand Sport' form it had two overhead camshafts and gave 184 bhp.

In 1927 M. Delage went back to 6-cylinders with the 3-litre DM and DMS; and in 1930 he offered the 4-litre, 8-cylinder D8.

Meanwhile, the firm had not been idle in the Grand Prix field. In 1923 they made a 2-litre V-12 of unprecedented complexity, with bore and stroke $51 \cdot 3 \times 80$ mm. Each bank had two overhead camshafts and the whole engine was constructed with ball and roller bearings. In unblown form it developed 120 bhp at 6000 rpm, and in 1924, when supercharged, it achieved 195 bhp at 7000 rpm, and was the Champion of Europe. One of these survives. Another racing V-12 Delage which survives is the $10\frac{1}{2}$-litre which took the world speed record in 1923 at 143 mph and also had a successful sprint and Brooklands career.

In 1926 came the even more successful $1\frac{1}{2}$-litre, straight eight Grand Prix car, of equal complication, with bore and stroke $55 \cdot 8 \times 76$ mm. This was even more efficient, and developed 170 bhp at the then unprecedented speed of 8000 rpm. In 1927 it carried all before it, and even ten years later, Richard Seaman, with one car only, swept the $1\frac{1}{2}$-litre class, winning three major races running, without the engine being touched.

Manufacturers are seldom equally successful with touring and racing cars, but in both these fields, the vintage Delage had few rivals, if any.

Year: 1919	*Valves:* side
Maker's HP: 24	*Wheelbase:* 11′ 3″
R.A.C. Rating: 23·8 hp	*Forward Speeds:* 4
Number of Cylinders: 6	*Final Drive Ratio:*
Bore and Stroke: 80 × 150 mm	·*Tyres:* 895 × 135
Engine Capacity: 4·5 litres	

Year: 1922	*Valves:* side
Maker's HP: 11	*Wheelbase:* 9′ 10″
R.A.C. Rating: 12·8 hp	*Forward Speeds:* 4
Number of Cylinders: 4	*Final Drive Ratio:* 4·1 or 4·9 to 1
Bore and Stroke: 72 × 130 mm	*Tyres:* 765 × 105
·*Engine Capacity:* 2·1 litres	

Year: 1922
Maker's HP: 15
R.A.C. Rating: 15·9 hp
Number of Cylinders: 4
Bore and Stroke: 80 × 150 mm
Engine Capacity: 3 litres
Valves: side
Wheelbase: 10' 5"
Forward Speeds: 4
Final Drive Ratio: 3·7 to 1
Tyres: 895 × 135

Year: 1924
Model: GL
Maker's HP: 40/50
R.A.C. Rating: 33·5 hp
Number of Cylinders: 6
Bore and Stroke: 95 × 140 mm

Engine Capacity: 6 litres
Valves: overhead
Wheelbase: 12' 10"
Forward Speeds: 4
Final Drive Ratio:
Tyres: 895 × 135

Year: 1924
Models: DI, DIS, DISS
Maker's HP: 14
R.A.C. Rating: 13·9 hp
Number of Cylinders: 4
Bore and Stroke: 75 × 120 mm
Engine Capacity: 2·2 litres

Valves: overhead
Wheelbase: 9' 10" or 10' 6"
Forward Speeds: 4
Final Drive Ratio: 4·08 or 4·45 or
4·8 to 1
Tyres: 820 × 120

Year: 1927
Model: DMS
Maker's HP: 21
R.A.C. Rating: 20·9 hp
Number of Cylinders: 6
Bore and Stroke: 75 × 120 mm

Engine Capacity: 3·1 litres
Valves: overhead
Wheelbase: 10' 7"
Forward Speeds: 4
Final Drive Ratio:
Tyres: 21 × 4½

above 1926 DISS—a short-chassis version of the DI with a close-ratio gearbox

left 1929 DM 3-litre with body by Felber of Paris

Year: 1930
Model: D8
Maker's HP: 30
R.A.C. Rating: 29·4 hp
Number of Cylinders: 8
Bore and Stroke: 77 × 109 mm
Engine Capacity: 4 litres
Valves: overhead
Wheelbase: 10′ 10″ or 11′ 11″
Forward Speeds: 4
Final Drive Ratio: 3·9 to 1
Tyres: 7 × 18

1½-litre straight eight: Malcolm
Campbell winning the 1928 Boulogne
Grand Prix

Delahaye   France

Delahaye was one of the select band who set up in the nineteenth century.
Throughout the Edwardian and vintage eras the Company concentrated on
refined and well-made touring cars. It was not until 1936 that Delahaye had
the bright idea of building a sports car round a slightly developed form of their
3½-litre, pushrod ohv, lorry engine. These simple and robust cars were
immensely successful and are among the best of what are now called 'Post-
Vintage Thoroughbreds'.

All vintage models were based on the 1922 programme.

Year: 1919
Maker's HP: 14/18
R.A.C. Rating: 15·9 hp
Number of Cylinders: 4
Bore and Stroke: 80 × 130 mm
Engine Capacity: 2·6 litres

Valves: side
Wheelbase: 10′ 6″
Forward Speeds: 4
Final Drive Ratio:
Tyres: 820 × 120

Year: 1922
Maker's HP: 10/12
R.A.C. Rating: 12·1 hp
Number of Cylinders: 4
Bore and Stroke: 70 × 120 mm
Engine Capacity: 1·8 litres
Valves: side
Wheelbase: 9′ 9″
Forward Speeds: 4
Final Drive Ratio:
Tyres: 765 × 105

1929 16CV straight eight with a
1902 De Dion Bouton

Year: 1922
Maker's HP: 20/30
R.A.C. Rating: 26·9 hp
Number of Cylinders: 6
Bore and Stroke: 85 × 130 mm
Engine Capacity: 4·5 litres

Valves: side
Wheelbase: 12' 0"
Forward Speeds: 4
Final Drive Ratio: 3·8 to 1
Tyres: 895 × 135

Delaunay-Belleville   France

The Edwardian Delaunay-Belleville was one of the most splendid cars of its day—beautifully made, extremely refined, and in appearance as aristocratic as its name.

The circular radiator of the Edwardians was continued in vintage days, but with the sharp edges rounded off, which just took off the real beauty of the thing. In fact, although it tried to keep pace with the march of time with a 2-litre overhead camshaft model, this fine old firm remained Edwardian at heart. Good as their vintage cars were, they could not, in the end, compete with their more progressive competitors.

In a report of 1920 we are told that 'The late Tsar had in his garage many Delaunay-Bellevilles, two of which, fitted with dual control and constructed specially regardless of cost, are now used by MM. Lenin and Trotsky'.

Year: 1919
Maker's HP: 20
R.A.C. Rating: 22·6 hp
Number of Cylinders: 6
Bore and Stroke: 78 × 140 mm
Engine Capacity: 4 litres

Valves: side
Wheelbase: 11' 0"
Forward Speeds: 4
Final Drive Ratio: 4·1 to 1
Tyres: 880 × 120

Year: 1919
Maker's HP: 25
R.A.C. Rating: 24·8 hp
Number of Cylinders: 4
Bore and Stroke: 100 × 140 mm
Engine Capacity: 4·4 litres

Valves: side
Wheelbase: 11' 0½"
Forward Speeds: 4
Final Drive Ratio: 3·8 to 1
Tyres: 880 × 120

Year: 1919
Maker's HP: 40/50
R.A.C. Rating: 39·8 hp
Number of Cylinders: 6
Bore and Stroke: 103 × 160 mm
Engine Capacity: 7·8 litres

Valves: side
Wheelbase: 12' 2"
Forward Speeds: 4
Final Drive Ratio: 3·6 to 1
Tyres: 935 × 135

Year: 1922
Maker's HP: 12
R.A.C. Rating: 12·8 hp
Number of Cylinders: 4
Bore and Stroke: 72 × 120 mm
Engine Capacity: 1·8 litres
Valves: side
Wheelbase: 10' 0"
Forward Speeds: 4
Final Drive Ratio: 4·4 to 1
Tyres: 765 × 105

1924 2·6-litre P4B 12CV coupé, with single ohc engine

D.F.P. France

The Societé Anonyme des Automobiles Doriot, Flandrin et Parant is perhaps mostly remembered by the reflected glory of W. O. Bentley's association with the firm, whose English representative he was in the just pre-1914 days. He has told in his autobiography how surprised Messrs Doriot, Flandrin & Parant were at the speeds he extracted from their machines, and it was at Bentley's instigation that in 1913 their cars became the first in the world to contain aluminium pistons.

They had not much new to say after 1918 and did not last very far into the vintage decade. The 12/40 was really the W. O. Bentley edition of the Edwardian 12/15.

Year: 1919
Maker's HP: 12/40
R.A.C. Rating: 12·1 hp
Number of Cylinders: 4
Bore and Stroke: 70 × 130 mm
Engine Capacity: 2 litres

Valves: side
Wheelbase: 9' 7½"
Forward Speeds: 4
Final Drive Ratio: 4·25 to 1
Tyres: 765 × 105

1923 12/40 tourer. The company stopped production in 1926

Year: 1922
Maker's HP: 10/12
R.A.C. Rating: 10·4 hp
Number of Cylinders: 4
Bore and Stroke: 65 × 120 mm
Engine Capacity: 1·6 litres

Valves: side
Wheelbase: 9′ 2″
Forward Speeds: 3
Final Drive Ratio: 4·45 to 1
Tyres: 760 × 90

Diatto

Italy

The Societa Anonima Autocostruzioni Diatto was founded in 1902. Its most popular model in Edwardian times was the 15·9 hp 4-cylinder model. In 1920 the Company was under the control of the Gnome and the Rhone aviation group. During the 1923–24 period the Maserati brothers experimented with the 2-litre overhead camshaft model to such an extent that it competed fairly successfully in several of the Grands Prix of the time, eventually evolving into the Maserati car in 1926.

1924 2-litre tourer. Diatto were well-known as coachbuilders before they turned to manufacturing cars. They lasted until 1930

Year: 1920
Maker's HP: 10
R.A.C. Rating: 8·9 hp
Number of Cylinders: 4
Bore and Stroke: 60 × 90 mm
Engine Capacity: 1 litre

Valves: side
Wheelbase: 7′ 11″
Forward Speeds: 3
Final Drive Ratio: 4·46 to 1
Tyres: 700 × 85

Year: 1921
Model: 4.D.C.
Maker's HP: 20
R.A.C. Rating: 17·8 hp
Number of Cylinders: 4
Bore and Stroke: 85 × 120 mm

Engine Capacity: 2·1 litres
Valves: overhead
Wheelbase: 9′ 10″
Forward Speeds: 4
Final Drive Ratio: 4·16 to 1
Tyres: 820 × 120

Year: 1922
Model: '25'
Maker's HP: 15
R.A.C. Rating: 15·9 hp
Number of Cylinders: 4
Bore and Stroke: 80 × 100 mm

Engine Capacity: 2 litres
Valves: overhead
Wheelbase: 9' 10"
Forward Speeds: 4
Final Drive Ratio: 4·16 to 1
Tyres: 820 × 120

Year: 1925
Model: '20.SS'
Maker's HP and R.A.C. Rating:
15·5 hp
Number of Cylinders: 4
Bore and Stroke: 79·7 × 100 mm

Engine Capacity: 2 litres
Valves: overhead
Wheelbase: 8' 10"
Forward Speeds: 4
Final Drive Ratio: 4·16 to 1
Tyres: 820 × 120

Dodge
America

Year: 1920
Maker's HP: 17/24
R.A.C. Rating: 24 hp
Number of Cylinders: 4
Bore and Stroke: $3\frac{7}{8}'' \times 4\frac{1}{2}''$
Engine Capacity: 3·4 litres

Valves: side
Wheelbase: 9' 6"
Forward Speeds: 3
Final Drive Ratio: 4·16 to 1
Tyres: 32 × 3½

Year: 1928
Model: 'Senior Six'
Maker's HP: 20/35
R.A.C. Rating: 25·35 hp
Number of Cylinders: 6
Bore and Stroke: $3\frac{1}{4}'' \times 4\frac{1}{2}''$

Engine Capacity: 3·6 litres
Valves: side
Wheelbase: 9' 8"
Forward Speeds: 3
Final Drive Ratio: 4·75 to 1
Tyres: 32 × 6

1929/30 'Standard 6'. The company became part of the Chrysler Corporation in 1928

Donnet Zedel　　　　　　　　　　　　　France

Prior to 1925 known as Zedel, q.v.

1926 14/40. In 1929 the company joined forces with Delahaye, Unic and
Chenard-Walcker, but still it only lasted until 1933

Year: 1925
Maker's HP: 10/20
R.A.C. Rating: 9·5 hp
Number of Cylinders: 4
Bore and Stroke: 62 × 91 mm
Engine Capacity: 1·1 litres

Valves: side
Wheelbase: 8′ 6″
Forward Speeds: 4
Final Drive Ratio: 5 to 1
Tyres: 715 × 115

Year: 1925
Maker's HP: 14/40
R.A.C. Rating: 13·9 hp
Number of Cylinders: 4
Bore and Stroke: 75 × 120 mm
Engine Capacity: 2·1 litres

Valves: side
Wheelbase: 9′ 7½″
Forward Speeds: 4
Final Drive Ratio: 4 to 1
Tyres: 765 × 105

Year: 1927
Maker's HP: 18/60
R.A.C. Rating: 18·2 hp
Number of Cylinders: 6
Bore and Stroke: 70 × 110 mm
Engine Capacity: 2·5 litres

Valves: side
Wheelbase: 10′ 6″
Forward Speeds: 4
Final Drive Ratio: 4·4 to 1
Tyres: 775 × 145

Douglas　　　　　　　　　　　　　England

Originally devoted to the manufacture of bootmaking appliances, the
Douglas Company turned before 1914 to motor-cycles. They produced 25,000
of the famous horizontally opposed twin, and also a 10·5 hp, horizontally

opposed, water-cooled engine which was used as a generator for mobile wireless transmitters. This engine was subsequently installed in a light car which was current from 1920 to 1922. The gearbox was in unit construction and there were helical coil springs for the back wheels.

The Company continued to market a horizontally-opposed twin until 1957, but with the engine set across the frame, instead of in line with it, as in the original model.

Year: 1920
Maker's HP and R.A.C. Rating:
10·5 hp
Number of Cylinders: 2
Bore and Stroke: 92 × 92 mm
Engine Capacity: 1·2 litres
Valves: side
Wheelbase: 8′ 0″
Forward Speeds: 3
Final Drive Ratio: 4·6 to 1
Tyres: 700 × 80

1919 2-seater coupé. The Vintage model was 200 lb heavier than the 1070 cc pre-war car

Duesenberg   America

F. S. Duesenberg made Bugatti aero-engines under licence in the 1914 war and in 1921 he won the Grand Prix with a 3-litre straight eight. This car had a single overhead camshaft operating three valves per cylinder, but opposite to Bugatti practice, there were one inlet and two exhaust. The brakes were truly hydraulic, being operated by water. Duesenberg later developed the Grand Prix car into a production model of 4·3 litres, and from this in turn he evolved the far more famous Model J.

1930 Model J. The chassis price was $8,500—or £1,750 (1930), which increased to about £4,000 for a coachbuilt saloon

This was intended to give the maximum in the way of performance, luxury, and owner drivability and certainly the specification covered all these aims.

While one has learnt to be somewhat sceptical about the capabilities of American horses, both now as then, the Model J must nevertheless have produced a fair proportion of its claimed 265, since one was allegedly timed at 129 mph; and was said to accelerate from 0 to 100 mph in twenty seconds. When fitted with a centrifugal supercharger, and known as the 'SJ', no less than 320 bhp was claimed.

The engine was of excellent design. The cylinders and top half of the crankcase were cast integral and the two camshafts were mounted in a separate head. The whole engine was stove-enamelled green and was rubber mounted.

The chassis was made extremely deep and copiously cross braced, but in view of the flexible engine mounting the resulting rigidity could not be carried through to the front part of the car where it is most needed.

There was a three-speed gearbox with a silent second on which over 100 m.p.h. was claimed for the blown car.

The brakes were hydraulic.

Yet the car failed to catch on. Perhaps the American market was not yet discerning enough to pay the high price of such high quality, while European purchasers would be put off by the uncompromisingly brash appearance of the machine. It seems doubtful, anyway, if it was quite as good as it set out to be.

Year: 1928	*Engine Capacity:* 6·8 litres
Models: J and SJ (supercharged)	*Valves:* overhead
Maker's HP: 45/265	*Wheelbase:* 11' 10½″
R.A.C. Rating: 44·9 hp	*Forward Speeds:* 3
Number of Cylinders: 8	*Final Drive Ratio:* 3·5 to 1
Bore and Stroke: 95 × 121 mm	*Tyres:* 700 × 19

Duplex   England

If the Duplex had a short life it was at least of considerable technical interest, as it had eight very small cylinders arranged in pairs, with a siamesed head

A contemporary catalogue illustration of 1920

carrying a communal sparking plug. One cylinder of each pair carried the inlet sleeve valve and the other contained the exhaust sleeve valve. With a total capacity of only 1·5 litres the then (1920) quite considerable output of 33 bhp was claimed at 3000 rpm. It was in production only for the years 1920 and 1921.

Year: 1920
Maker's HP: 10
R.A.C. Rating: 10·5 hp
Number of Cylinders: 8
Bore and Stroke: 56 × 75 mm
Engine Capacity: 1·5 litres

Valves: sleeve
Wheelbase: 8' 10"
Forward Speeds: 3
Final Drive Ratio:
Tyres: 710 × 90

DuPont   America

The DuPont was made from 1920 to 1932.

The 1920 model was a 4-cylinder, and there was a 6-cylinder model from 1923 to 1927. Then came the most famous DuPont; the straight eight, Model G. This was one of America's nearest attempts at a vintage sports car, with its

above 1927 26/80 with 6-cylinder 'Wisconsin' engine and Lockheed hydraulic brakes on all four wheels
below 1929 Model G 'Speedster', with 'Continental' engine giving 114 bhp thus making the Model G America's third most powerful car at that time after the Duesenberg and the blown Stutz

large engine, and the option of a quite close-ratio four-speed gearbox. About 700 of this type were made, of which about twenty-three survive in America, but none is known of in England.

The Model G was raced at Indianapolis in 1930, qualifying at 89 mph lap-speed, and in 1929 one ran at Le Mans but had to retire when the required ballast broke loose, fell through the floor, hit the propeller shaft and cracked the gearbox casing.

Year: 1923	*Valves:* overhead
Maker's HP: 26/80	*Wheelbase:* 10′ 5″
R.A.C. Rating: 26·9 hp	*Forward Speeds:* 3 or 4
Number of Cylinders: 6	*Final Drive Ratio:* 4·75 to 1
Bore and Stroke: $3\frac{3}{8}'' \times 5''$	*Tyres:* 32×6
Engine Capacity: 4·3 litres	

Year: 1928	*Engine Capacity:* 5·2 litres
Model: G.	*Valves:* side
Maker's HP and R.A.C. Rating:	*Wheelbase:* 10′ 5″ or 12′ 6″
36·45 hp	*Forward Speeds:* 3 or 4
Number of Cylinders: 8	*Final Drive Ratio:* 3·75 or 4·25 to 1
Bore and Stroke: $3\frac{3}{8}'' \times 4\frac{1}{2}''$	*Tyres:* $32 \times 6·50$

Enfield-Allday   England

Enfield-Allday's chief claim to fame is that during the early vintage years they were designed by A. C. Bertelli, later of Aston Martin fame. Indeed, the Renwick and Bertelli car—the prototype of the 'International' Aston Martin —bore a marked resemblance to the contemporary Enfield-Allday.

The typical Enfield-Allday is a 10 hp side-valve light car, though of a rather more robust variety than many of its kin. An enlarged version ran in the voiturette class of the 1922 Tourist Trophy race, but without success.

In 1921, however, the Company distinguished itself by threatening to produce an exceptionally unconventional design, best described in the words of its maker's specification:

"The 5-cylinder radial engine of 63×80 mm cylinder dimensions has a capacity of 1·4 litres. The valves are the super-imposed, hollow mushroom slide-poppet type. The three-speed gearbox drives through a multi-disc clutch. The frame is delta-shaped and made of small diameter tubular members. The wheelbase is 8′ 9″ and tyres are 810×90 mm. Cantilever springs are used all round. The adjustable steering column has a hinged handwheel. The brakes are of the expanding ring type together with a fabric covered cone running brake."

A head-on view of the chassis and engine of the 1919 radial-engined two-seater

The more conventional product of the Company was the 10/20 light car, shown here as a three-seater sports-tourer

Year: 1921
Maker's HP: 10/20
R.A.C. Rating: 10 hp
Number of Cylinders: 4
Bore and Stroke: 63·5 × 117·5 mm
Engine Capacity: 1·5 litres

Valves: side
Wheelbase: 9' 0"
Forward Speeds: 3
Final Drive Ratio: 4·75 to 1
Tyres: 30 × 3½

Ensign

England

After producing an indifferent selection of motor-cars for a short time before the war, the post-war programme of the British Ensign Motor Company of Willesden came as an unexpected surprise. The Company misguidedly decided to compete in the luxury class and in 1920 produced a 6-cylinder car of 7-litres capacity. It had, however, an extremely advanced specification and deserved greater popularity and financial backing than it gained.

The engine, according to the best war-time aeroplane practice had 6

The 1919 38·4 hp, 6-cylinder—before the advent of Entz magnetic transmission. (*See* Crown Magnetic)

cylinders, cast in pairs, the overhead 'tulip' valves operated by a single camshaft driven by a vertical shaft. The crankshaft was supported on seven pressure lubricated bearings, everything on the engine was of polished aluminium and apparently bore an outward resemblance to the later Mercedes models.

The performance was well up to the standard of its contemporaries, as it lapped Brooklands in standard form at 80 mph consistently for five or six hours. In 1920, however, in the face of an impending financial crisis, the Company was taken over by Harry Crown and the remaining chassis were installed with his electric transmission and renamed the 'Crown Ensign'.

But by far the most interesting development of the Company was the 'V-12' —two banks of the 6-cylinder on a common crankcase. This project was designed to develop 250 hp at 2000 rpm; but unfortunately it did not even reach prototype stage.

Year: 1920
Maker's HP and R.A.C. Rating:
38·4 hp
Number of Cylinders: 6
Bore and Stroke: 101·6 × 139·7 mm
Engine Capacity: 7 litres

Valves: overhead
Wheelbase: 12' 4"
Forward Speeds: variable
Final Drive Ratio:
Tyres: 895 × 135

Eric Campbell   England

The Eric Campbell had considerable sporting qualities. The Coventry Simplex engine had high-lift cams and lightened reciprocating parts, and drilled, cast-iron pistons. It was also a good-looking little car, with its Rolls-Royce-like little radiator and light polished aluminium body. 23 bhp and upwards of 60 mph were claimed and the car certainly had some Brooklands successes.

1920 10 hp sporting 2-seater at Brooklands

However, the Company were in low water by 1924 when they were taken over by the Vulcan Iron Company.

Year: 1919	*Valves:* side
Maker's HP: 10	*Wheelbase:* 7' 3"
R.A.C. Rating: 10·8 hp	*Forward Speeds:* 3
Number of Cylinders: 4	*Final Drive Ratio:* 4·2 to 1
Bore and Stroke: 66 × 109·5 mm	*Tyres:* 710 × 90
Engine Capacity: 1·5 litres	

Essex   America

The Essex car never made any pretensions as to quality, but in the early vintage Model A managed to obtain a little more than usual performance from a slightly smaller engine than was customary in America. After 1923 Essex reverted to six cylinders and side-valves, including the popular but uninteresting 'Super-Six' introduced in 1928.

Year: 1919
Model: A
Maker's HP and R.A.C. Rating: 18·2 hp
Number of Cylinders: 4
Bore and Stroke: 85·7 × 127 mm
Engine Capacity: 2·9 litres
Valves: ioe
Wheelbase: 9' 0½"
Forward Speeds: 3
Final Drive Ratio: 4·6 to 1
Tyres: 815 × 105

4-cylinder tourer at Shelsley Walsh hill-climb in 1922

1929 'Super Six' 6-cylinder 'Speedabout' model with bodywork by Biddle & Smart, at $945 (£189) when new. This car is in the Harrah Collection at Reno, Nevada

Excelsior

Belgium

Not many cars have come out of Belgium, but such as have were almost uniformly of high quality. The Excelsior lived up to this high tradition. Before embarking on private car manufacture the Company made some formidable Grand Prix and *Coupe de l'Auto* racing cars between 1912 and 1914. In production form the first Excelsior consisted of a large refined side-valve machine, but in 1927 this engine acquired a shaft-driven overhead camshaft operating inclined valves, to which the mixture was supplied by the then very unusual number of three carburettors. In this form the Excelsior was good for 90 mph, and at any rate one specimen survives in this country. It is a most imposing machine and the craftsmanship is of a very high order.

The overhead camshaft model had considerable racing success and won the Belgian 24-hour touring car race.

Year: 1925	*Engine Capacity:* 5·4 litres
Model: C	*Valves:* side
Maker's HP: 35	*Wheelbase:* 11′ 10½″
R.A.C. Rating: 30·1 hp	*Forward Speeds:* 3
Number of Cylinders: 6	*Final Drive Ratio:* 3·75 to 1
Bore and Stroke: 90 × 140 mm	*Tyres:* 895 × 135

Year: 1928	*Forward Speeds:* 4
Model: 'Supersports'. As Model C but *Valves* overhead.	*Final Drive Ratio:* 3·75 to 1
Wheelbase: 10′ 10″	*Tyres:* 33 × 5

1921 30 hp tourer. The Company started making cars in 1902 and were taken over by Imperia in 1929

Farman

France

This superb chassis was made by the Farman brothers of early aviation fame. The aluminium block had cast-iron cylinder liners and a vertical shaft drove the overhead camshaft.

Rear springing was by short cantilever springs, and a transverse semi-elliptic, together with an anti-rolling device.

The model remained current throughout the vintage decade, the stroke later being increased to 150 mm, giving a capacity of 7 litres.

Year: 1920
Maker's HP: 40
R.A.C. Rating: 37·2 hp
Number of Cylinders: 6
Bore and Stroke: 100 × 140 mm
Engine Capacity: 6·6 litres
Valves: overhead
Wheelbase: 11′ 9″
Forward Speeds: 4
Final Drive Ratio: 3·25 to 1
Tyres: 895 × 135

1925 A6B 6·6-litre. The early examples were as fast as a Hispano-Suiza and had the advantage of a four-speed gearbox. The similar 7-litre model was called the NF

Fiat   Italy

Originally appearing as F.I.A.T., this famous firm has been known as Fiat since 1906.

In Edwardian days Fiat had a distinguished history of luxury touring cars and very advanced racing cars. When racing was still a matter of brute force, Fiats were about the first to make racing cars of handsome lines and fine finish, and as early as 1905 they matched these with such advanced features as inclined overhead valves. They were rewarded in 1907 when they swept the board in all the important races. In 1911 they won the G.P. de France (admittedly against slight opposition) with a 10½-litre overhead camshaft engine,

In 1922, 2-litre 6-cylinder Fiats driven by Felice Nazarro and Pietro Bordino won the French and Italian Grand Prix respectively

having four valves per cylinder, whose design may have owed a good deal to Ettore Bugatti. In 1914 the G.P. Fiats had two overhead camshafts and were among the few who pioneered front-wheel brakes for racing, but they were not to meet with further success in racing until 1922 when their 6-cylinder, 2-litre, twin ohc machines were the undisputed European champions. Fiat largely abandoned racing after 1924, though they had one win in 1927 with a supercharged 12-cylinder 1½-litre, and they also experimented with a 6-cylinder, supercharged, 1½-litre two-stroke, with two crankshafts and twelve opposed pistons. But it was never made to work satisfactorily.

Production Fiats during the twenties were predominantly economical

The Type 501S, manufactured between 1921 and 1926, is seen here with 'torpedo sport' bodywork

family outfits with few claims to high performance. Unfortunately there were also a great multiplicity of models, which cannot be traced comprehensively in the space available here.

Undoubtedly the most famous and successful was the 501, which was introduced in 1919 and continued in production until 1926. Like nearly all vintage Fiats, it was excessively low-geared to counteract its considerable weight and inconsiderable power output. But for those who are not in a hurry this was balanced by sound design, fine finish, good handling qualities and excellent reliability. The Fiat Register knows of thirty survivors in Great Britain.

Contemporary with the '501' were the '505', 4-cylinder, '15/20' and the '510', 6-cylinder, 20/30, of which the latter only is listed below, the bore and stroke being identical.

Although Fiat toyed with a luxury, 7-litre, V-12, their only serious effort at vintage luxury was the so-called 40 hp type 519 (which was, however, rated at 27 hp and developed 80 bhp).

In 1926 came the baby 7 hp, type 509, which also had considerable success despite a final drive ratio of 6·1 to 1.

In 1926 started a downward trend, typical of the late vintage years. The last of the handsome brass pear-shaped radiators gave way to an undistinguished flat-topped affair and most of the type-numbers had two added to them to signify a general cheapening. Simultaneously a new range of 6-cylinder, side-valve models was introduced with type numbers from 520 to 527, too complex to retail here; the '525' has been selected as typical to include in the following specifications. They were all quite worthy but uninteresting.

It was 1933 before Fiats recovered from this general lapse, with their Tipo 508S 'Balilla' model.

The 510S sports model had a shorter wheelbase than the 510, and 53 bhp against the latter's 46

Year: 1919. Type 501
Maker's HP: 10/15
R.A.C. Rating: 10·4 hp
Number of Cylinders: 4
Bore and Stroke: 65 × 110 mm
Engine Capacity: 1·5 litres
Valves: side
Wheelbase: 8' 8¼"
Forward Speeds: 4
Final Drive Ratio: 5·1 to 1
Tyres: 760 × 90

Year: 1921. Type 510.
Maker's HP: 20/30
R.A.C. Rating: 20·9 hp
Number of Cylinders: 6
Bore and Stroke: 75 × 130 mm
Engine Capacity: 3·4 litres
Valves: side
Wheelbase: 10' 2"
Forward Speeds: 4
Final Drive Ratio: 4·82 to 1
Tyres: 895 × 135
(Type 505, 15/20 hp, generally similar, but 4 cylinders)

The Type 519 saloon. This model was made from 1922 to 1927

Year: 1922. Type 519
Maker's HP: 40
R.A.C. Rating: 26·8 hp
Number of Cylinders: 6
Bore and Stroke: 85 × 140 mm
Engine Capacity: 4·8 litres

Valves: overhead
Wheelbase: 11′ 9¾″
Forward Speeds: 4
Final Drive Ratio: 4·08 to 1
Tyres: 895 × 135

Year: 1926. Type 509
Maker's HP: 7
R.A.C. Rating: 8 hp
Number of Cylinders: 4
Bore and Stroke: 57 × 97 mm
Engine Capacity: 1 litre

Valves: overhead
Wheelbase: 8′ 4⅜″
Forward Speeds: 3
Final Drive Ratio: 6·1 to 1
Tyres: 715 × 115

Year: 1927. Type 525
Maker's HP: 20/70
R.A.C. Rating: 25 hp
Number of Cylinders: 6
Bore and Stroke: 82 × 118 mm
Engine Capacity: 3·7 litres

Valves: side
Wheelbase: 10′ 8⅜″
Forward Speeds: 4
Final Drive Ratio: 4·7 to 1
Tyres: 32 × 6·75

Ford   America

The 'T' Model Ford had a run of nearly nineteen years, and while this is by no means a record, there is probably no other model which was in production so long, with so little modification.

Henry Ford made cars under various guises in the nineties and in 1902 came his world-speed-record '999', but the Ford Company as it is known today was not formed until 1903. The first models had a mid-chassis, horizontally opposed twin engine, but Ford also experimented with an air-cooled vertical four, and produced one splendid luxury car, the 6-cylinder, 6·6-litre Model K of 1906. With the rakish coachwork of the 'Gentleman's Speedster' it was one of the most imposing Edwardian cars. It had the extremely unusual firing order of 123654 which nevertheless works surprisingly well.

All Edwardian Fords had a two-speed epicyclic gearbox, but in 1906 came the Models N, R and S, which in most ways anticipated the famous 'T'. The latter was the first to be constructed by fully mass-production methods and it was on sale by the end of 1908. The aim was to produce a car 'combining the qualities of strength, lightness, power, speed and hill-climbing ability with those of endurance and economy of upkeep', and in this Henry Ford certainly succeeded. Although a power output of some 22 bhp from 2·9 litres may not seem excessive, it was more per litre than the contemporary Rolls-

Royce. With becoming modesty, Mr Ford remarked: 'There are excellent features in other cars, but better features or as high-grade materials as are used in the Model 'T' Ford cannot be found in any other car at any price. A better car is not and cannot be made.'

The specification comprised a splash-lubricated 4-cylinder engine with detachable head; ignition was by flywheel alternator, which supplied current to four separate trembler coils. The gearbox was two-speed epicyclic and suspension was by transverse leaf springs at front and rear.

In 1917 the handsome, flat-sided brass radiator gave way to 'the streamline hood, large radiator and enclosed fan, crown fenders, black finish and nickel trimmings'. In 1919 came electric lighting and starting.

The model continued until 1927, still with wooden-spoked wheels and still without front-wheel brakes. In all, 15,000,000 were made.

In 1928 it was followed by the 4-cylinder Model A, of either 2- or 3·2-litre capacity. These had a conventional three-speed gearbox, but it was not until the V-8 that Ford again produced a model of outstanding importance. The Model 'T' must be accounted as one of the great cars of motoring history.

above 1920 Model T. The Company sold no less than 15,007,003 'Tin Lizzies' in the 19 years of her production life . . .

. . . after which she was followed by the more conventional Model A in 1928 *(below)*

Year: 1908
Model: T
Maker's HP: 20
R.A.C. Rating: 22·4 hp
Number of Cylinders: 4
Bore and Stroke: $3\frac{3}{4}'' \times 4''$

Engine Capacity: 2·9 litres
Valves: side
Wheelbase: 8' 4"
Forward Speeds: 2
Final Drive Ratio: 3·64 to 1
Tyres: 760 × 90

Year: 1928
Model: A
Maker's HP and R.A.C. Rating:
24 hp
Number of Cylinders: 4
Bore and Stroke: $3\frac{7}{8}'' \times 4\frac{1}{4}''$

Engine Capacity: 3·2 litres
Valves: side
Wheelbase: 8' 4"
Forward Speeds: 3
Final Drive Ratio: 3·78 to 1
Tyres: 30 × 4·5

Year: 1928
Model: AF
Maker's HP and R.A.C. Rating:
14·9 hp
Number of Cylinders: 4
Bore and Stroke: 3·05" × 4·25"

Engine Capacity: 2 litres
Valves: side
Wheelbase: 8' 7½"
Forward Speeds: 3
Final Drive Ratio: 4·6 to 1
Tyres: 30 × 4·5

Franklin
America

The origin of the Franklin car can be traced to 1901 when a Mr J. Wilkinson built three air-cooled cars on which to test and develop a compressed air starting device. He was commissioned by Mr H. Franklin to design the Franklin car which appeared later in the year. This car had a 4-cylinder engine and the rear axle being located solely by its fully elliptical springs, the latter feature surviving until the mid-thirties.

In 1905 the first 6-cylinder Franklin was introduced with an air-cooled

1926 Series 11 coupé. Being light in weight thanks to its air-cooling, the Franklin was economical for its size on both fuel and tyres

engine. The air was conducted to the cylinders by means of flywheel fans which forced the air into jackets enclosing the individual cylinders encased in copper cooling fins. There was also a partition plate half-way up the cylinder jackets and, above, an airtight bonnet—the principle being for air from the fan to pass along the fins and down the cylinders.

In 1912 'individual recirculating pressure-fed lubrication' was adopted and in 1922 an ingenious device for centrifugally air cleansing the carburettor was adopted. Duralumin con-rods were another feature introduced by the Franklin Company. The 6-cylinder model continued throughout the vintage period culminating in the 1930 'Speedster'.

Year: 1928	*Valves:* overhead
Maker's HP: 26	*Wheelbase:* 9' 11"
R.A.C. Rating: 25·3 hp	*Forward Speeds:* 3
Number of Cylinders: 6	*Final Drive Ratio:* 4·73 to 1
Bore and Stroke: $3\frac{1}{4}'' \times 4\frac{3}{4}''$	*Tyres:* 32 × 6
Engine Capacity: 3·9 litres	

Year: 1930	*Engine Capacity:* 4·5 litres
Model: 'Speedster'	*Valves:* overhead
Maker's HP: 29·4	*Wheelbase:* 11' 0"
R.A.C. Rating: 29·4 hp	*Forward Speeds:* 4
Number of Cylinders: 6	*Final Drive Ratio:* 3·6 to 1
Bore and Stroke: $3\frac{1}{2}'' \times 4\frac{3}{4}''$	*Tyres:* 31 × 6·50

Frazer Nash England

It is a pity that F comes before G, since the article on the G.N. should really be read before this one on the Frazer Nash. The G.N. was parent to the Frazer Nash and the two are basically alike. The unconventional transmission by

1925 1½-litre Anzani-engined car with aluminium body, which belongs to Nigel Arnold-Forster, a Past President of the Vintage Sports Car Club

chains and dogs is the outstanding feature of both, and for a description of it the reader is referred to G.N.

Production of the Frazer Nash started in early 1925 with an overhead-valve 'Powerplus' engine, of which only one example survives, but this was soon supplanted by the 1·5-litre, side-valve Anzani engine, whose simplicity and lightness were fully in keeping with the rest of the machine. With a power output of some 40 bhp and an all-up weight of only 13 cwt the Frazer Nash had a power-weight ratio which very few vintage cars could equal, and on acceleration up to about 60 mph, the Frazer Nash could leave most of them. Although the maximum speed rarely exceeded 70 mph, the high gearing gave a cruising speed of at least 60 mph, and the ratios could be easily and quickly altered to taste.

The power output could not be greatly increased, though it is said that an unblown Anzani was finally made to yield 55 bhp. For sprint use a supercharger was added in 1928, but the engine was too light in construction to take it without impaired reliability. Therefore, in 1929 the Anzani finally gave way to the ohv Meadows, type 4ED engine which continued to be fitted until about 1938. At the same time, four forward speeds became standard and the weight increased to 15 cwt.

The characteristics of the vintage Frazer Nash are lightness, simplicity, brisk acceleration, high cruising speed, accurate steering, instantaneous gear-changing, and silence on all gears. It was one of the most outstanding vintage sports cars.

Contrary to universal belief, a shaft-driven Frazer Nash with Anzani engine and artillery wheels was listed in 1924 and at least one was actually made.

1929 Meadows-engined 'Boulogne' Model. The pundits insist that Captain Archie Frazer-Nash's name has a hyphen, but that his cars do not . . .

Year: 1925
Maker's HP and R.A.C. Rating: 11·9 hp
Number of Cylinders: 4
Bore and Stroke: 69 × 100 mm
Engine Capacity: 1·5 litres

Valves: side
Wheelbase: 8' 0"
Forward Speeds: 3
Final Drive Ratio: Usually 3·5 or 4·1 to 1
Tyres: 710 × 90

Year: 1929
Maker's HP and R.A.C. Rating:
11·9 hp
Number of Cylinders: 4
Bore and Stroke: 69 × 100 mm
Engine Capacity: 1·5 litres

Valves: overhead
Wheelbase: 8′ 3″
Forward Speeds: 4
Final Drive Ratio: Usually 4·1 to 1
Tyres: 27 × 4·4

G.N.   England

H. R. Godfrey and A. Frazer-Nash started making cycle-cars in 1910 and by the war they had already achieved considerable success, working with the most rustic sort of equipment.

The Edwardian G.N.'s had belt drive, but for immediate post-war production the manufacturers devised a form of chain transmission which was at once unconventional, light, simple and highly efficient.

8·7 hp model in France. The bearded French driver is thought to be René David, sometime editor of the magazine *L'Auto*

At the front of the car was an air-cooled V-twin engine with a single-plate clutch and shaft ending in a bevel box about under the driver's seat. This drove a cross-shaft running the full width of the chassis. Keyed to this shaft were four sliding dog-clutches and running loose upon it were four chain-sprockets, also fitted with dog-clutches. Keyed to the solid back axle were four sprockets connected by light chains to the sprockets on the countershaft. The gear-selector mechanism enabled any one of the sliding dogs to be meshed with its opposite dog on one of the sprockets, whereupon drive from the engine to the back axle, via the chain in question, was established. The sprockets on the back axle could be speedily changed, so that the ratios could be altered to taste or for special requirements. The reverse gear had an intermediate pair of spur gears to make it go the other way.

Thus equipped, the G.N. was alternatively the best of the touring cycle-cars, or about the most formidable sprint car of its day, invariably driven in competition by one or other of its intrepid manufacturers. In 1919, a touring model ran from London to Edinburgh without stopping the engine, and averaged 20 mph and 60 mpg.

In 1923 a 4-cylinder, water-cooled model was attempted, which was not successful and Messrs Godfrey and Nash left the Company, Frazer-Nash then setting up on his own to make the Frazer Nash car.

The V-twin G.N. was also made in France by the Salmson Company, under licence.

The G.N. Company continued as a servicing station and still exists.

Year: 1919
Maker's HP and R.A.C. Rating:
8·7 hp
Number of Cylinders: 2
Bore and Stroke: 84 × 98 mm
Engine Capacity: 1·1 litre

Valves: side or overhead
Wheelbase: 8′ 6″
Forward Speeds: 3
Final Drive Ratio: to choice
Tyres: 650 × 65

Year: 1923
Maker's HP: 12/25
R.A.C. Rating: 11·9 hp
Number of Cylinders: 4
Bore and Stroke: 69 × 100 mm
Engine Capacity: 1·5 litres

Valves: side
Wheelbase: 8′ 6″
Forward Speeds: 3
Final Drive Ratio: to choice
Tyres: 700 × 80

Guy   England

When the Guy motor-car was introduced in 1919 it was described by its manufacturers as being ten years ahead of its time.

The engine was one of the first if not the first British 'V-8'. The cylinders were arranged in two banks of four at an angle of 90 degrees, and bore a marked resemblance to the 4-cylinder commercial lorry produced by the Company both before and after the war. Unusual features of the vehicle were that the engine was mounted by ball-joints on a sub-frame—the forerunner of flexibly mounted engines. The chassis was automatically lubricated, the system coming into operation when full right 'lock' was operated. The brakes on all four wheels were operated by rods.

The car was capable of 75–80 mph, and about fifty were made though none are known to exist today. A Guy engine, however, formed the basis of a special evolved by an extremely well-known English Bugatti engineer in his bedroom. Unhappily on completion it was found the car had to be dismantled before he could get it out.

Year: 1919
Maker's HP: 20
R.A.C. Rating: 25·7 hp
Number of Cylinders: 8
Bore and Stroke: 72 × 125 mm
Engine Capacity: 4 litres
Valves: side
Wheelbase: 10' 10"
Forward Speeds: 4
Final Drive Ratio: 4·06 to 1
Tyres: 820 × 120

1920 20 hp touring car. About 150 of
the V-8 model were made

G.W.K. England

Messrs Grice Wood and Keiller may fairly be said to have devised the only
simple, successful and efficient infinitely variable gear ever applied to a
motor-car. It could only transmit a very moderate amount of power, which is
why it has not survived; nevertheless, the Company did so for twenty years,
from 1911 to 1931.

A normal propeller shaft terminated in a large flat wheel. Its backward-
facing side had a friction surface. On the back axle was another wheel which
was connected to the gear lever and could be slid from side to side. Its peri-
phery was in contact with the friction face of the large wheel on the end of the
propeller shaft. Thus, when the driven wheel was near the centre of the driving
wheel the gear ratio was low and vice versa. In other respects the design was
conventional, and the engine developed about 22 bhp.

The efficacy of the system was shown by the success of the G.W.K. in early
reliability trials. At least one specimen survives in active use.

Year: 1919
Maker's HP and R.A.C. Rating:
10·8 hp
Number of Cylinders: 4
Bore and Stroke: 66 × 100 mm
Engine Capacity: 1·4 litres
Valves: side
Wheelbase: 8' 10"
Forward Speeds: variable
Tyres: 700 × 80

1921 10·8 hp two-seater coupé. It
was built in what later became a jam
factory, at Maidenhead

Gwynne

England

The 8 hp Gwynne first appeared in 1922. It seems to have been evolved from the Spanish Victoria. It was manufactured by Gwynnes Pumps Ltd., of Chiswick. The engine was a 4-cylinder of 950 cc and would exceed 3000 rpm. The overhead valves were in a detachable head and operated by pushrods. On the inlet side there was a remarkable contrivance whereby water could be conveyed to the 'hot spot' in summer and exhaust gas in winter; this system gave over 40 mpg.

The Gwynne was usually offered in 2-seater and the better known 'hip bath' form. A sports version was also available with a Brooklands lap speed certificate for 65 mph. Later in 1924 a 4-seater Gwynne made best performance in the 1924 Small Car Trials.

The 10 hp succeeded the '8' in 1927, but this model survived only two years.

Several Gwynne engines found favour with G.N.-based special builders, as the engine readily lent itself to tuning.

Year: 1922	*Valves:* overhead
Maker's HP: 8	*Wheelbase:* 7' 3"
R.A.C. Rating: 7·5 hp	*Forward Speeds:* 3
Number of Cylinders: 4	*Final Drive Ratio:* 4 to 1
Bore and Stroke: 55 × 100 mm	*Tyres:* 700 × 80
Engine Capacity: 1 litre	

Year: 1927	*Valves:* overhead
Maker's HP: 10	*Wheelbase:* 8' 0"
R.A.C. Rating: 9·8 hp	*Forward Speeds:* 3
Number of Cylinders: 4	*Final Drive Ratio:* 5 to 1
Bore and Stroke: 63 × 100 mm	*Tyres:* 27 × 4·40
Engine Capacity: 1·2 litres	

1924 8 hp with a special skiff-tailed sporting body by Compton

Hampton

England

The Hampton car was first made in 1911, but in vintage form it was mainly notable for its light-alloy, ohv engine, the cylinder block being aluminium with cast-iron liners. It had a considerable reputation for reliability; but in 1928 came the inevitable symptom of decline—a small 6-cylinder side-valve. Nevertheless, the Company survived until 1933, and its expiring effort was the more enterprising one of an ohv straight-eight.

Year: 1920
Maker's HP and R.A.C. Rating:
11·9 hp
Number of Cylinders: 4
Bore and Stroke: 69 × 120 mm
Engine Capacity: 1·8 litres

Valves: overhead
Wheelbase: 9′ 0″
Forward Speeds: 3
Final Drive Ratio: 4 to 1
Tyres: 710 × 90

Year: 1928
Maker's HP: 15/45
R.A.C. Rating: 14·8 hp
Number of Cylinders: 6
Bore and Stroke: 63 × 90 mm
Engine Capacity: 1·7 litres
Valves: side
Wheelbase: 9′ 6″
Forward Speeds: 4
Final Drive Ratio: 4·5 to 1
Tyres: 28 × 4·95

1927 11·9 hp 2-seater. During the Vintage years, Hamptons were made at Stroud in Gloucestershire, and enjoyed a good reputation in the West Country

H.E.

England

The Herbert Engineering Company started life in 1920 with a fairly uninteresting side-valve touring car, which was soon increased from 69 mm to 72·5 mm bore. However, in 1922 came a most elegant sporting model with a three-seater canoe-shaped body. The engine was mainly as before, so that the maximum speed was not much more than 65 mph. Nevertheless, with sensible gear ratios and a multi-plate clutch a quite useful overall performance was achieved.

In 1927 came the conventionally fashionable side-valve 6-cylinder, though of rather more than average merit; which was as well, since it was extremely difficult to work on if the block had to be removed.

The firm also experimented, in 1923, with a 16-valve, 4-cylinder ohv engine and, in about 1928, with a supercharged 1½-litre six; but neither went into serious production.

Year: 1920
Maker's HP: 14/20
R.A.C. Rating: 11·9 hp
Number of Cylinders: 4
Bore and Stroke: 69 × 120 mm
Engine Capacity: 1·8 litres

Year: 1922
Model: Sports
Maker's HP: 14/40
R.A.C. Rating: 13 hp
Number of Cylinders: 4
Bore and Stroke: 72·5 × 120 mm
Engine Capacity: 2 litres
Valves: side
Wheelbase: 9′ 6″
Forward Speeds: 4
Final Drive Ratio: 4·2 to 1
Tyres: 815 × 105

Year: 1926
Maker's HP: 16/55
R.A.C. Rating: 15·7 hp
Number of Cylinders: 6
Bore and Stroke: 65 × 115 mm
Engine Capacity: 2·3 litres

Valves: side
Wheelbase: 9′ 6″
Forward Speeds: 4
Final Drive Ratio: 4·5 to 1
Tyres: 810 × 90

1924 14/40: a well-built 2-litre sporting tourer but somewhat over-priced at about £500

Valves: side
Wheelbase: 10′ 6″
Forward Speeds: 4
Final Drive Ratio: 4·7 to 1
Tyres: 820 × 120

1928 16/55: the 2·3-litre model had an aluminium cylinder head and inclined valves

Hillman   England

The vintage Hillman was a well-made, if undistinguished car, and certainly on a very much higher plane than the early Hillman 'Minx' which was one of the more unpleasant manifestations of the mid-thirties.

In addition to the immediately post-1918 model listed below there was available a 63 × 90 mm 'Speed Model' which is mainly of interest because Raymond Mays started his career on one.

Later, instead of the inevitable side-valve six, Hillmans had the initiative to produce a 2·6-litre, overhead-valve, straight-eight, which was quite a handsome and effective car.

Year: 1918
Maker's HP: 11
R.A.C. Rating: 10·4 hp
Number of Cylinders: 4
Bore and Stroke: 65 × 120 mm
Engine Capacity: 1·6 litres
Valves: side
Wheelbase: 8' 6"
Forward Speeds: 3
Final Drive Ratio: 4·2 to 1
Tyres: 700 × 85

'Speed Model': Raymond Mays competing at Tring hill-climb in 1921

Year: 1926
Maker's HP: 14
R.A.C. Rating: 12·8 hp
Number of Cylinders: 4
Bore and Stroke: 72 × 120 mm
Engine Capacity: 2 litres
Valves: side
Wheelbase: 9' 4"
Forward Speeds: 4
Final Drive Ratio: 4·77 to 1
Tyres: 29 × 4·40

1927 Fourteen saloon. The model first appeared in 1926 and was continued after the Rootes Brothers took over in 1928

Year: 1929
Maker's HP: 20
R.A.C. Rating: 19·7 hp
Number of Cylinders: 8
Bore and Stroke: 63 × 105 mm
Engine Capacity: 2·6 litres
Valves: overhead
Wheelbase: 10' 0½"
Forward Speeds: 4
Final Drive Ratio: 5 to 1
Tyres: 29 × 5·15

Hispano-Suiza   France and Spain

The success and renown of Hispano-Suiza may owe something to its aristo-cratic sounding name, but it had a more solid backing as well, in the shape of Marc Birkigt (pronounced Birkisht, more or less), unquestionably one of the finest and most versatile designers in all automobile history.

The firm started life in Barcelona, in 1904, making a luxurious 20/24 and a $7\frac{1}{2}$-litre 40 hp. The only advanced feature was the use of unit construction for the gearbox.

In 1909 the firm entered for the *Coupe de l'Auto* race and in 1910 they won it with a long-stroke, T-head, 4-cylinder machine. This was shortly put into production, and by royal patronage was allowed to be called the 'Type Alfonso XIII'. In production form this famous model, one of the first specific-ally sporting cars, had an 80×180 mm, 3·6-litre, T-head engine developing 64 bhp; the then quite respectable figure of 18 hp per litre. Like nearly all Birkigt's designs it was hampered by a wide-ratio three-speed gearbox which seems to have been the one blind spot in his equipment.

Count Louis Zborowski's 1922 37·2 hp two-seater with coachwork by Kellner of Paris

In 1911 the French factory was opened and in 1912 the firm experimented for the *Coupe de l'Auto* race with a supercharger consisting of a 2-cylinder reciprocating pump; but it never appeared in public.

During the war Birkigt and Hispano-Suiza produced a highly successful V-8, 140×150 mm ohc aero engine. After it, the Barcelona factory produced for a time a 4-cylinder, ohc, 85×130 mm machine, but the main effort was the 37·2 hp produced from the French factory in 1919. This may really be said to have set the pace for the vintage decade. The 6-cylinder, ohc $6\frac{1}{2}$-litre engine had a light alloy cylinder block with screwed-in liners. Despite a compression ratio of only $4\frac{1}{2}$ to 1 it was claimed to produce 135 bhp at 3500 rpm, and on this low compression ratio its three widely spaced ratios were really quite adequate. It was only when the compression was increased, and other makers began to catch up, that the three speeds began to show some inadequacy. To match this advanced engine was a rigid chassis, affording unsurpassed road-holding and steering; and the first really efficient four-wheel braking, operated by the famous mechanical servo mechanism, later adopted by Rolls-Royce. An axle ratio of 3·37 to 1 was used at first, but in most if not all surviving '37's' the ratio is 3·5 to 1.

In 1922–23 came the slightly mysterious and highly elusive short chassis 'Monza', but in 1924 appeared the magnificent 'Boulogne' with the 6½ litres and 37·2 hp of the standard model increased to 8 litres and 45 hp. With a compression ratio of 6 to 1 the 'Boulogne' was the outstanding car of the mid-twenties.

In the meantime, the Barcelona factory had dropped its 4-cylinder machine in favour of a scaled-down, 3·7-litre version of the 37·2 hp French car, to be known as the 'Barcelona'. This was usually fitted with a prodigiously low axle ratio which gave it remarkable top-gear acceleration but a much-restricted cruising speed. On Spanish roads this probably did not matter.

By 1930 Birkigt considered that the '37·2' and its derivatives had had their day and produced perhaps the most magnificent production car of all time; the 9·4-litre V-12. This had a 100 × 100 mm, pushrod ohv engine of remarkable smoothness, power and flexibility. Even with heavy saloon bodies, 100 mph was readily attained. But although his final masterpiece remained an essentially vintage car it is very doubtful if any came on the market before 1931. It was followed by a less distinguished 6-cylinder, 100 × 110 mm machine, while the Barcelona factory produced a 3-litre, 80 × 100 mm, 6-cylinder pushrod model, both of these appearing in 1934.

In 1931 Hispano-Suiza bought up the Ballot concern and for a time the Ballot factory produced a 4½-litre, 90 × 120 mm model of mixed parentage, called the 'Junior'.

Birkigt's great achievements undoubtedly are the Edwardian 'Alfonso'; the vintage '37·2' and 'Boulogne'; and the most fabulous of all V-12; a post-vintage-thoroughbred if ever there was one.

1927 3·7-litre Model I6, or 'Barcelona', as it was made at the Spanish factory

Year: 1919
Maker's HP: 40
R.A.C. Rating: 37·2 hp
Number of Cylinders: 6
Bore and Stroke: 100 × 140 mm
Engine Capacity: 6·6 litres

Valves: overhead
Wheelbase: 12′ 1″
Forward Speeds: 3
Final Drive Ratio: 3·5 to 1
Tyres: 895 × 135

Year: 1922
Model: 'Barcelona'
Maker's HP: 16
R.A.C. Rating: 17·9 hp
Number of Cylinders: 4
Bore and Stroke: 85 × 130 mm

Engine Capacity: 3 litres
Valves: overhead
Wheelbase: 10′ 8″
Forward Speeds: 4
Final Drive Ratio:
Tyres: 820 × 120

Year: 1925
Model: 'Barcelona'
Maker's HP: 20
R.A.C. Rating: 26·9 hp
Number of Cylinders: 6
Bore and Stroke: 85 × 110 mm

Engine Capacity: 3·7 litres
Valves: overhead
Wheelbase: 12′ 1″
Forward Speeds: 3
Final Drive Ratio: 4·23 or 4·91 to 1
Tyres: 835 × 135

1928 8-litre H6C Sport, or
'Boulogne', model, with Gurney
Nutting coachwork, when it was
owned by Peter Hampton

Year: 1925
Model: 'Boulogne'
Maker's HP and R.A.C. Rating:
45 hp
Number of Cylinders: 6
Bore and Stroke: 110 × 140 mm
Engine Capacity: 8 litres
Valves: overhead
Wheelbase: 11′ 0″
Forward Speeds: 3
Final Drive Ratio: 3·3 to 1
Tyres: 895 × 135

Horstman
England

There has been considerable controversy as to whether the name of this car is spelt with one or two 'n's'. However, a compromise has been reached on agreeing that the Horstman car was designed by a Mr Horstmann, who owned a garage in Bath. In fact, the second 'n' was omitted after 1922.

The first car was made in 1914 and had the unusual feature of valves arranged horizontally and diagonally across the head and diagonally above each other.

Despite the advantages of easy access, through valve caps at the side of the head, and a claimed smoothness and silence, this model was produced only for a very short time after the war.

Vintage Horstmen had a choice of Coventry Simplex and Anzani engines and also sported a 'kick starter' which was claimed to be 'a simple Archimedian arrangement operated by a pedal'. This may have been so, but nevertheless the authors know of at least one person who still bears the scars of an encounter with this device. During the early 1920's Horstman was a consistent performer in the 200-mile race with the Anzani-engined model having two carburettors on the exhaust side in 1922 and a supercharger in 1923—the first British car to be so equipped. They were also one of the first British cars to have hydraulic brakes.

There is a very representative selection of Horstman surviving including an Edwardian horizontal valve car; the flat and V-shaped radiatored vintage touring models, and there is also a rumour of one of the 200-mile race cars in existence. These cars are distinguished by a Daimler-like finning on the top of the radiator.

Year: 1920
Maker's HP and R.A.C. Rating: 10·4 hp
Number of Cylinders: 4
Bore and Stroke: 65 × 100 mm
Engine Capacity: 1·3 litres
Valves: side
Wheelbase: 9′ 4″
Forward Speeds: 3
Final Drive Ratio: 4 to 1
Tyres: 710 × 85 mm

A contemporary factory photograph of the 1921 'Super Sports' model. It was listed at £472 10s

Year: 1924
Maker's HP: 12/30
R.A.C. Rating: 11·8 hp
Number of Cylinders: 4
Bore and Stroke: 69 × 100 mm
Engine Capacity: 1·5 litres
Valves: side
Wheelbase: 9′ 6″
Forward Speeds: 3
Final Drive Ratio: 4·34 to 1
Tyres: 710 × 90

Hotchkiss   France

The Edwardian and early vintage Hotchkiss was characterized by a very handsome round radiator.

The chief interest of the Company was the manufacture of quick-firing guns and machine guns. It is curious how many arms manufacturers produced cars as a side-line.

After the war the first model made was the ohv 4-cylinder '18/22', quickly followed by a 16 hp model. Overhead-valves were introduced in 1922 for the 16 hp but for some reason were not retained for more than a year. These cars were available with some extremely handsome boat-shaped bodies—one example of which is known to survive.

In 1922 the model 'AR' was introduced, and proved to be an exceedingly interesting design. It was intended for the luxury market and is a typical example of the early vintage high speed luxury car. The $6\frac{1}{2}$-litre ohc engine gave 130 bhp at 3000 rpm and was set in a substantially deep 12-foot long chassis with restricted cantilever rear springs and four-wheel brakes. A chassis of this type survives in the Conservatoire des Arts et Métiers, Paris, but it is doubtful if further models were made.

The Company evidently frightened themselves so much with the 'AR' that a string of rather dreary side-valve models followed until 1928, when the ohv 'AM.80' was introduced. This model formed the basis of all subsequent models and proved to be a fast and reliable car, winning the Monte Carlo Rally outright in 1933, 1934 and 1939.

The 12CV (15·9 hp) AM2 was introduced in 1926 and had pushrod overhead valves. Saloons would do 66 mph

Year: 1919	*Engine Capacity:* 4 litres
Model: 'AF'	*Valves:* side, prior to 1922
Maker's HP: 18/22	*Wheelbase:* 10′ 10″
R.A.C. Rating: 22·4 hp	*Forward Speeds:* 4
Number of Cylinders: 4	*Final Drive Ratio:* 3·5 to 1
Bore and Stroke: 95 × 140 mm	*Tyres:* 880 × 120

Year: 1922	*Valves:* overhead
Model: 'AR'	*Wheelbase:* 12′ 0″
R.A.C. Rating: 37·2 hp	*Forward Speeds:* 4
Number of Cylinders: 6	*Final Drive Ratio:* 4·0 to 1
Bore and Stroke: 100 × 140 mm	*Tyres:* 895 × 135
Engine Capacity: 6·6 litres	

Year: 1923
Model: 'AM'
Maker's HP and R.A.C. Rating:
15·9 hp
Number of Cylinders: 4
Bore and Stroke: 80 × 120 mm
Engine Capacity: 2·4 litres
Valves: overhead
Wheelbase: 10′ 0″
Forward Speeds: 4
Final Drive Ratio: 3·5 to 1
Tyres: 820 × 120

1930 AM80, with seven-bearing
crankshaft

Year: 1929
Model: 'AM.80'
Maker's HP and R.A.C. Rating:
23·8 hp
Number of Cylinders: 6
Bore and Stroke: 80 × 100 mm

Engine Capacity: 3 litres
Valves: overhead
Wheelbase: 10′ 1″ or 10′ 10″
Forward Speeds: 4
Final Drive Ratio: 4·55 to 1
Tyres: 32 × 6

Hudson

Canada

The first production model Hudson appeared in 1909 and due to its low price, useful specification and an intensive advertising campaign, attained immediate popularity. The '20' model, as it was known, had 'sliding gear transmission (selective type)', the motor being 4-cylinder, four-cycle water-cooled—known as the 'Renault type'.

In 1910 the first die-cast bearings and 'fluid cushion' clutch to be used in the industry were offered in the Hudson and in 1911 the model 33 had four cylinders cast 'en bloc'. The 1916 6-cylinder model had a compression ratio of 5 to 1, quite high for the period, and a fully balanced crankshaft.

After this sound Edwardian grounding, Hudson, rather strangely, relied for the vintage market solely on the 30 hp 'Super-Six' which remained virtually unchanged to the end of the vintage period, a 'Great Eight' being introduced in 1930.

Year: 1918
Model: Super-Six
R.A.C. Rating: 29·4 hp
Number of Cylinders: 6
Bore and Stroke: 88·9 × 120 mm
Engine Capacity: 4·6 litres

Valves: side
Wheelbase: 10′ 5½″
Forward Speeds: 3
Final Drive Ratio: 4·45 to 1
Tyres: 880 × 120

1926 Hudson 'Super Six': the model first appeared in 1916 and it sold briskly throughout the Vintage decade

Humber

England

Whether it was applied to bicycles, motor-cycles or cars, until the end of the vintage period the name 'Humber' has always been synonymous with good quality and excellent workmanship.

Humber built a wide and varied range of cars before the war ranging from the early Beeston Humber forecars to the later 28 hp 4-cylinder luxury cars and the twin cylinder 'Humberette'. This Edwardian era culminated, surprisingly enough, in the Henry-inspired Burgess-designed twin ohc T.T. car of 1914. Unhappily, unlike its fellow contestant in that race, the Sunbeam, the Company failed to follow up this design with a vintage sporting car.

After the war Humbers embarked on a range of models to appeal to a wide

1922 15·9 hp touring car. Note the two separate windscreens for the rear seat passengers attached to 'decking' over their legs

market. In 1920 10·5 hp and 15·9 hp models were introduced, both with 4-cylinder side-valve engines and cone leather-covered clutches. In 1922 came the 8/18 model which set the style for the rest of the vintage Humber cars. The 8/18 had an engine whose inlet valves were overhead and exhaust valves at the side—a practice continued by Rolls-Royce until 1959. This model at once gained a name for lively performance, ease of control and a remarkable degree of finish for a car of this type. The ioe engine was adopted on the rest of the Humber range which continued virtually unchanged until 1926 when the 9/20 superseded the 8/18.

The Company was strongly adverse to front-wheel brakes and even in 1925 only grudgingly supplied Humber-Perrot type front-wheel brakes as an extra.

In 1927 Humber ventured into the luxury class with the 6-cylinder 20/55, a single-plate clutch replacing the earlier cone type. In 1928 it gained a Dewandre servo-assisted braking system and a 'twin' Zenith carburettor. This model was developed into the popular 'Snipe' in 1930.

1923 8/18 hp 'chummy' listed at £275 when it was introduced in that year

Year: 1919
Maker's HP: 10
R.A.C. Rating: 10·5 hp
Number of Cylinders: 4
Bore and Stroke: 64 × 120 mm
Engine Capacity: 1·6 litres

Valves: side
Wheelbase: 8' 9½"
Forward Speeds: 4
Final Drive Ratio: 4·33 to 1
Tyres: 710 × 90

Year: 1920
Maker's HP: 15·9
R.A.C. Rating: 15·9 hp
Number of Cylinders: 4
Bore and Stroke: 80 × 140 mm
Engine Capacity: 2·8 litres

Valves: side
Wheelbase: 10' 3½"
Forward Speeds: 4
Final Drive Ratio: 4·3 to 1
Tyres: 815 × 105

Year: 1923
Maker's HP: 8/18
R.A.C. Rating: 7·8 hp
Number of Cylinders: 4
Bore and Stroke: 56 × 100 mm
Engine Capacity: 1 litre

Valves: ioe
Wheelbase: 7' 10½"
Forward Speeds: 3
Final Drive Ratio: 4·9 to 1
Tyres: 700 × 80

Year: 1925
Maker's HP: 12/25
R.A.C. Rating: 11·8 hp
Number of Cylinders: 4
Bore and Stroke: 69 × 120 mm
Engine Capacity: 1·8 litres

Valves: ioe
Wheelbase: 9' 1"
Forward Speeds: 4
Final Drive Ratio: 4·5 to 1
Tyres: 765 × 105

Year: 1925
Maker's HP: 15/40
R.A.C. Rating: 15·9 hp
Number of Cylinders: 4
Bore and Stroke: 80 × 140 mm
Engine Capacity: 2·8 litres

Valves: ioe
Wheelbase: 10' 3½"
Forward Speeds: 4
Final Drive Ratio: 4·3 to 1
Tyres: 820 × 120

Year: 1927
Maker's HP: 20/55
R.A.C. Rating: 20·9 hp
Number of Cylinders: 6
Bore and Stroke: 75 × 116 mm
Engine Capacity: 3 litres

Valves: ioe
Wheelbase: 10' 6"
Forward Speeds: 4
Final Drive Ratio: 4·6 to 1
Tyres: 31 × 5·25

Year: 1930
Model: 'Snipe'
Maker's HP: 25/72
R.A.C. Rating: 23·8 hp
Number of Cylinders: 6
Bore and Stroke: 80 × 116 mm

Engine Capacity: 3·5 litres
Valves: ioe
Wheelbase: 10' 0"
Forward Speeds: 4
Final Drive Ratio: 4·5 to 1
Tyres: 29 × 5·5

Contemporary catalogue illustration of the 1930 'Snipe'

Hupmobile

America

Year: 1919
Maker's HP: 15/18
R.A.C. Rating: 16·9 hp
Number of Cylinders: 4
Bore and Stroke: 82·55 × 139·7 mm
Engine Capacity: 3 litres

Valves: side
Wheelbase: 9′ 4″
Forward Speeds: 3
Final Drive Ratio: 4·87 to 1
Tyres: 815 × 105

Year: 1925
Maker's HP and R.A.C. Rating:
27 hp
Number of Cylinders: 8
Bore and Stroke: 73·5 × 120 mm
Engine Capacity: 4 litres

Valves: side
Wheelbase: 9′ 10¼″
Forward Speeds: 3
Final Drive Ratio: 4·64 to 1
Tyres: 33 × 6

Year: 1926
Maker's HP and R.A.C. Rating:
23·2 hp
Number of Cylinders: 6
Bore and Stroke: 79·4 × 108 mm
Engine Capacity: 3·2 litres

Valves: side
Wheelbase: 9′ 6″
Forward Speeds: 3
Final Drive Ratio: 4·64 to 1
Tyres: 30 × 5·25

1932 15/18 4-cylinder coupé, with an earlier touring version on the left

Invicta

England

The Invicta was a late-comer in vintage affairs but earned itself a considerable following, some of which it still enjoys.

The original 2·6-litre (soon increased to 3 litres) was a nicely made, pushrod ohv 6-cylinder which was joined in 1928 by a similar but less attractive 4½-litre, both having Meadows engines. However, in 1930 the 4½-litre appeared in much fiercer shape, described as 100 mph, which speed it would, in fact, approach or even attain. Reasonably light, it also had formidable acceleration. Its very low build was not, however, an unmixed blessing as its makers had not found out that a low centre of gravity coupled with a high roll-centre makes for somewhat unpredictable handling characteristics under large applications of lateral 'g'. Perhaps wisely, the Company went in more for endurance records than for racing, but they also did well in sprints, and won the Monte Carlo Rally in 1931. In post-vintage times a 1½-litre model was introduced whose prodigious avoirdupois was dragged along by a hard-worked 6-cylinder, ohc Blackburne engine with a really unpardonable back axle ratio. Production stopped in 1934 after which various ideas were toyed with and after the war on advanced design, with 2 ohc, completely automatic variable gearing and four-wheel independent suspension was carried to an advanced stage and at least twenty were actually built.

It was called the 'Black Prince'.

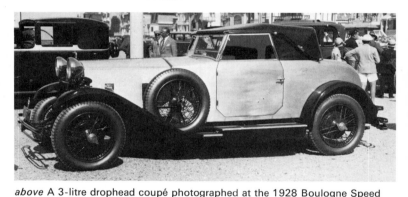

above A 3-litre drophead coupé photographed at the 1928 Boulogne Speed Week
below 1930 4½-litre S-type, often referred to as the '100 mph' model. It cost £1,345 with the bodywork shown here

Year: 1925	*Valves:* overhead
Maker's HP and R.A.C. Rating:	*Wheelbase:* 10′ 0″
19·5 hp	*Forward Speeds:* 4
Number of Cylinders: 6	*Final Drive Ratio:* 3·61 or 3·9 to 1
Bore and Stroke: 72·5 × 120 mm	*Tyres:* 28 × 4·95
Engine Capacity: 3 litres	

Year: 1928	*Valves:* overhead
Maker's HP and R.A.C. Rating:	*Wheelbase:* 9′ 4″ or 10′ 0″
29·1 hp	*Forward Speeds:* 4
Number of Cylinders: 6	*Final Drive Ratio:* 3·61 or 3·9 to 1
Bore and Stroke: 88·5 × 120 mm	*Tyres:* 30 × 5·25
Engine Capacity: 4·5 litres	

Isotta Fraschini   Italy

The firm of Isotta Fraschini was founded in 1899 and since 1910 every Isotta Fraschini made has been fitted with four-wheel braking. From 1919 they were the first serious vendors of a straight-eight. Although the vintage straight-eight is widely, and deservedly known, probably their finest model was the 1913 and 1914, 4-cylinder, 16-valve, ohc, 130 × 200 mm, 10½-litre, 100 hp model. With an imposing V-radiator and, of course, front brakes, this must have been the most exciting production car of the Edwardian era. One or two survive in America. At the other end of the scale was their 1908 Voiturette Grand Prix car (possibly designed by Bugatti and certainly the basis of his famous 'type 13'), of which a specimen survives in Australia.

Shortly after 1918 came the 5·9-litre, straight-eight with pushrod ohv, whose main peculiarity was a single casting for the cylinder block, but with two four-cylinder heads. The firing order was also the (at any rate theoretically) inferior one of two 4-cylinder engines joined end to end. The ratios of the three-speed gearbox were even more widely spaced than those of the contemporary Hispano-Suiza with which on nearly all counts, the Isotta Fraschini has always suffered by comparison.

The standard model claimed only a modest 80 bhp but in 1925 came the enlarged, 7·4-litre, 'Tipo Spinto', with 140 bhp.

Year: 1919. 'Tipo 8'	*Valves:* overhead
Maker's HP: 35/50	*Wheelbase:* 12′ 1″
R.A.C. Rating: 35·8 hp	*Forward Speeds:* 3
Number of Cylinders: 8	*Final Drive Ratio:* 3·75 to 1
Bore and Stroke: 85 × 130 mm	*Tyres:* 895 × 135
Engine Capacity: 5·9 litres	

Year: 1925. 'Tipo Spinto'
Maker's HP: 50/100
R.A.C. Rating: 44·3 hp
Number of Cylinders: 8
Bore and Stroke: 95 × 130 mm
Engine Capacity: 7·4 litres

Valves: overhead
Wheelbase: 11′ 2½″ or 12′ 1″
Forward Speeds: 3
Final Drive Ratio: 3·25 to 1
Tyres: 895 × 150

top 1927 Tipo 8-ASS (Super Spinto) 'Cella' four-seater fixhead coupé
above 1928 Tipo 8-A with coachwork by Castagne of Milan

Itala   Italy

The Itala concern was founded in 1904 and immediately entered the racing
field with considerable impact, winning the Targa Florio in 1906. Later they
sponsored rotary valves with at least considerable success, and a rotary-valve
model was still listed in 1922. Itala again competed in the Targa Florio in 1923
and as late as 1926 the firm contemplated a return to Grand Prix racing with a
1·1- and 1·5-litres V-12.

In 1925 a highly effective 2-litre, 6-cylinder model was introduced. The firm
survived until 1935.

Year: 1920
Maker's HP: 16/20
R.A.C. Rating: 17·1 hp
Number of Cylinders: 4
Bore and Stroke: 83 × 130 mm
Engine Capacity: 2·8 litres

Year: 1922
Maker's HP: 26/40
R.A.C. Rating: 26·9 hp
Number of Cylinders: 6
Bore and Stroke: 85 × 130 mm
Engine Capacity: 4·5 litres
Valves: rotary
Wheelbase: 12' 2"
Forward Speeds: 4
Final Drive Ratio:
Tyres: 895 × 135

Valves: side
Wheelbase: 10' 6"
Forward Speeds: 4
Final Drive Ratio: 4·7 to 1
Tyres: 820 × 120

1928 Model 61 2-litre 6-cylinder,
designed by the eminent engineer
Giulio Cesare Cappa

Jowett   England

The Jowett story started in 1901 when the concern made a water-cooled 'V'
twin intending to compete with the contemporary de Dion and Aster engines.
In 1906 the Company was engaged with the manufacture of Scott-Jowett
motor-cycles and also made an interesting air-cooled, 3-cylinder-in-line
engine with overhead inlet valves. By 1910 Jowett had disassociated themselves
with the Scott motor-cycle concern and concentrated on producing their light
car with a water-cooled flat twin engine, the prototype having tiller steering.
It can be seen from this earlier history that the engine might easily have been

The early 'Seven' models had fixed-head engines of 907 cc and dubious
brakes, but flexibility and acceleration were good

either a vertical, 'V' or 'in line' engine. The Company chose the 'flat' engine because of its adaptability to the thermosyphon cooling system. This model with three-speed gearbox, and engine of 907 cc, continued almost unchanged in a variety of chassis sizes and body shapes until 1939 and was extremely popular even to the extent of a Jowett owners' club being formed in 1923. In post-war years the twin-cylinder engine was used in the 'Bradford' vans and the company marketed the extremely good 'Javelin' and 'Jupiter' 'flat-four' cars.

Several examples of the vintage Jowett are still to be seen and still impress when entered in hill-climbing trials, confirming their advertising slogan 'The little engine with the big pull'.

Year: 1920
Maker's HP: 7
R.A.C. Rating: 7 hp
Number of Cylinders: 2
Bore and Stroke: 75·4 × 101·5 mm
Engine Capacity: 0·9 litre

Valves: side
Wheelbase: 7' 0"
Forward Speeds: 3
Final Drive Ratio: 4·5 to 1
Tyres: 700 × 80

Lagonda England

Lagonda go back to 1898 as manufacturers of motor-cycles and produced a somewhat out-of-date tri-car in 1904. During Edwardian days the Company made an excellent 20 hp torpedo which gained an award in the highly improbable 2000 mile reliability trial and race, the course of which was Petrograd–Kiev–Moscow–Petrograd. Shortly before the war an 11·1 hp light car was produced and was carried on after the war changing into the 11·9 and finally ending up as the 12/24. It was this model that was successfully driven from London to Capetown in 1954 overcoming alarming difficulties *en route*.

In 1925 for no apparent reason Lagonda drastically changed their policy, replacing the 12/24 by the handsome and refined 2-litre which met with immediate success and in 1928 this was supplemented by a speed model. A few of these were also supercharged. The car was very popular as a sort of poor man's Bentley and many survive in active use.

The 2-litre continued in production until 1932, but in 1929 it was supplemented by a Meadows-engined, 6-cylinder, pushrod ohv 3-litre.

In post-vintage days, under the leadership of W. O. Bentley, the Company kept in prominence with the 4½-litre Meadows-engined models and later the very remarkable ohc, V-12, 4½-litre. After the war came W. O. Bentley's last design, an advanced 2½-litre whose engine was the basis of the highly successful David Brown Aston Martin power unit.

Year: 1913–19
Maker's HP: 11
R.A.C. Rating: 11·1 hp
Number of Cylinders: 4
Bore and Stroke: 67 × 95 mm
(*Bore:* 69 mm in 1921)
Engine Capacity: 1·1 litres
Valves: ioe
Wheelbase: 7′ 9″
Forward Speeds: 3
Final Drive Ratio: 4·6 to 1
Tyres: 700 × 80

The 11·9 hp was introduced in 1920.
Advanced features included a
monocoque body, an anti-roll bar and
possibly the first-ever fly-off
handbrake

Year: 1925
Maker's HP: 14/60
R.A.C. Rating: 12·9 hp
Number of Cylinders: 4
Bore and Stroke: 72 × 120 mm
Engine Capacity: 2 litres

Valves: overhead
Wheelbase: 10′ 0″
Forward Speeds: 4
Final Drive Ratio: 4·6 to 1
Tyres: 31 × 4·75

Year: 1927
Maker's HP: 16/65
R.A.C. Rating: 17·7 hp
Number of Cylinders: 6
Bore and Stroke: 69 × 120 mm
Engine Capacity: 2·7 litres

Valves: overhead
Wheelbase: 10′ 0″
Forward Speeds: 4
Final Drive Ratio: 4·6 to 1
Tyres: 30 × 4·75

Year: 1928. 'Speed Model'
As 14/60 but *Final Drive Ratio*

4·2 to 1
Tyres: 21 × 5·25

1929 2-litre 'Speed Model', a development of the 14/60, with twin
carburettors and 6·8:1 compression ratio

Year: 1929
Model: 'Three litre'
Maker's HP and R.A.C. Rating: 19·3 hp
Number of Cylinders: 6
Bore and Stroke: 72 × 120 mm
Engine Capacity: 3 litres
Valves: overhead
Wheelbase: 11′ 6″
Forward Speeds: 4
Final Drive Ratio: 4·7 or 5·3 to 1
Tyres: 21 × 4½

1930 Meadows-engined 3-litre, considered by some to be the best Lagonda of all

Lanchester   England

Probably the most brilliant brain that has ever been applied to automobile design was that of F. W. Lanchester. He approached all problems from first principles and after some five years of experiment his first production car in 1900 was unusual in almost every important particular; yet it was not unusual from mere waywardness, and worked with great efficiency and refinement, while in such matters as wire wheels, mechanically operated valves, direct drive in top gear and disc brakes it was many years ahead of its time.

When F. W. partially relaxed his control over the motor-car design side of the business his hardly less brilliant brother George took over, and while Lanchester cars gradually conformed more and more with convention, they remained highly individual to the end.

Veteran and Edwardian Lanchesters differed so fundamentally from contemporary trends that it would be impossible to describe them here, and

1921 40 hp tourer—the 'Forty' was in the Rolls-Royce class in both refinement and price

fortunately they embarked on an entirely new design in 1919. This was the famous 'Forty' which was powered by an ohc, 6-cylinder, 6-litre engine. Its modest 80 bhp was nevertheless ahead in output of the larger contemporary Rolls-Royce 'Silver Ghost' engine and it was little if at all behind it in refinement.

Like all its predecessors, the 'Forty' had a three-speed epicyclic gearbox. The model remained in production until 1929 and was fitted with front brakes from 1925. It is fortunate that among the few survivors of this famous car are one of the first and one of the last ever made.

George VI, as Duke of York, was an enthusiastic Lanchester owner, and had two 'Forty's'.

In 1923 came a 21 hp, in convenient competition with the newly announced 20 hp Rolls-Royce, which it could comfortably out-perform, and out-stop, having large front brakes from the first, which the Rolls-Royce had not. In general, the '21' was a scaled-down edition of the '40' but a deplorable pandering to the populace was found in the gearbox which contained a lot of conventional cogwheels providing four widely spaced ratios. The bore of the '21' was at first 74·5 mm but this was shortly increased to 78·7 mm.

The last true Lanchester was the 4½-litre straight-eight of 1928; a very fine car indeed to end a series of outstanding achievements. It was in effect a '21' with two extra cylinders. In 1931 the high engineering ideals of the Lanchesters could not withstand the world depression: the Company was taken over by the B.S.A. group and this great name was dragged through a series of drab and uninspired designs.

Year: 1919
Maker's HP: 40
R.A.C. Rating: 38·4 hp
Number of Cylinders: 6
Bore and Stroke: 4″ × 5″
Engine Capacity: 6·2 litres

Valves: overhead
Wheelbase: 11′ 9″ or 12′ 6″
Forward Speeds: 3
Final Drive Ratio: 3·3 to 1
Tyres: 895 × 135

1925 21 hp saloon. In 1926 the bore was enlarged to give 3·3 litres, when this model was sometimes referred to as the '23'

Year: 1923
Maker's HP: 21
R.A.C. Rating: 20·6 hp
Number of Cylinders: 6
Bore and Stroke: 74·5 × 114 mm
Engine Capacity: 3 litres
Valves: overhead
Wheelbase: 10′ 9″
Forward Speeds: 4
Final Drive Ratio: 4·37 to 1
Tyres: 820 × 120

Year: 1928
Maker's HP: 30
R.A.C. Rating: 31 hp
Number of Cylinders: 8
Bore and Stroke: 78·7 × 114 mm
Engine Capacity: 4·4 litres

Valves: overhead
Wheelbase: 11' 10½"
Forward Speeds: 4
Final Drive Ratio: 4 to 1
Tyres: 32 × 6

1928 30 hp straight-eight saloon with George Lanchester and trophies

Lancia

Italy

Lancias have always been refreshingly different and remain so to this day.

Edwardian Lancias consisted of large 4-cylinder side-valves, rather low geared. The last of these was the 'Theta' (Lancia models were all known by Greek letters up to the end of vintage times) which was continued in the vintage 'Kappa', the latter only differing materially in having a detachable cylinder head. This was further developed as the 'Di-Kappa' which then confusingly turned into a 'Tri-Kappa' which, however, had a 4½-litre ohv, V-8 engine, quite unlike any previous subdenomination of 'Kappa'. It is doubtful if any example of this interesting model survives in Britain but of its

1926 Sixth Series 'Lambda' torpedo tourer with the long chassis of 11ft 2⅝in wheelbase, but an enormous steering lock as well

just-vintage successor, the massive V-8 'Di-Lambda', quite a number are still to be seen. The 'Tri-Kappa' was the first Lancia to have the narrow, 22-degree V-arrangement of the cylinders which remained a Lancia characteristic for many years.

However, interesting as are the 'Kappa's' and 'Di-Lambda's', the model which carried the name of Lancia highest during the vintage decade was the 'Lambda'. In prototype form, with a radiator looking very like a Bugatti, the 'Lambda' existed as early as 1918, but it did not get into production until 1922, shortly after the 'Tri-Kappa'.

The 'Lambda' was characterized by its short and very rigid narrow V-4-cylinder ohc engine with its Zenith carburettor fixed on to the back of the block. Power output was restricted by the porting dictated by the V formation, but a good deal could be done by lightening the flywheel and other engine parts whereby the safe engine speed could be raised from 3000 rpm (in the gears) to nearly 5000. The chassis consisted of welded steel struts which also

1930 'Dilambda' with Weymann bodywork. In spite of a weight of around 2½ tons depending on the body, it was possible to go from 9 to 90 mph in top gear

formed the long, flat-sided touring body. Rear suspension was normal semi-elliptic but the independent front suspension was by vertical coil springs. The whole arrangement was highly effective and the road-holding powers of vintage Lancias were proverbial.

In saloon form a box-shaped lid was simply dropped on top of the touring body and could always be detached at will.

The 'Lambda' appeared in series-numbers, and having run very quickly through the first three series, the remainder conveniently arrived at roughly yearly intervals, the 4th in 1924, 5th in 1925, and so forth. The first three had three speeds and few survive. The 4th series had four speeds and did not differ materially from the 5th, which was the most popular in this country. A fashionable treatment was to cut quite a long piece out of the middle of the motor-car and then weld the two remaining halves together again. The 6th series differed only from the 5th in its electrical equipment and very few came to Britain. Up to this series the cylinder bore was 75 mm. In the 7th series the bore was increased to 79·37 mm (2·3 litres) and in the 8th there was a further increase to 82·55 mm (2·5 litres). Also in the 8th the monocoque construction was given up in favour of a normal chassis, and many of these carried a very effective Weymann saloon body. The 8th survives in considerable numbers and differed very little from the 9th which was the last 'Lambda' and of which at any rate one survives in this country in almost mint condition.

Stamina, good roadholding, good brakes, and fine mechanical finish, rather than very high performance, are the qualities which have endeared the Lancia to its enthusiastic owners.

Year: 1919	*Engine Capacity:* 5 litres
Model: 'Kappa'	*Valves:* side
Maker's HP: 35	*Wheelbase:* 11' 1½"
R.A.C. Rating: 30 hp	*Forward Speeds:* 4
Number of Cylinders: 4	*Final Drive Ratio:* 3·46 to 1
Bore and Stroke: 110 × 130 mm	*Tyres:* 895 × 135

Year: 1922	*Engine Capacity:* 4·6 litres
Model: 'Tri-Kappa'	*Valves:* overhead
Maker's HP: 28/80	*Wheelbase:* 11' 1½"
R.A.C. Rating: 27·8 hp	*Forward Speeds:* 4
Number of Cylinders: 8	*Final Drive Ratio:* 3·9 to 1
Bore and Stroke: 75 × 130 mm	*Tyres:* 895 × 135

Year: 1922	*Engine Capacity:* 2·1 litres
Model: 'Lambda' (First Series)	*Valves:* overhead
Maker's HP: 14/40	*Wheelbase:* 10' 2"
R.A.C. Rating: 13·9 hp	*Forward Speeds:* 3
Number of Cylinders: 4	*Final Drive Ratio:* 4·16 to 1
Bore and Stroke: 75 × 120 mm	*Tyres:* 765 × 105

Year: 1929	*Engine Capacity:* 4 litres
Model: 'Di-Lambda'	*Valves:* overhead
Maker's HP and R.A.C. Rating: 31·2 hp	*Wheelbase:* 11' 5"
	Forward Speeds: 4
Number of Cylinders: 8	*Final Drive Ratio:* 4·25 to 1
Bore and Stroke: 79·37 × 100 mm	*Tyres:* 16 × 50

Lea-Francis   England

The firm of Lea-Francis is usually thought of solely in connection with the vintage era and later, but it was founded in 1895 and in 1903 marketed a 3-cylinder model with connecting rods reputedly two feet long. It is not known if any Edwardian Lea-Francis survives.

The vintage history starts with a quite sedate little side-valve, in 1923, and an air-cooled V-twin, but a Meadows-engined Sports model in 1925 gained immediate popularity, having excellent steering and a range of handsome bodies. This was later supercharged as the 'Hyper' model. With its raked-back radiator this was an extremely effective car, and won the 1928 T.T. race. Privately entered Lea-Francis's also performed creditably at Le Mans in 1928 and 1930. The only chronic fault seems to have been erratic lubrication to the vane-type supercharger.

In conformity with late-vintage fashion, various small 6-cylinder models were toyed with, and might have been quite good had they not all been too heavy, culminating in the complicated 2-litre, ohc 'Ace of Spades' which finally broke the Company in 1930, although it has since revived on various occasions.

Year: 1923
Maker's HP and R.A.C. Rating:
8·9 hp
Number of Cylinders: 4
Bore and Stroke: 60 × 95 mm
Engine Capacity: 1·1 litres
Valves: side
Wheelbase: 7′ 6″
Forward Speeds: 3
Final Drive Ratio: 4·78 to 1
Tyres: 700 × 80

above 'Hyper' or S-type. In the 1928 Ulster Tourist Trophy race one of these cars, driven by Kaye Don, won at 64·06 mph for the 410 miles
below 12/40 hp 'P-type'. Introduced in 1928, this model had semi-elliptic springs at the rear, in place of the quarter-elliptics found on the earlier 12/22 'J-type'

Year: 1925
Model: 'Sports'
Maker's HP: 12/40
R.A.C. Rating: 11·9 hp
Number of Cylinders: 4
Bore and Stroke: 69 × 100 mm

Engine Capacity: 1·5 litres
Valves: overhead
Wheelbase: 8′ 9″
Forward Speeds: 4
Final Drive Ratio: 3·9 or 4·7 to 1
Tyres: 27 × 4·4

Year: 1927
Model: 'Hyper-Sports'
Maker's HP and R.A.C. Rating:
11·9 hp
Number of Cylinders: 4
Bore and Stroke: 69 × 100 mm

Engine Capacity: 1·5 litres
Valves: overhead. Supercharged
Wheelbase: 9′ 3″
Forward Speeds: 4
Final Drive Ratio: 3·75 or 4·7 to 1
Tyres: 27 × 4·4

Year: 1927
Maker's HP: 14/40
R.A.C. Rating: 13·4 hp
Number of Cylinders: 6
Bore and Stroke: 60 × 100 mm
Engine Capacity: 1·7 litres

Valves: overhead
Wheelbase: 9′ 9″
Forward Speeds: 4
Final Drive Ratio: 5 to 1
Tyres: 28 × 4·95

Year: 1928
Maker's HP: 16/60
R.A.C. Rating: 15·7 hp
Number of Cylinders: 6
Bore and Stroke: 65 × 100 mm
Engine Capacity: 2 litres

Valves: overhead
Wheelbase: 9′ 9″
Forward Speeds: 4
Final Drive Ratio: 5 to 1
Tyres: 28 × 4·95

Léon Bollée   France

Founded in 1842, as bell-founders and general engineers, Léon Bollée first
turned to steam cars in 1873, and were pioneers of the mechanically propelled
road-vehicle in France. After a short excursion into the realms of calculating
machines in 1878, this versatile firm next produced, in 1895, a stark three-
wheeled petrol-engined machine with a performance far ahead of its time. In
1900 came the first four-wheeler, but after these promising starts the Léon
Bollée relapsed into mediocrity, surviving until the end of the vintage decade.

1923 12/16 2-litre saloon. Vintage models were well-engineered but
old-fashioned in design, and the company's Le Mans factory was taken over by
Sir William Morris at the end of 1924

Year: 1922	*Valves:* side
Maker's HP: 16/20	*Wheelbase:* 10′ 3″
R.A.C. Rating: 15·9 hp	*Forward Speeds:* 4
Number of Cylinders: 4	*Final Drive Ratio:*
Bore and Stroke: 80 × 130 mm	*Tyres:* 815 × 105
Engine Capacity: 2·6 litres	

Year: 1923	*Valves:* overhead
Maker's HP: 12/16	*Wheelbase:* 9′ 10″
R.A.C. Rating: 12·8 hp	*Forward Speeds:* 4
Number of Cylinders: 4	*Final Drive Ratio:* 4 to 1
Bore and Stroke: 72 × 120 mm	*Tyres:* 765 × 105
Engine Capacity: 2 litres	

Leyland   England

The Leyland Eight was designed by Parry Thomas so that although it was intended solely as a luxury car it had a power-output and performance far above average.

First shown in 1920 the straight-eight engine comprised such unusual features as valves operated by an overhead camshaft and controlled by canti-lever leaf springs. The back axle had two spiral bevel gears whereby the two axle shafts could be inclined to counteract the steep camber of continental roads. Later, Thomas used this to effect on the banked surface of Brooklands by turning the axle upside down—perhaps this was even what he had in mind in introducing such an unusual feature.

It is strange that such an advanced design should have had only rear-wheel

Four-seater touring model. Some other examples of the 18 cars which were built had radiator shells which tapered from bottom to top and squarish headlamps with circular lenses. When the 'Eight' appeared at the 1920 Motor Show, the Press christened it the 'Lion of Olympia'. At £3,050 it was the most costly British car of the day brakes, even though they were vacuum-servo-assisted. Front springing was normal semi-elliptic but the back springs were quarter-elliptic mounted on torsion bars inside the frame. There were anti-roll bars at back and front.

In full touring trim the Leyland had a maximum of 90 mph which was far ahead of anything else in the luxury class prior to the 'Boulogne' Hispano-Suiza. As finally developed by Parry Thomas it took the Brooklands Lap Record at 129·36 mph and held it up to the time of his death in 1927.

Of the eighteen made, probably only one survives, happily in the hands of the Leyland Company, where it has been restored to mint condition by Leyland apprentices.

Year: 1920
Maker's HP: 40
R.A.C. Rating: 39·2 hp
Number of Cylinders: 8
Bore and Stroke: 89 × 146 mm
Engine Capacity: 7·2 litres

Valves: overhead
Wheelbase: 10′ 6″, 11′ 9″ or 12′ 6″
Forward Speeds: 4
Final Drive Ratio: 2·8 or 3·2 to 1
Tyres: 895 × 135

Le Zèbre   France

In a motoring journal under the heading of 'Le Zèbre' we read the sole rather enigmatic comment that 'it is a small French car of some note'. In the following specification it appears to be a perfectly normal side-valve, 4-cylinder light car with no exceptional mechanical features. It was available in French torpedo, English torpedo, and 2-seater de luxe form.

The remarks of an ex-owner of one of these cars, however, are interesting. It appears that the engine, clutch and gearbox were cast in one unit, and this method was satisfactory until oil began to run back through the clutch to the gearbox, necessitating its draining every fifty miles. It also suffered from the distressing habit of losing wheelnuts, and axle shafts broke regularly every 200 miles.

Year: 1920
Maker's H.P.: 8/10
R.A.C. Rating: 7·5 hp
Number of Cylinders: 4
Bore and Stroke: 55 × 105 mm
Engine Capacity: 1 litre
Valves: side
Wheelbase: 8′ 3″
Forward Speeds: 4
Final Drive Ratio: 5 to 1
Tyres: 710 × 90

1920 8/10. Its designers, Messrs. Salomon and Lamy, were later partly responsible for the 5CV Citroen and Amilcars respectively

Lincoln

When the Lincoln firm got into financial difficulties it was taken over by Henry Ford, who was thus able to revive his interest in making luxury cars which he had last had an opportunity of exploiting in the K Model Ford, twenty years previously.

The Lincoln was one of the highest quality American vintage cars, and its L-head, V-8 engine operated with extreme smoothness and reliability. It was, moreover, of handsome and dignified appearance, often with quite a number of European characteristics.

In 1932, Henry Ford produced an even more fabulous and expensive 7½-litre V-12 which had a top gear performance from 2 to nearly 100 mph, and was undoubtedly one of the great cars of the thirties.

1928 Sport-Phaeton and 1929 convertible coupé by Brunn. The original L-head V-8 engine was designed by Henry M. Leland after his departure from Cadillac in 1917

Year: 1923
Maker's HP and R.A.C. Rating:
36·4 hp
Number of Cylinders: 8
Bore and Stroke: 3½″ × 5″
Engine Capacity: 6·2 litres

Valves: side
Wheelbase: 11′ 4″
Forward Speeds: 4
Final Drive Ratio: 4·58 to 1
Tyres: 33 × 5

Lorraine-Dietrich   France

Known at different times as Lorraine-Dietrich and de Dietrich, the key to this confusing behaviour is found in the name of the Company which was 'Ste. Lorraine des Anciens Ets de Dietrich et Cie'. At one time metal workers to Louis XIV, the Company survived until shortly before the 1939 war. Their first car was made in 1897 to the design of Amédée Bollée, junior.

In early de Dietrich days the firm tended to employ free-lance designers among whom was the youthful Bugatti. Later they featured actively in racing and their 1912, 15-litre chain-driven Lorraine-Dietrich was among the last of the 'giants' in Grand Prix racing, being conclusively beaten by the 7½-litre Peugeot in that year. One of these cars came over to Brooklands and raced there until 1930, known as 'Vieux Charles Trois'. It subsequently appeared in Vintage Sports-Car Club events but its cylinder blocks are in a parlous state, so that its competition future seems doubtful.

Nineteen hundred and twenty saw two useful 6-cylinder Lorraine-Dietrichs in production, known as 'The Silken Six'. They had unit construction and aluminium pistons. But the outstanding vintage model was the 3½-litre sports car of 1925, which won the 24-hour race at Le Mans in both 1925 and 1926. The design was quite straightforward but the engine presented an unusual appearance, the overhead valves being operated by exposed pushrods of great length and hardly thicker than knitting needles. For some extraordinary reason only three speeds were fitted until 1930 when, as the B.36, it acquired four.

The handsome, round-topped radiator carries on its enamelled badge the two-headed cross of Lorraine; but unfortunately very few of these fine cars survive. The Company survives as road engineers.

Year: 1920
Maker's HP: 15
R.A.C. Rating: 20·9 hp
Number of Cylinders: 6
Bore and Stroke: 75 × 130 mm
Engine Capacity: 3·4 litres
Valves: overhead
Wheelbase: 10' 6"
Forward Speeds: 3
Final Drive Ratio: 3·9 to 1
Tyres: 815 × 105

Le Mans, 1925: floral tributes bedeck the winning 3½-litre car of de Courcelles/Rossignol. (Note also on the right the strange front end of Senechal's 1·1-litre Chenard et Walcker which won the Triennial Cup)

Year: 1920	*Valves:* side
Maker's HP: 30	*Wheelbase:* 10' 11½"
R.A.C. Rating: 30·1 hp	*Forward Speeds:* 4
Number of Cylinders: 6	*Final Drive Ratio:* 3·9 to 1
Bore and Stroke: 90 × 160 mm	*Tyres:* 895 × 135
Engine Capacity: 6·1 litres	

Year: 1925	*Engine Capacity:* 3·4 litres
Model: 'Sports'	*Valves:* overhead
Maker's HP: 20/70 (later 20/80)	*Wheelbase:* 9' 6"
R.A.C. Rating: 20·9 hp	*Forward Speeds:* 3
Number of Cylinders: 6	*Final Drive Ratio:* 3·5 to 1
Bore and Stroke: 75 × 130 mm	*Tyres:* 820 × 120

Le Mans, 1926: the 3·4-litre Bloch/Rossignol car which won, storms past the 1·2-litre E.H.P. (Ets. H. Precloux) of de Costier/Bussienne which came eighth

Marendaz Special   England

D. K. Marendaz was one-half of the firm who made the Marseal car—the other half being a Mr Seelhaft. It was from the 75 mph sports Marseal that the Marendaz Special was developed in 1926. It had the well-known 4-cylinder Anzani engine but later models had 8-cylinder engines of Miller origin, and all models were available with supercharger.

A Continental or Erskine engine could also be fitted. The Company survived until 1936.

Year: 1926	*Engine Capacity:* 1·5 litres
Maker's HP: 11/55 (when	*Valves:* side
supercharged 12/120)	*Wheelbase:* 8' 6" or 9' 4"
R.A.C. Rating: 11·9 hp	*Forward Speeds:* 3 or 4
Number of Cylinders: 4	*Final Drive Ratio:* 3·5 or 4·5 to 1
Bore and Stroke: 69 × 100 mm	*Tyres:* 700 × 80

Year: 1929
Maker's HP: 14/55 (when supercharged 14/125)
R.A.C. Rating: 13·3 hp
Number of Cylinders: 8
Bore and Stroke: 52 × 88 mm

Engine Capacity: 1·5 litres
Valves: overhead
Wheelbase: 9′ 3″
Forward Speeds: 4
Final Drive Ratio:
Tyres: 27 × 4·40

1927, 11/55 at £495. In 1928 the company took the 24-hour record for the 1100 and 1500 cc classes at Montlhéry track

Marmon   America

Howard Marmon was a millstone manufacturer before entering the car manufacturing business in 1902. In 1904 a V-4 engined car was produced, followed in 1906 by an air cooled 'V-8' with pushrod operated overhead valves.

During the vintage period two models were produced—a 6-cylinder model and a straight-8. Alloy was again extensively employed in engine construction and a particularly substantial frame was used; in fact, Marmons stated in a somewhat curious advertising slogan of the period that of 11,000 Model 34's delivered, only twelve had been returned with cracked chassis frames.

After a rather indifferent L-head 8-cylinder the most notable of all Marmon designs was produced in 1931—the V-16. Again it was a pushrod engine almost entirely made of aluminium with steel cylinder liners and claimed to develop over 200 bhp. This vehicle was intended to compete with the Duesenberg, Cadillac class but never quite attained the popularity it deserved. It was succeeded by a V-12-engined car of extremely advanced specification. The engine was the V-16 with the middle four cylinders taken out, but the chassis was of the tubular backbone type, in the best Austro-Daimler style. Independent rear suspension was adopted by the use of a de Dion axle but the car was introduced in the teeth of the world depression when the price of a car was the chief factor to consider rather than its design. The V-12 was the last of the Marmons and production ended in 1933.

left 1923 6-cylinder. Model 34. The ohv 5·6 litre engine produced 84 bhp at 2,450 rpm in 1920
right 1928 straight-8 coupé. The 8-cylinder engine came in two sizes that year —3·1-litres in the Model 68 and 3·5-litres in the Model 78

Year: 1925
Maker's HP and R.A.C. Rating:
33·7 hp
Number of Cylinders: 6
Bore and Stroke: $3\frac{3}{4}'' \times 5\frac{1}{8}''$
Engine Capacity: 5·6 litres

Valves: overhead
Wheelbase: 11' 4"
Forward Speeds: 3
Final Drive Ratio: 4·1 to 1
Tyres: $32 \times 4\frac{1}{2}$

Year: 1927
Maker's HP and R.A.C. Rating:
24·2 hp
Number of Cylinders: 8
Bore and Stroke: $2\frac{3}{4}'' \times 4''$
Engine Capacity: 3·1 litres

Valves: overhead
Wheelbase: 9' 8"
Forward Speeds: 3
Final Drive Ratio: 4·7 or 5·1 to 1
Tyres: $29 \times 5·25$

Maserati   Italy

The name of Maserati first became associated with racing in connection with Isotta Fraschini and Diatto cars.

From 1922 until 1925 Alfieri Maserati modified a Diatto to run in Grands Prix of the period, but without any notable success. He did, however, cause a mild sensation at the Grand Prix at San Sebastian in 1924, when he made some particularly pointed remarks about the similarity between the Sunbeam and Fiat designs.

The first Maserati racing car appeared (without success) as a supercharged 8-cylinder in 1926, but the car was gradually developed until in 1930–31 it was considered a likely winner in any race for which it was entered. 1930 was the *marque's* best season when it carried off five major road race victories. In

1929 the first of the 'Sedici Cilindri' was evolved—this fearsome machine consisted of two supercharged 2-litre 8-cylinder engines installed side by side in a special chassis, the crankshafts being geared together. The car proved unmanageable on twistier circuits except in the hands of the most experienced drivers but was timed at 152 mph over 10 kilometres at Cremona. Fortunately a unique Sports version still survives.

Although Maserati seldom listed production models until its later years, it kept to the highly commendable policy of offering new racing and sports-racing cars to the public.

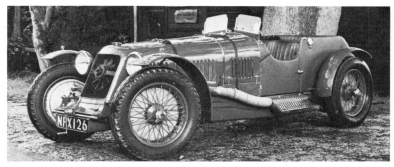

top 1928 Targa Florio: Luigi Fagioli sweeps through Campo Felice in a Tipo 26B, which had a maximum speed of about 125 mph. The 2-litre engine gave 145 bhp at 5,300 rpm
above 1930 Tipo 26M 2½-litre supercharged straight-8 sports-racing two-seater. The cooling fan has been fitted in the radiator cowl to cope with modern traffic conditions and is not original

Year: 1930	*Valves:* overhead
Maker's HP:	*Wheelbase:*
R.A.C. Rating: 21 hp	*Forward Speeds:* 4
Number of Cylinders: 8	*Final Drive Ratio:*
Bore and Stroke: 65 × 94 mm	*Tyres:*
Engine Capacity: 2·5 litres	

Mathis

France

Emile Mathis was an early protagonist of the small, multi-cylinder engine and marketed a small 4-cylinder as early as 1911. In this, he probably took his inspiration from Ettore Bugatti, whom he engaged in 1904 to design the Hermes car (for some mysterious reason sold in England as a 'Burlington').

His earliest vintage model was a fairly uninteresting 1140 cc, side-valve four, credited with 17 bhp at 2100 rpm. But in 1922 there appeared an even smaller, 800 cc model, and in the following year this acquired two additional cylinders to give a capacity of 1200 cc, which was then remarkably small for a 6-cylinder engine.

In 1925 this model (as listed below) was reorganized with the altered bore and stroke of 60 × 70 mm, giving almost the same capacity, and having overhead valves. In this form, with a pointed-tail two-seater body it was capable of 70 mph.

Year: 1921
Maker's HP: 8–10
R.A.C. Rating: 8·9 hp
Number of Cylinders: 4
Bore and Stroke: 60 × 100 mm
Engine Capacity: 1·1 litres

Valves: side
Wheelbase: 8' 0"
Forward Speeds: 4
Final Drive Ratio: 4·5 to 1
Tyres: 710 × 90

Year: 1922
Maker's HP: 6/8
R.A.C. Rating: 7·5 hp
Number of Cylinders: 4
Bore and Stroke: 55 × 80 mm
Engine Capacity: 0·8 litre

Valves: side
Wheelbase: 7' 6"
Forward Speeds: 4
Final Drive Ratio: 5 to 1
Tyres: 700 × 80

Year: 1923
Maker's HP: 12/14
R.A.C. Rating: 11·2 hp
Number of Cylinders: 6
Bore and Stroke: 55 × 80 mm
Engine Capacity: 1·2 litres

Valves: side
Wheelbase: 9' 0"
Forward Speeds: 4
Final Drive Ratio: 5 to 1
Tyres: 700 × 80

The 1,800 cc 'Emysix' appeared first in 1928. Weighing-in at just under 19 cwt, it went much better than it stopped

Maudslay England

Maudslay is the third company that was noted for commercial vehicle production, but also turned to motor-car production in the vintage period.

Before World War I Maudslay were noted for refined touring cars, the extraordinary feature of the design being a single overhead camshaft engine. After the war the Company again turned to private car manufacture and designed a vehicle that was not only the first British 2 ohc production car but also had specification comparable with the sports car practice of today.

The engine was a 6-cylinder of 2-litres capacity. The cylinder head was detachable carrying overhead valves in a hemispherical head. Valves were operated by twin overhead camshafts driven by a Y-shaped connecting rod at the back of the engine. Twenty-two roller bearings were used in the engine including the crankshaft, big-end and camshaft. They were lubricated by an eccentric plunger-type oil pump.

The ignition was by coil and the two Solex carburettors were fed by Autovac. A single-plate clutch and four-speed gearbox were used and the front half of the Perrot-type four-wheel brake system was servo-assisted and rod operated. The chassis was notably robust, the joints being flanged rather than brazed and the wheels were the centre lock (knock-off) Rudge Whitworth wire type.

Unhappily the Motor Show chassis was completely destroyed by fire at the coachbuilders, so the test chassis was hastily substituted causing considerable interest. However, the Company decided to concentrate on commercial vehicle business so one of the most interesting of the vintage period car designs was shelved, leaving us only to imagine what a 1930 Maudslay might have been like had production been allowed to continue.

Year: 1923
Model: 2-L.6
Maker's HP: 15/80
R.A.C. Rating: 15·7 hp
Number of Cylinders: 6
Bore and Stroke: 65 × 100 mm

Engine Capacity: 2 litres
Valves: overhead
Wheelbase: 10′ 3″
Forward Speeds: 4
Final Drive Ratio:
Tyres: 34 × 4½

A Gordon Crosby cut-away drawing of the 1923 2-LS, or 15/80, chassis, which was to cost £825 without bodywork

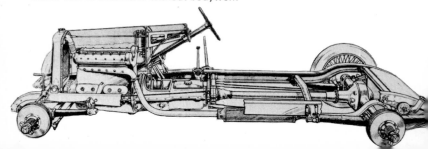

Maxwell   Canada

Maxwell had only one vintage model which was in production from 1920 to 1925 after which the firm was merged with the Chrysler Corporation.

Year: 1920	*Valves:* side
Maker's HP: 18/22	*Wheelbase:* 9′ 1″
R.A.C. Rating: 20·9 hp	*Forward Speeds:* 3
Number of Cylinders: 4	*Final Drive Ratio:* 3·58 to 1
Bore and Stroke: 92 × 114 mm	*Tyres:* 30 × 3½
Engine Capacity: 3 litres	

Maxwell-Chalmers Show Display of 1924. In fact the Maxwell Company (and its associate Chalmers) had been taken over by Walter P. Chrysler in 1923

Mercedes-Benz   Germany

The pioneer German firm of Daimler changed its name in 1901 to avoid sales-resistance on the important, but anti-German French market. Thenceforward all models were known as Mercedes. In 1925 Mercedes amalgamated with the equally ancient firm of Benz since when the style of the Company has been Daimler-Benz.

The Company is generally credited with having produced the first 'modern' motor-car in its 1901 35 hp, which had a pressed steel frame, honeycomb radiator, silent and flexible engine, and gate-change gears. In 1903, this was followed by the first 'sports' car, the famous 9-litre '60', a 4-cylinder, 140 × 150 mm

143

machine; later came the '90' and '120'.

If these were the sporting ideal of the Edwardian young blood, even more so were the vintage series, which seem to have been designed specifically to appeal to the mental adolescent. They had an arrogantly pointed radiator, outside exhaust pipes of enormous size, howling supercharger, and generally, coachwork to match.

However, the earliest vintage models were quite innocuous, including the excellent 28/95, intended for luxury coachwork.

In 1923, the 2·6-litre, 4-cylinder 10/40 became available with a supercharger which raised its modest maximum speed from 60 to 74 mph. While this was by no means the first supercharged car, it was the first supercharged car to be offered and sold in any numbers and until the advent of the supercharged Bugatti models in 1927, Mercedes-Benz had a virtual monopoly of this apparatus as fitted to production models. The supercharger was a Roots type. Whereas all other exponents of supercharging have placed the instrument between the carburettor and the engine, Mercedes-Benz preferred to pump air into the carburettor, and they persisted in this mistaken practice until as late as 1937. Their primary reason, at least initially, was that the engine would not stand up to supercharging for long, and they therefore had to apply it in such a way that the blower could be cut in at will, for short bursts of acceleration. This involved placing it outside the carburettor and it was driven by a clutch which was engaged by depressing the accelerator beyond the full throttle position. This layout also accounts for the excessive noise made by a supercharged Mercedes and enthusiasts spoke with bated breath of the surge of power and the exhilarating scream which the supercharger produced. About the scream there could be no doubt; the surge of power was more questionable. Thus, the 1927 6·1-litre model, claiming 180 bhp, could only manage 88 mph during an *Autocar* road test, and took twenty seconds to accelerate from 0 to 60 mph—figures which could be beaten by a 1920, 4½-litre, side-valve Vauxhall 30/98. In keeping with this pathetic performance were singularly ineffective brakes, a very temperamental clutch, and unmentionable fuel consumption.

When works-prepared for racing, however, some outstanding results were achieved, and a 'works' 38/250 with extra-large blower could certainly approach 150 mph. They also handled very well for such large machines.

The '38/250' was the last vintage model, and its place was taken in the later thirties by some even less effective straight-eights with four-wheel independent suspension.

Against this mostly rather undistinguished history must be set an entirely successful record in racing. Mercedes-Benz have only gone in for racing when it suited them from the point of view of politics, or publicity, and with minor exceptions they have always overwhelmingly attained their objective, whether in 1908, 1914, 1934–39, or 1954. To many people the 1937 straight-eight, 5·6-litre, 15 cwt Grand Prix Mercedes is the greatest racing car of all time.

Year: 1921
Maker's HP: 28/95
R.A.C. Rating: 41 hp
Number of Cylinders: 6
Bore and Stroke: 105 × 140 mm
Engine Capacity: 7·4 litres
Valves: overhead
Wheelbase: 11' 0$\frac{3}{8}$"
Forward Speeds: 4
Final Drive Ratio: 3·8 to 1
Tyres: 935 × 135

1922 Scheveningen Trials. No. 5:
6-cylinder 28/95; No. 3: Talbot

Year: 1922
Maker's HP: 6/20
R.A.C. Rating: 11·5 hp
Number of Cylinders: 4
Bore and Stroke: 68 × 108 mm
Engine Capacity: 1·5 litres

Valves: overhead
Wheelbase: 9' 1"
Forward Speeds: 4
Final Drive Ratio: 4 to 1
Tyres: 760 × 100

Year: 1922
Maker's HP: 10/35
R.A.C. Rating: 15·9 hp
Number of Cylinders: 4
Bore and Stroke: 80 × 130 mm
Engine Capacity: 2·6 litres

Valves: overhead (1923 with
supercharger)
Wheelbase: 10' 2"
Forward Speeds: 4
Final Drive Ratio:
Tyres: 820 × 120

Year: 1922
Maker's HP: 16/50
R.A.C. Rating: 24·8 hp
Number of Cylinders: 4
Bore and Stroke: 100 × 130 mm
Engine Capacity: 4·1 litres

Valves: sleeve
Wheelbase: 10' 9"
Forward Speeds: 4
Final Drive Ratio:
Tyres: 895 × 135

Year: 1925
Maker's HP: 33/140
R.A.C. Rating: 32·9 hp
Number of Cylinders: 6
Bore and Stroke: 94 × 150 mm
Engine Capacity: 6·1 litres

Valves: overhead
Wheelbase: 12' 4"
Forward Speeds: 4
Final Drive Ratio: 4·3 to 1
Tyres: 895 × 135

Year: 1927
Maker's HP: 33/180. Specification
as 33/140 but supercharged

Year: 1928
Maker's HP: 36/220
R.A.C. Rating: 35·7 hp
Number of Cylinders: 6
Bore and Stroke: 98 × 150 mm
Engine Capacity: 6·8 litres

Valves: overhead (supercharged)
Wheelbase: 11' 2"
Forward Speeds: 4
Final Drive Ratio: 2·5, 2·76 or
3·08 to 1, optional
Tyres: 895 × 135

Year: 1930
Maker's HP: 38/250
R.A.C. Rating: 37·2 hp
Number of Cylinders: 6
Bore and Stroke: 100 × 150 mm
Engine Capacity: 7·1 litres

Valves: overhead (supercharged)
Wheelbase: 11' 4"
Forward Speeds: 4
Final Drive Ratio: 2·76 to 1
Tyres: 20 × 6·5

top 1927 33/180 6·1-litre supercharged touring car. It was good for about 85 mph and cost £1,300 in Britain or 26,000 marks at home
above 1930 38/250 Type SS or 'Super Sports', supercharged 7·1-litre with 225 bhp on tap and a maximum speed around 115 mph

Mercer   America

In Edwardian times America produced some extremely fine sports cars, and none was finer than the Mercer. The make first went into production in 1909 and achieved its greatest fame with the four-speed, T-head model 35J of 1912.

With a bore and stroke of $4\frac{3}{8}'' \times 5''$ the engine had a capacity of 5 litres. It was mounted on a sub-frame and pulled a top gear ratio of 2·52 to 1, giving it a maximum of 75 mph at the peak engine speed of 2000 rpm.

These beautifully made and extremely handsome cars handled as well as the best Europeans of the period and were unusual in that the engine did not like operating on wide throttle openings at low revs. Their competition successes between 1911 and 1914 were numerous and important.

In 1915 Mercer abandoned the sub-frame and went over to a very long-stroke, L-head engine. Despite its 171 mm stroke it was capable of 2800 rpm and claimed to develop 72 bhp. This represents the then very high piston speed of 3150 feet per minute. Even so, the back axle ratio was as low as 3·87 to 1.

The model was known as the 22/70 and it remained in production until 1923, when it was replaced by an ohv six.

American enthusiasts dispute hotly as to the relative merits of the T- and L-head Mercers, but we believe the earlier T-head to be very much the better car. In any case, after the war, there was practically no sale for sports cars in the United States, and the survival of the Company even until 1925 was a considerable achievement.

Year: 1915
Maker's HP: 22/70
R.A.C. Rating: 22·4 hp
Number of Cylinders: 4
Bore and Stroke: $3\frac{3}{4}'' \times 6\frac{3}{4}''$
Engine Capacity: 4·8 litres

Valves: side
Wheelbase 11' 0" (also available shorter)
Forward Speeds: 4
Final Drive Ratio: 3·87 to 1
Tyres: $32 \times 4\frac{1}{2}$

1922 L-head 4-cylinder 'Raceabout', designed by A. C. Schultz who came to the Company from Locomobile

Métallurgique — Belgium

The Societé Anonyme des Automobiles Métallurgique began manufacturing cars in 1900. Their cars soon became popular and by 1908 a wide range of cars from 12 hp to 80 hp were produced. The firm also dabbled in Grand Prix racing as was the custom of most large concerns of that time, but without any notable success. In 1909 the famous 'V'-shaped radiator appeared; a shape that was to continue until the demise of the Company in 1926.

The vintage Métallurgique at first was of obvious Edwardian parentage but around 1924 the single chain-driven overhead camshaft 2-litre was evolved. Despite an unladen weight of 27 cwt this car could comfortably reach 75 mph with good road-holding. Later models had the letters F.N. cast on the cylinder block indicating a connection with the famous Fabrique Nationale engineering concern.

There are known to be three Métallurgique in existence—a 1910 12 hp phaeton, a 1925 ohc 2-litre tourer and the incomparable 1907 car with 1912, 21-litre, Maybach engine.

1924 2-litre single ohc skiff-tail four-seater, with aluminium 'engine-turned' bodywork by Compton. The Company was taken over by Minerva in 1927

Year: 1920
Maker's HP: 26
R.A.C. Rating: 24·8 hp
Number of Cylinders: 4
Bore and Stroke: 100 × 160 mm
Engine Capacity: 5 litres

Valves: side
Wheelbase: 12' 2½"
Forward Speeds: 4
Final Drive Ratio: 3 to 1
Tyres: 835 × 135

Year: 1921
Maker's HP: 14
R.A.C. Rating: 15·9 hp
Number of Cylinders: 4
Bore and Stroke: 80 × 130 mm
Engine Capacity: 2·6 litres

Valves: side
Wheelbase: 10' 7"
Forward Speeds: 4
Final Drive Ratio: 4·15 to 1
Tyres: 820 × 120

Year: 1922
Maker's HP: 18
R.A.C. Rating: 20 hp
Number of Cylinders: 4
Bore and Stroke: 90 × 140 mm
Engine Capacity: 3·6 litres

Valves: side
Wheelbase: 11' 4"
Forward Speeds: 4
Final Drive Ratio: 4·15 to 1
Tyres: 880 × 120 mm

Year: 1924
Maker's HP: 12/40
R.A.C. Rating: 12·1 hp
Number of Cylinders: 4
Bore and Stroke: 70 × 128 mm
Engine Capacity: 2 litres

Valves: overhead
Wheelbase: 10′ 2″
Forward Speeds: 4
Final Drive Ratio: 4·25 to 1
Tyres: 765 × 105

M.G.   England

M.G. stands for Morris Garages, of which Cecil Kimber was the general
manager. When he decided to build a sports car to his own design, mainly of
Morris parts, he called it an M.G.

The 1922–23 cars had a Hotchkiss ohv engine and a light pointed-tail body.
With the ordinary Morris bull-nose radiator it was a very handsome car.

In 1924 the M.G. went into limited production, although it was not until
1927 that it was made in any quantity. In production form the Morris side-
valve, 14/28 engine was used, in 1927 becoming known as the 14/40 with a
straight-edged Morris radiator. It was a good car, except for the quite useless
three-speed Morris gearbox.

In 1928 came the 18/80, which was an entirely M.G. design incorporating
only the ohc Morris 'Isis' engine. This again was a very good design and a
really handsome car, but the chassis was rather flexible for its 80 mph maximum, and once again there was the dreadful three-speed gearbox. In 1930,
therefore, the 18/80 Mark I was supplemented by the Mark II which had a
more substantial chassis and a useful four-speed gearbox, and also two carburettors. The slight loss in performance owing to additional weight was offset
by improved handling and the four-speed box. In 1930 five more highly tuned
versions were made for Le Mans, known as the Mark III, or 'Tiger'. As racing
cars they were not very successful, but at least one of them survives.

But it was the 'Midget' which really made the fame of the Company, first
introduced in 1928. The 'M' type had a fabric-covered two-seater body with
slightly pointed tail, joined in 1931, by the metal-covered 'D' type which was
otherwise basically similar. The engine was the ohc Morris 'Minor' unit, still
with a wide-ratio three-speed box, which vitiated the performance even more
drastically than on the 14/40 and 18/80. Nevertheless, the M.G. 'Midget' was
a thoroughly useful performer in its day and although it only developed about
20 bhp (the maker's 8/33 seems to have had no factual foundation) this was a
substantial advance over the contemporary Austin '7'.

For 750 cc class competition the 'Midget' could be had with the stroke
reduced to 73 mm, and with a four-speed gearbox with a short, remote-
control lever that pushed forward into top like many Bugattis. This 'C' type,
or 'Montlhéry Midget' was really a splendid car for its date, and when super-

charged (as was optional) it was said to develop 60 bhp—a sobering thought with a two-bearing crankshaft.

1925 'bull-nose' 14/28 sports-tourer, which sold for £360. About 400 were produced between 1924 and 1926

Year: 1924
Maker's HP: 14/28 (from 1927, 14/40)
R.A.C. Rating: 13·9 hp
Number of Cylinders: 4
Bore and Stroke: 75 × 102 mm
Engine Capacity: 1·8 litres
Valves: side
Wheelbase: 8' 10½"
Forward Speeds: 3
Final Drive Ratio: 4·4 to 1
Tyres: 27 × 4·4. (14/40 Mark IV introduced 1927)

The M-type 'Midget', of which over 3,000 were made, first appeared at the 1928 Motor Show priced at £175. It was in production from 1928 to 1932

Year: 1928
Model: 'M'
Maker's HP: 8/33
R.A.C. Rating: 8·05 hp
Number of Cylinders: 4
Bore and Stroke: 57 × 83 mm
Engine Capacity: 0·85 litre (for 'C' type, 57 × 73 mm = 0·75 litre)
Valves: overhead
Wheelbase: 6' 6"
Forward Speeds: 3 (for 'C': 4)
Final Drive Ratio: 4·89 to 1
Tyres: 27 × 4

The 18/80 Six (Mks. I, II and III) were in production from 1928 to 1933. The early versions were good for around 80 mph with first-rate acceleration—excellent performance for the day

Year: 1928. 'Mark I'
Maker's HP: 18/80
R.A.C. Rating: 17·7 hp
Number of Cylinders: 6
Bore and Stroke: 69 × 110 mm
Engine Capacity: 2·4 litres

Valves: overhead
Wheelbase: 9' 6"
Forward Speeds: 3
Final Drive Ratio: 4·27 to 1
Tyres: 29 × 5

Year: 1930. 'Mark II'. As Mark I
but four speeds

Minerva
Belgium

The Belgian firm of Minerva made motor-cycles from 1900 and motor-cars from 1902. They continued in the production of large high-quality cars up to 1939.

In the Edwardian era they occasionally went in for racing, their only notable success being to win the 1907 Kaiserpreis race in the hands of the late Lord Brabazon. As it was not a particularly good car the victory was mainly of Man over Machine. In 1909 they espoused the cause of the sleeve-valve and in 1914 they entered for the T.T. race. The sleeve-valve was considered, at that time, to gain over the poppet valve not only in silence, but to the extent of 12 per cent in actual power output and this was attributed to the fact that 'in the sleeve motor the flow sections are more favourable and owing to this the charging capacity is higher'. But be that as it might at low speeds, the sleeve valve had a pronounced tendency to seize at high revs, and to overcome this the racing Minerva had an excess oil supply arranged to operate at full throttle openings. The resultant smoke-screen gave extreme offence to the other competitors, and despite its 'higher charging capacity' the Minerva did not win the race.

1928 6-cylinder 32 hp 'AK' drophead coupé. Minervas were built in Antwerp from 1900 to 1939

For the vintage market the Minerva was available in 4- or 6-cylinder **form,** and the latter gradually increased in capacity from 5·3 to 6 litres. One of the latter performed creditably at Brooklands, and they were very good cars. Finally, in 1930, came a superlative straight-eight which continued into the post-vintage era.

With its highly distinctive radiator, with a curved top and raised centre-section whose contours were carried out into the bonnet line, the Minerva was as handsome as any luxury car of the vintage era.

Year: 1921
Maker's HP: 20
R.A.C. Rating: 20·1 hp
Number of Cylinders: 4
Bore and Stroke: 90 × 140 mm
Engine Capacity: 3·6 litres

Valves: sleeve
Wheelbase: 11' 2"
Forward Speeds: 4
Final Drive Ratio: 3·9 to 1
Tyres: 880 × 120

Year: 1921
Maker's HP: 30
R.A.C. Rating: 30·1 hp
Number of Cylinders: 6
Bore and Stroke: 90 × 140 mm
Engine Capacity: 5·4 litres

Valves: sleeve
Wheelbase: 11' 11"
Forward Speeds: 4
Final Drive Ratio: 3·4 to 1
Tyres: 880 × 120

Year: 1930
Maker's HP: 40
R.A.C. Rating: 40·1 hp
Number of Cylinders: 8
Bore and Stroke: 90 × 130 mm
Engine Capacity: 6·6 litres

Valves: sleeve
Wheelbase: 12' 9½"
Forward Speeds: 4
Final Drive Ratio: 3·73 to 1
Tyres: 32 × 6

Moon

America

Year: 1920
Maker's HP: 20
R.A.C. Rating: 25·6 hp
Number of Cylinders: 6
Bore and Stroke: 3¼" × 4½"
Engine Capacity: 3·9 litres
Valves: side
Wheelbase: 9' 10"
Forward Speeds: 3
Final Drive Ratio: 4 5/11 to 1
Tyres: 33 × 4½

1923 6-cylinder Sport-Phaeton tourer. Aimed at the luxury market, its radiator was a copy of that of the Rolls-Royce. The Moon rose in 1905 and set in 1930

Year: 1929
Maker's HP: 29
R.A.C. Rating: 28 hp
Number of Cylinders: 8
Bore and Stroke: 3" × 4¾"
Engine Capacity: 4·4 litres

Valves: side
Wheelbase: 10' 5½"
Forward Speeds: 3
Final Drive Ratio: 4·4 to 1
Tyres: 31 × 6·2

Morgan England

Although not strictly within the terms of reference of this book, the Morgan is included to represent the various vintage three-wheelers of which it was pre-eminently the best.

Morgans made only three-wheelers from 1910 up to 1936, when the Morgan 4/4 was introduced.

The make-up consisted of a tubular chassis; a choice of various V-twin engines, and two-speed chain drive by dog-clutches, much on the lines of the G.N. Until 1926 the only brake was on the back wheel. Independent front suspension by vertical coil springs has been used on all models from first to latest.

Even an Edwardian Morgan was capable of over 60 mph, and the early vintage models with J.A.P., Precision or M.A.G. engines of around 1000 cc capacity, and an all-up weight of 4 cwt, had really powerful acceleration. They all seemed, however, to be rather unnecessarily low geared.

In 1924 came the first of the various 'Aero' models with J.A.P., Anzani or Blackburne engine, and in 1927 the lower-built, wickedly handsome 'Super-aero' which could be made to do nearly 100 mph. A Morgan has covered a flying kilometre at 116 mph.

Morgan addicts claim that it is one of the safest things on wheels; lesser mortals think the addicts are just very brave.

1924 'Aero' model, with water-cooled Blackburne engine and Compton body. About 70 mph and 45 mpg were available

Year: 1920	*Valves:* side
Maker's HP: 8	*Wheelbase:* 6′ 0″
R.A.C. Rating: 8·96 hp	*Forward Speeds:* 2
Number of Cylinders: 2	*Final Drive Ratio:* 4·5 to 1
Bore and Stroke: 85 × 85 mm	*Tyres:* 700 × 80
Engine Capacity: 0·9 litre	

Year: 1924	*Engine Capacity:* 1·1 litres
Model: 'Aero'	*Valves:* overhead
Maker's HP: 8	*Wheelbase:* 6′ 0″
R.A.C. Rating: 8·96 hp	*Forward Speeds:* 2
Number of Cylinders: 2	*Final Drive Ratio:* 4·5 to 1
Bore and Stroke: 85 × 96·8 mm	*Tyres:* 27 × 4
(Blackburne engine)	

Morris England

From inconspicuous beginnings in 1912, Morris cars became vintage best-sellers. Not that they were very much better than the best of their rivals, such as the Clyno; but W. R. Morris built up an efficient assembly-line system of manufacture which enabled him to make startling price-reductions in 1922, to which his less efficiently produced competitors had no answer.

The early vintage Morris 'Cowley' and 'Oxford' had an engine partly of Morris's own design, and made for him in the Coventry factory of Hotchkiss. This was a surprisingly lively and practically indestructible unit and drove through a cork-insert clutch which was extremely smooth in action, though reluctant to disengage when cold.

The 'Cowley' was merely a cheap edition of the 'Oxford', but in 1923 the 'Oxford' was supplied with a large-bore engine. There was also a very rare bull-nosed 6-cylinder model, which can only have been in production for a very short time.

In 1927, the famous 'bull-nose' radiator gave way to the far less distinguished flat-fronted and straight-sided radiator which remained current on Morris cars until 1939.

W. R. Morris had always maintained that as long as you used only two valves per cylinder, there was no advantage to be gained from overhead valves. It was, therefore, a matter of some surprise, in 1928, when the Morris suddenly appeared, not only with overhead valves, but also an overhead camshaft, as the 'Minor' and 'Isis'. While in Morris form but little advantage was taken of this potentially high-efficiency fitment, it was at least of great advantage to the M.G. as may be read in the section on that make.

Year: 1919
Model: 'Oxford' and 'Cowley'
Maker's HP and R.A.C. Rating:
11·9 hp
Number of Cylinders: 4
Bore and Stroke: 69·5 × 102 mm
Engine Capacity: 1·5 litres
Valves: side
Wheelbase: 8' 6"
Forward Speeds: 3
Final Drive Ratio: 4·75 to 1
Tyres: 710 × 90 (Cowley: 700 × 80)

above 1921 'Oxford' with gilled-tube radiator and 'Doctor's Coupé' bodywork, originally owned by Lord Sandwich, and sold at auction for £225 in 1962
below 1928 'Isis' 6-cylinder tourer at £385

Year: 1923
Model: 'Oxford'. As for 1919 but
Bore and Stroke 75 × 102 mm, and

Engine Capacity 1·8 litres
Tyres: 26 or 28 × 3·5

Year: 1928
Model: 'Minor'
Maker's HP: 8
R.A.C. Rating: 8·05 hp
Number of Cylinders: 4
Bore and Stroke: 57 × 83 mm
Engine Capacity: 0·9 litre
Valves: overhead
Wheelbase: 6' 6"
Forward Speeds: 3
Final Drive Ratio: 4·9 to 1
Tyres: 27 × 4

1930 ohc 'Minor' with coachbuilt saloon bodywork

Year: 1928 Engine Capacity: 2·4 litres
Model: 'Isis' Valves: overhead
Maker's HP: 18 Wheelbase: 9′ 6″
R.A.C. Rating: 17·7 hp Forward Speeds: 3
Number of Cylinders: 6 Final Drive Ratio: 4·8 to 1
Bore and Stroke: 69 × 110 mm Tyres: 29 × 5·5

Mors   France

The Mors was one of France's finest makes in veteran and Edwardian times and this held good into their vintage model which, however, made no serious attempt to keep abreast of the times and the firm ceased manufacture in 1927.

Founded in 1895, Mors entered into racing in 1897 and by 1901 they were the first to provide an effective challenge to Panhard et Levassor supremacy. Soon they, in turn, were passed over by more progressive Italian and German designs and they retired from racing in 1908.

The vintage Mors was a 3·6-litre, 4-cylinder, sleeve-valve, developing 50 bhp at 2000 rpm. The radiator, with its raised centre section—not very distinguished in Edwardian form—had been moulded into a thing of real beauty, and in the corner of the honeycomb were the letters SSS, standing for 'Sans Soupapes Silencieuse'. A popular body was a comfortable two-seater with down-swept, pointed tail, of extremely elegant appearance. The car performed with that combination of considerable briskness and great refinement which characterized so many fine cars in the first vintage years, yet which is so rarely found from 1924 onwards.

Year: 1921 Engine Capacity: 3·6 litres
Model: 'SSS' Valves: sleeve
Maker's HP: 14/20 Wheelbase: 10′ 6″
R.A.C. Rating: 20·1 hp Forward Speeds: 4
Number of Cylinders: 4 Final Drive Ratio: 3·5 to 1
Bore and Stroke: 90 × 140 mm Tyres: 820 × 120

1925 tourer, seen here at the National Motor Museum at Beaulieu, alongside an Austro-Daimler of the same date

Motobloc France

The Motobloc's main claim to fame, both in vintage and Edwardian times, was that its flywheel was situated in the centre of the engine, between the two middle cylinders. This system gave an extremely vibration-free performance at all speeds. The valve layout was inlet over exhaust. The multi-plate clutch, gearbox and engine were all cast in one unit and lubricated by the same oil—hence the name 'Motobloc'. A 12 hp model survived after the war until the end of the vintage period, when the firm disappeared from the list of car manufacturers.

Year: 1920
Maker's HP: 12
R.A.C. Rating: 15·9 hp
Number of Cylinders: 4
Bore and Stroke: 80 × 120 mm
Engine Capacity: 2·4 litres

Valves: ioe
Wheelbase: 9' 10½"
Forward Speeds: 4
Final Drive Ratio: 4·8 to 1
Tyres: 820 × 120

12CV 4-cylinder with four-wheel-brakes, outside the London coachbuilding works of Louis Maffre who made the bodywork, c1922. Motoblocs acquired independent front suspension in 1928

Napier England

Montague Napier was the third generation of his family to practise as an engineer, and Napiers had been engineers for eighty or ninety years when he made his first motor-car in 1900.

This was largely based on the contemporary Panhard, and in 1900 it competed with success in the 1000-mile trial. From this time the business prospered and a lucky win in the 1902 Gordon Bennett race brought increased fame.

In 1904 Napier turned to the 6-cylinder engine and was perhaps just ahead of Sunbeam to be the first to market a production 'six'. Backed by S. F. Edge's flair for publicity and considerable racing success, the business prospered increasingly.

In 1919 an entirely new model was put on the market. The overhead camshaft operated slightly inclined valves, but like so many cars of the period, the potential advantages of this camshaft layout were stultified by very much restricted inlet manifolding, so that the 6·1-litre engine only produced 80 bhp. It was thus little if any faster than the contemporary Rolls-Royce 'Silver Ghost' and not quite as refined.

The cylinder block and crankcase were aluminium with pressed-in steel liners. The suspension was by semi-elliptic springs at the front, and cantilever at the back with an anti-roll device.

The 40/50 continued in production until 1925, the last few chassis having front brakes. Thereafter the factory turned over entirely to aero-engines, and various of these were subsequently used with great success in a variety of record-breaking racing cars.

In 1931, when the Bentley Company went into liquidation, Napiers made arrangements for buying the assets and had arranged with W. O. Bentley to

top 1921 40/50 hp with 'All-Weather' body by the Regent Carriage Company
above 1921 40/50 tourer by Cunard, with individual hoods for the front and rear seats

design and build a 6¼-litre machine based upon the 8-litre Bentley. From the showing of the 8-litre this would undoubtedly have been one of the finest British cars of all time. Whether they got wind of the project is not known, but Rolls-Royce certainly stepped in with surprising suddenness at the last moment and out-bid Napier in the slightly distressing circumstances which Mr Bentley has told in his splendid autobiography. Rolls-Royce thus strangled at birth what, with the combined genius of Bentley and prestige of Napier, might have proved to be an exceedingly embarrassing competitor. In doing so they robbed England of a motor-car which would certainly have redounded greatly to her credit.

Year: 1919
Maker's HP: 40/50
R.A.C. Rating: 38·4 hp
Number of Cylinders: 6
Bore and Stroke: 4″ × 5″
Engine Capacity: 6·1 litres

Valves: overhead
Wheelbase: 11′ 5″
Forward Speeds: 4
Final Drive Ratio: 3·3 or 3·75 to 1
Tyres: 895 × 135

Nash   America

Before finally appearing as the 'Nash' in 1917, the Company marketed cars known as the 'Jeffery' in 1914 and the 'Rambler' in 1901.

The prototype 1901 'Rambler', having a forward mounted engine and a steering wheel, was rejected as being too radical. Production was started in 1902, the car finding favour with the public and 1500 being made during that year. A satisfied customer is reputed to have written to the Company that 'it starts immediately and runs like a Jack-rabbit'—a somewhat questionable recommendation.

By 1910 the height of luxury was attained, the limousine being equipped with speaking tube, mirror, clock, cigar case and broom holder.

1926 Model 21 'Light Six', with John Davidson

During the vintage period a 6-cylinder car was produced and in 1930 the inevitable 'Eight' appeared—a vogue similar to the 'Light Six' period so popular in England a few years earlier.

Year: 1920	*Valves:* overhead
Maker's HP: 20/25	*Wheelbase:* 10' 1"
R.A.C. Rating: 25·35 hp	*Forward Speeds:* 3
Number of Cylinders: 6	*Final Drive Ratio:* 4·5 to 1
Bore and Stroke: $3\frac{1}{4}'' \times 5''$	*Tyres:* 33 × 4
Engine Capacity: 4 litres	

Year: 1930	*Valves:* overhead
Maker's HP and R.A.C. Rating: 33·8 hp	*Wheelbase:* 10' 4" or 11' 1"
	Forward Speeds: 3
Number of Cylinders: 8	*Final Drive Ratio:* 4·5 to 1
Bore and Stroke: 82·5 × 114·3 mm	*Tyres:* 32 × 6
Engine Capacity: 5 litres	

Newton-Ceirano England

This make and model is identical with the Model S.150 Italian Ceirano (q.v. and **illustration**).

Year: 1927	*Valves:* overhead
Maker's HP: 14	*Wheelbase:* 8' 9"
R.A.C. Rating: 10·4 hp	*Forward Speeds:* 4
Number of Cylinders: 4	*Final Drive Ratio:* 4·5 to 1
Bore and Stroke: 65 × 110 mm	*Tyres:* 730 × 130
Engine Capacity: 1·4 litres	

Oldsmobile America

The Oldsmobile was designed by Ransom E. Olds. He had received an engineering grounding by working for his father, Pliny F. Olds, in a company manufacturing gas engines. In 1891 a steam passenger vehicle was made, very similar in design to the contemporary Amédée Bollée. The first petrol driven car was made in 1897, quickly followed by the famous 'Curved dash'' model. The 'Curved dash' is one of the best-known early American cars, and was the first of the modern fashion of manufacturing replicas.

After 1923 the Company, with the majority of the rest of the American car manufacturing firms, persevered with one model, an 18 hp, 6-cylinder.

Year: 1920
Maker's HP: 18·9
R.A.C. Rating: 19·2 hp
Number of Cylinders: 6
Bore and Stroke: 72 × 120 mm
Engine Capacity: 2·6 litres
Valves: side
Wheelbase: 9′ 4″
Forward Speeds: 3
Final Drive Ratio: 4·3 to 1
Tyres: 815 × 105

Town Sedan: the 6-cylinder Model 30 was introduced in 1923, and 44,000 cars were sold

O.M. Italy

The O.M. managed to produce an almost indecent amount of power from a relatively uninteresting side-valve engine. Indeed until 1933 when the Company were told to turn to commercial vehicle manufacture by Mussolini, the O.M. dogmatically adhered to side-valves in a country whose high performance cars generally sported at least one, or more often two, overhead camshafts.

The Company, whose initials stand for Officine Mecchaniche, built ships, locomotives, and lorries in 1918 on a very large scale. In 1920 there appeared a 10/30 hp car with the familiar side-valves, that ran in modified form in the 1921 Targa Florio. In 1918 O.M. took over the Zust factory and the early Targa Florio cars had a rounded, bull-nose, Zust-like radiator.

In 1923 a 6-cylinder of 2-litres capacity was introduced, the engine developing 45 bhp. These cars had excellent handling qualities and very light and accurate steering due to precise weight distribution.

In competitions about this time the O.M. was very successful, gaining first, second and third places in the first Mille Miglia, and winning the Rudge Whitworth cup at Le Mans. The 15/60 sports model with triple diffuser Zenith carburettor was developed from these cars, and developed 60 bhp at 4000 rpm.

Meanwhile the English concessionaires L. C. Rawlence & Co. produced an ohv head and several minor alterations such as right hand gear change. These ohv cars may be distinguished by their smaller, narrower radiator. At the end of the vintage period came the 2·2-litre supercharged model—a very handsome car with sloping radiator and Zagato-type coachwork. With the Rawlence head it developed 95 bhp. In 1935 the factory was requisitioned to build lorries for the Italo-Abyssinian war.

O.M. attempted an entry into G.P. racing in 1927 with two 1½-litre 8-cylinder supercharged cars. A three-speed gearbox made the cars quite unsuitable for road racing at a time when Delage had five and Bugatti four speeds. They did nevertheless obtain very creditable second and fourth places in the G.P. d'Europe at Monza in 1927.

Year: 1920
Maker's HP: 10/30
R.A.C. Rating: 11·9 hp
Number of Cylinders: 4
Bore and Stroke: 69 × 100 mm
Engine Capacity: 1·5 litres
Valves: side
Wheelbase: 9′ 2″
Forward Speeds: 4
Final Drive Ratio: 5·2 to 1
Tyres: 765 × 105

Treasure Hunt: the Tipo 665 6-cylinder 4-seater tourer. The 2-litre O.M.s had first-class brakes and a fast gear-change

Year: 1924
Maker's HP: 15/45
R.A.C. Rating: 15·7 hp
Number of Cylinders: 6
Bore and Stroke: 65 × 100 mm
Engine Capacity: 2 litres
Valves: side
Wheelbase: 10′ 2″
Forward Speeds: 4
Final Drive Ratio: 5 to 1
Tyres: 765 × 105

Overland

Nationality various

This confusing make had, at different times, factories in America, England and Canada.

Year: 1919. Nationality, America
Maker's HP: 19
R.A.C. Rating: 18·2 hp
Number of Cylinders: 4
Bore and Stroke: $3\frac{3}{8}″ \times 5″$
Engine Capacity: 2·9 litres
Valves: side
Wheelbase: 8′ 4″
Forward Speeds: 3
Final Drive Ratio: 4·5 to 1
Tyres: 30 × $3\frac{1}{2}$

1927 'Whippet Coach' 2·2-litre 4-cylinder. The earlier Model 4 sold well in Britain. To avoid duty, its mechanical parts were made in Toronto and the cars were assembled in Manchester where the bodies were made

Year: 1924. Nationality, British
Maker's HP and R.A.C. Rating:
13.9 hp
Number of Cylinders: 4
Bore and Stroke: 75 × 102 mm
Engine Capacity: 1·8 litres

Valves: side
Wheelbase: 8′ 10″
Forward Speeds: 3
Final Drive Ratio: 4·5 to 1
Tyres: 31 × 4·4

Year: 1928. Nationality, Canada
Model: 'Whippet'
Maker's HP: 21
R.A.C. Rating: 21·6 hp
Number of Cylinders: 6
Bore and Stroke: 3″ × 4″

Engine Capacity: 2·7 litres
Valves: side
Wheelbase: 9′ 1½″
Forward Speeds: 3
Final Drive Ratio: 5·11 to 1
Tyres: 29 × 4·75

Packard
America

It is not sufficiently realized in England what almost uniformly superb cars were made by Packards from the earliest years at least up to 1939. The firm was founded in 1899 and by Edwardian times was making a thumping 4-cylinder with considerable sporting capabilities.

In 1915 came the 'Twin-Six', which was a 6·9-litre V-12 and which proved to be a formidable answer to the Cadillac V-8. Developing 75 bhp, and not unduly heavy, it is probable that a 'Twin-Six' could see off a 1919 'Silver Ghost' or 40/50 Napier and with at least equal smoothness and flexibility. They were, moreover, very expensive and correspondingly well made, if not always in a way to please European aesthetic taste.

The 'Twin-Six' remained in production until 1923 by which time over 35,000 had been made. It was then replaced by the first straight eight; a six had been offered since 1920. The latter seems to have been supplied with various back axle ratios of which the higher, 4·08 to 1, gave it an acceptably high cruising speed, while the flexibility and smoothness of the engine was little inferior to the 'Twin-Six'. With its rigidly mounted engine, quite high-geared and very positive steering, and reasonably effective front brakes the vintage Packard straight-eight is a machine which any connoisseur of fine cars could be proud to own.

Nor did the standard fall off in the thirties when (subsidized by a line of cheaper 'pot-boilers') the Company continued to build prestige cars whose overall excellence was second to none. These were the 'Super-eight' and the 'Twelve', which was a return to the V-12 layout, of over 7 litres capacity.

American collectors avidly import Continental vintage cars; it would be nice to see a few more Packards in Europe. A 'Twin-Six' would be an outstanding possession, but it is doubtful if one exists outside America.

Year: 1915
Model: 'Twin-Six'
Maker's HP and R.A.C. Rating:
43·2 hp
Number of Cylinders: 12
Bore and Stroke: 3″ × 5″

Engine Capacity: 6·9 litres
Valves: side
Wheelbase: 11′ 4″
Forward Speeds: 3
Final Drive Ratio: 4·36 to 1
Tyres: 35 × 5

Year: 1921
Maker's HP and R.A.C. Rating:
27·3 hp
Number of Cylinders: 6
Bore and Stroke: 3⅜″ × 5″
Engine Capacity: 4·3 litres

Valves: side
Wheelbase: 10′ 6″
Forward Speeds: 3
Final Drive Ratio: 4·33 to 1
Tyres: 33 × 4½

Year: 1923
Maker's HP and R.A.C. Rating:
36·4 hp
Number of Cylinders: 8
Bore and Stroke: 3⅜″ × 5″
Engine Capacity: 5·9 litres

Valves: side
Wheelbase: 11′ 6″
Forward Speeds: 3
Final Drive Ratio: 4·08 or 4·33 to 1
Tyres: 33 × 5

top 1921 'Twin Six', the first 12-cylinder car to go into series production and the first American touring car to have aluminium pistons
above 1930 Model 734 'Speedster'. These 8-cylinder sporting models had a high axle ratio, 4-speed gearboxes and 145 bhp

Palladium
England

An Edwardian chain-driven, 2-cylindered car was Palladium's first venture into motor car production. In 1922 a light car with a Hotchkiss engine was offered and was tested at 47 mph over the mile at Brooklands. A Dorman engine was substituted in 1923 together with front-wheel brakes—an unusual feature for light cars at that time. The Dorman engine apparently provided a substantial increase in power as we are told that 60 mph could be reached. The make attained considerable popularity but was unable to cope with the large number of orders placed, and the Company ceased manufacture in 1925.

Year: 1922
Maker's HP: 12
R.A.C. Rating: 11·9 hp
Number of Cylinders: 4
Bore and Stroke: 69 × 100 mm
Engine Capacity: 1·5 litres

Valves: side
Wheelbase: 9′ 3″
Forward Speeds: 3
Final Drive Ratio: 4·66 to 1
Tyres: 760 × 90

The 1923 Palladium was unusual for a British light car in having efficient four-wheel brakes, but it was rather expensive at £395

Panhard et Levassor
France

At first representing German Daimler interests in France, Panhard et Levassor rapidly assumed pre-eminence in their own right. By 1890 they had established the layout of the conventional modern motor-car with its engine at the front, driving through a sliding-pinion gearbox. In 1895 a Panhard won the world's first motor race, from Paris to Bordeaux and back, averaging 15 mph over the total distance of 732 miles. Panhards continued to dominate the racing scene until 1902, but after this they failed to keep abreast of progress, although the great reputation which they had won for themselves in the early years continued to stand them in good stead in the retail market, where they concentrated mostly on high-quality luxury cars.

In the vintage decade they employed sleeve-valve engines almost exclusively, which developed a power output per litre comparable with the best poppet valve engines of the period. This was in part due to the pioneer use of light steel valves, in place of cast iron. In 1922 came a 6½-litre straight-eight which later grew to 8 litres (for record work only), and one of the latter took the world's hour record at Brooklands, as late as 1934, at 133 mph.

1923 18/30 4-cylinder coupé de ville by Hooper

Year: 1920
Maker's HP: 14/20
R.A.C. Rating: 12·8 hp
Number of Cylinders: 4
Bore and Stroke: 72 × 140 mm
Engine Capacity: 2·3 litres

Valves: side
Wheelbase: 9′ 4″
Forward Speeds: 4
Final Drive Ratio: 4·5 to 1
Tyres: 765 × 105

Year: 1920
Maker's HP: 18/30
R.A.C. Rating: 17·9 hp
Number of Cylinders: 4
Bore and Stroke: 85 × 140 mm
Engine Capacity: 3·2 litres

Valves: sleeve
Wheelbase: 10′ 9″
Forward Speeds: 4
Final Drive Ratio: 4 to 1
Tyres: 820 × 120

Year: 1920
Maker's HP: 28/40
R.A.C. Rating: 27·3 hp
Number of Cylinders: 4
Bore and Stroke: 105 × 140 mm
Engine Capacity: 4·9 litres

Valves: sleeve
Wheelbase: 11′ 4″
Forward Speeds: 4
Final Drive Ratio: 3·5 to 1
Tyres: 880 × 120

Year: 1922
Maker's HP: 40/50
R.A.C. Rating: 35·8 hp
Number of Cylinders: 8
Bore and Stroke: 85 × 140 mm
Engine Capacity: 6·4 litres

Valves: sleeve
Wheelbase: 12′ 4⅝″
Forward Speeds: 4
Final Drive Ratio: 3·5 to 1
Tyres: 895 × 135

Year: 1927
Maker's HP: 20/60
R.A.C. Rating: 20·9 hp
Number of Cylinders: 6
Bore and Stroke: 75 × 130 mm
Engine Capacity: 3·5 litres
Valves: sleeve
Wheelbase: 11′ 9″
Forward Speeds: 4
Final Drive Ratio: 4 to 1
Tyres: 835 × 135

1926 6·4-litre, sleeve-valve, straight-eight saloon with 'basket-work' body

1929 20CV, sleeve-valve, 4-cylinder sports-coupé

Peerless   America

Packard, Pierce-Arrow and Peerless were known as 'the three P's' and considered quite the aristocracy of American vintage motoring.

From 1916 to 1923 Peerless concentrated on a fine V-8 about which perhaps the most unusual feature, for an American car, was a multi-plate clutch. In

1925 6-cylinder, 2-seater, 6-80 Roadster at $2,335. Rather dreary-looking bodies did not help sales of the mid-1920s models, which were given a face-lift (fairly successfully) in 1929

1925 came a more conventional six (with single-plate clutch) and the Company finally passed out in 1931.

Year: 1922	*Valves:* side
Maker's HP and R.A.C. Rating:	*Wheelbase:* 10' 5"
33·8 hp	*Forward Speeds:* 3
Number of Cylinders: 8	*Final Drive Ratio:* 4·9 to 1
Bore and Stroke: $3\frac{1}{4}'' \times 5''$	*Tyres:* $34 \times 4\frac{1}{2}$
Engine Capacity: 5·4 litres	

Year: 1925	*Valves:* side
Maker's HP and R.A.C. Rating:	*Wheelbase:* 10' 6"
29·4 hp	*Forward Speeds:* 3
Number of Cylinders: 6	*Final Drive Ratio:* 4·64 to 1
Bore and Stroke: $3\frac{1}{2}'' \times 5''$	*Tyres:* 33×620
Engine Capacity: 4·7 litres	

Peugeot
France

Peugeot is one of the oldest names in the industry. The firm was founded in 1889, and a Peugeot is recorded as having travelled from Paris to Brest in 1891, while in the Paris–Rouen trials of 1894 the first place was shared by Panhard and Peugeot. In the first motor race, in 1895, from Paris to Bordeaux and back, a Peugeot came second to the winning Panhard.

These veteran Peugeots used the 15 degree V-twin Daimler engine, rear-mounted in a tubular chassis. They never made much of a mark in nineteenth-century racing, but in 1906 they returned to racing in the voiturette class which they dominated for a time with exceedingly crude but effective singles and twins of immensely long stroke.

Their next racing effort was the epoch-making 1912 Grand Prix winner, designed by the Swiss Ernest Henry. With its twin overhead camshafts and relatively high-efficiency engine, the racing Peugeot of 1912 and '13 laid down the lines of racing design for many years to come. In 1914, Peugeot were among the pioneers of front brakes for racing.

Edwardian touring Peugeots were mostly large side-valve cars, but in 1911 they engaged Ettore Bugatti to design their 'Bébé' which was probably the first 4-cylinder production car of less than 1000 cc. It was in fact only 850 cc, with a fixed T-head, 55×90 mm engine. These little cars enjoyed considerable popularity but in 1920 they were replaced by the even smaller, very high-spirited 'Quadrilette' of only 680 cc. At first with a very narrow, tandem two-seater body this graduated by degrees to a more serious conveyance and remained in production until 1930. With its transverse front spring and ball-main-bearing engine it probably had a considerable influence on the design of the Austin '7'.

Other early Peugeots were of conventional side-valve design but in 1922 the firm produced a 6-cylinder sleeve-valve, with the light steel sleeves pioneered by Panhard, and this model was known as the T.156. In 1923, the 3·8-litre 4-cylinder won the Touring Car Grand Prix at Tours and went into production about the same time. While it is impossible to accept the ridiculously high power outputs claimed for the sleeve-valve Panhards and Peugeots of this period, in relationship to their known performance, they undoubtedly compared favourably with poppet valve engines of the period, and Peugeots did extremely well in touring-car events throughout the vintage years. They were noted for their economical fuel consumption.

Another sleeve-valve Peugeot had a remarkably long racing history, from the 1922 Targa Florio to the 1931 French Grand Prix. It did not feature prominently in either, but in the 1930 Grand Prix at Spa it led until the last lap when it ran out of fuel.

Year: 1920
Model: 'Quadrilette'
Maker's HP: 4
R.A.C. Rating: 6·2 hp
Number of Cylinders: 4
Bore and Stroke: 50 × 85 mm
Engine Capacity: 0·7 litre
Valves: side
Wheelbase: 7' 7"
Forward Speeds: 3
Final Drive Ratio: 5·25 to 1
Tyres: 650 × 65

1920 16 hp four-seater tourer

1921 Type 161 'Quadrilette'. Its rear track of but thirty inches made 'tandem' (or 'staggered' in some versions) seating a necessity

Year: 1920
Maker's HP: 11
R.A.C. Rating: 10·8 hp
Number of Cylinders: 4
Bore and Stroke: 66 × 105 mm
Engine Capacity: 1·4 litres
Valves: side
Wheelbase: 8' 3¾"
Forward Speeds: 4
Final Drive Ratio: 5·25 to 1
Tyres: 710 × 90

Year: 1920
Maker's HP: 16
R.A.C. Rating: 16·7 hp
Number of Cylinders: 4
Bore and Stroke: 82 × 130 mm
Engine Capacity: 2·7 litres

Valves: side
Wheelbase: 10' 1¾"
Forward Speeds: 4
Final Drive Ratio: 4·6 to 1
Tyres: 820 × 120

Year: 1922
Type 156
Maker's HP: 32
R.A.C. Rating: 33·2 hp
Number of Cylinders: 6
Bore and Stroke: 95 × 140 mm

Engine Capacity: 6 litres
Valves: sleeve
Wheelbase: 12' 0½"
Forward Speeds: 4
Final Drive Ratio: 3·2 to 1
Tyres: 895 × 135

Year: 1923
Maker's HP: 23/65
R.A.C. Rating: 22·4 hp
Number of Cylinders: 4
Bore and Stroke: 95 × 135 mm
Engine Capacity: 3·8 litres

Valves: sleeve
Wheelbase: 11' 6"
Forward Speeds: 4
Final Drive Ratio: 3·7 to 1
Tyres: 896 × 135

Louis Wagner at the wheel of the 3·8-litre he shared with Dauvergne at
Le Mans in 1926. They retired due to electrical faults

Pierce-Arrow   America

Packard, Peerless and Pierce-Arrow are generally regarded in America as
their outstanding quality cars of the vintage era. Neither the Peerless nor
Pierce-Arrow, however, had the business ability of Packard to keep going
through the depression of the thirties. The vintage Pierce-Arrow had little of
of interest other than its high quality of manufacture and finish. It is rare even
in America and there is only one in England. It certainly did not compare

with its Edwardian predecessor, the monumental 13-litre, 6-cylinder 'Great Pierce-Arrow'.

Before they turned to motor manufacture, Pierce-Arrow appear to have made bird-cages.*

Year: 1920
Maker's HP: 38
R.A.C. Rating: 38·2 hp
Number of Cylinders: 6
Bore and Stroke: 4″ × 5½″
Engine Capacity: 6·9 litres

Valves: side
Wheelbase: 11′ 2″
Forward Speeds: 4
Final Drive Ratio
Tyres: 35 × 5

Year: 1930
Maker's HP and R.A.C. Rating:
39·2 hp
Number of Cylinders: 8
Bore and Stroke: 3½″ × 4¾″
Engine Capacity: 6 litres

Valves: side
Wheelbase: 11′ 1″
Forward Speeds: 3
Final Drive Ratio: 4·23 to 1
Tyres: 19 × 650

1923 Model 80 Coupé Sedan—whose 6·9-litre, L-head, 6-cylinder engine produced a rather sad 70 bhp

Renault   France

The Renault Company was founded in 1898, and until the death of Marcel Renault in the Paris–Madrid race of 1903, Renaults were active in light car racing where, owing to their more restrained appetite for tyres, they not infrequently kept up with, or even beat, the unrestrained monsters. Renaults

---

* According to the invaluable reference work *The World's Automobiles, 1880–1955*, by G. R. Doyle, published by Temple Press, Ltd.

were also champions from the first of the live axle and no Renault ever had chain drive.

In 1906, 1907 and 1908 Renaults were entered for the Grand Prix, which they won in 1906.

Edwardian touring Renaults were conventional side-valve machines (as indeed were the racing cars, from which they differed but little except as to power-weight ratio), famous for their almost complete indestructibility. The little 2-cylinder model, also, was one of the nicest Edwardian small cars.

The same qualities were found in all vintage Renaults whose performance varied exclusively as the size of the engine, from the little 8·3 hp to the giant '45'. In fact, so far as the engines are concerned, there is little to distinguish a vintage from an Edwardian specimen. The 7½-litre '40', which later had the bore increased from 100 mm to 110 mm to give it a capacity of 9·1 litres, as the '45' was undoubtedly the largest vintage car in serious production, and in nearly all respects it was an Edwardian design, even to wooden-spoked wheels. In 1925 a sporting version became available with a 3 to 1 axle ratio, and a considerable performance which was not matched by its cornering abilities. In 1926 a single-seater version took the 24-hour record at Montlhéry at 108·3 mph, covering its last lap at 119 mph—a considerable feat on that track.

The only serious shortcoming of the '45' was the inadequacy of its electric starting arrangements, and so that the owner could give these physical assistance, he was supplied with a decompressor control, and a starter-motor button, both conveniently adjacent to the starting handle.

The '45' continued in production until 1929 when it was replaced by a slightly smaller straight-eight. Until 1929, Renaults retained their radiator at the back of the engine, where they had put it in 1904.

Year: 1919
Maker's HP: 12
R.A.C. Rating: 15·9 hp
Number of Cylinders: 4
Bore and Stroke: 80 × 140 mm
Engine Capacity: 2·8 litres

Valves: side
Wheelbase: 10' 1"
Forward Speeds: 4
Final Drive Ratio: 4·3 to 1
Tyres: 815 × 105

Year: 1919
Maker's HP: 18
R.A.C. Rating: 22·4 hp
Number of Cylinders: 4
Bore and Stroke: 95 × 160 mm
Engine Capacity: 4·6 litres
Valves: side
Wheelbase: 10′ 11″
Forward Speeds: 4
Final Drive Ratio: 4·45 to 1
Tyres: 820 × 120

Year: 1919
Maker's HP: 40
R.A.C. Rating: 37·2 hp
Number of Cylinders: 6
Bore and Stroke: 100 × 160 mm
Engine Capacity: 7·5 litres

Valves: side
Wheelbase: 12′ 6″ or 13′ 2″
Forward Speeds: 3 or 4
Final Drive Ratio: 4 to 1
Tyres: 920 × 120

Year: 1923
Maker's HP and R.A.C. Rating:
8·3 hp
Number of Cylinders: 4
Bore and Stroke: 58 × 90 mm
Engine Capacity: 1 litre

Valves: side
Wheelbase: 8′ 0″
Forward Speeds: 3
Final Drive Ratio: 5·25 to 1
Tyres: 700 × 80

left White Elephant: the 1929 9·1-litre, fixed-head, 45 hp, seven-seater tourer had wooden wheels—and an eventual maximum speed of about 90 mph
top Other end of the scale—Renault's answer to the Citroën light car: 1924/5 6CV NN Type 8·3 hp saloon
above 1929 'Reinastella' straight-8, with conventional radiator for'ard, water pump and servo-assisted brakes. The four-door touring body is by Million-Guiet

173

Year: 1929
Maker's HP: 40
R.A.C. Rating: 40·2 hp
Number of Cylinders: 8
Bore and Stroke: 90 × 140 mm
Engine Capacity: 7·1 litres

Valves: side
Wheelbase: 12′ 0″
Forward Speeds: 3
Final Drive Ratio: 4 to 1
Tyres: 32 × 6·75

Year: 1930
Maker's HP and R.A.C. Rating:
12·5 hp
Number of Cylinders: 6
Bore and Stroke: 58 × 93 mm
Engine Capacity: 1·5 litres

Valves: side
Wheelbase: 8′ 8¼″
Forward Speeds: 3
Final Drive Ratio: 5·1 to 1
Tyres: 12 × 45

Rhode   England

From their introduction in 1921 Rhode cars had overhead valves, at first operated by a shaft-driven camshaft and later by pushrods. Although this factor undoubtedly gave more power to the engine—we are told in a contemporary report 'that the car can climb quite steep hills without issuing steam from its vent pipe'—it caused quite noticeable drumming and vibration. Lubrication was by the centrifugal principle. The flywheel dipped itself in the sump oil and flung it up a vertical pipe which fed to the overhead valve gear and thence to the rest of the engine.

As was the custom of most light car manufacturers of the period, a sports model was produced in 1924. It differed from standard by having a special camshaft, aluminium cylinder head, a four-speed gearbox and front-wheel brakes.

The semi-sporting 'Hawk' was introduced in 1928 and attained success in trials of the period.

Year: 1921
Maker's HP and R.A.C. Rating:
9·5 hp
Number of Cylinders: 4
Bore and Stroke: 62 × 90 mm
Engine Capacity: 1·1 litres
Valves: overhead
Wheelbase: 8′ 6″
Forward Speeds: 3
Final Drive Ratio: 4·2 to 1
Tyres: 700 × 80

Year: 1928
Model: 'Hawk'
Maker's HP: 12/50
R.A.C. Rating: 11·9 hp
Number of Cylinders: 4
Bore and Stroke: 69 × 100 mm

Engine Capacity: 1·5 litres
Valves: overhead
Wheelbase: 10′ 4″
Forward Speeds: 4
Final Drive Ratio: 5 to 1
Tyres: 28 × 4·95

Riley England

The Edwardian Riley was a V-twin light car, but in 1919 the firm produced a very sound long-stroke, 4-cylinder, 1½-litre which rapidly earned a good reputation. This was further enhanced in 1923 when it appeared in more sporting guise than hitherto, with extremely handsome two- or four-seater bodies in polished aluminium, always with red mudguards. From this the model became known as the 'Redwing'. Several still survive. The 'Redwing' continued in production until 1926 when the new 'Nine' was first shown, and the orders for it were so numerous that in order to cope with them at all, the 'Redwing' had to be withdrawn.

The 'Nine' was certainly an outstanding machine with overhead valves set at 90 degrees in a hemispherical head and operated by short pushrods from two camshafts carried high on each side of the block. In this way the light reciprocating parts of an ohc engine were obtained while yet retaining the easy maintenance of the pushrod layout. The crankshaft was very sturdy so the fact of the engine having no centre main bearing only became a defect with the very high power outputs later extracted from the engine.

Another advanced, though by no means novel, feature was the silent, constant-mesh third speed. The earliest, fabric-covered bodies nowadays look rather clumsy, but in their day they were thought outstandingly handsome, and as soon as the boot became smoothed into the main body lines

above 1920 10·8 hp Riley with alloy pistons, 35 bhp and full electtical
equipment, listed at £550
left London–Edinburgh Run, 1922: ohc 9·5 hp Rhode 'light car'

they really were so. Altogether, the Riley 'Nine' was something quite new in brisk, small car, luxury motoring.

The susceptibility of the engine to tuning attracted many racing men and racing Rileys soon became almost unbeatable in their class.

In 1928 came the very low-built, 90 mph 'Brooklands' nine, and also the 1·6-litre six of similar cylinder dimensions, whose considerable weight and very low axle ratio made it less satisfactory than might have been expected. Its engine was eventually developed into the E.R.A. of which several are still giving more modern designs a brisk run for their money in Historic Racing Car events.

Year: 1919
Maker's HP: 11
R.A.C. Rating: 10·8 hp
Number of Cylinders: 4
Bore and Stroke: 65·8 × 110 mm
Engine Capacity: 1·5 litres
Valves: side

Wheelbase: 9' 0"
Forward Speeds: 4
Final Drive Ratio: 4 to 1
Tyres: 710 × 90
(*Year:* 1924, sports model
'Redwing' of similar specification)

Year: 1927
Model: 'Nine'
Maker's HP and R.A.C. Rating:
9 hp
Number of Cylinders: 4
Bore and Stroke: 60·3 × 95·2 mm

Engine Capacity: 1·1 litres
Valves: overhead
Wheelbase: 9' 0"
Forward Speeds: 4
Final Drive Ratio: 5·2 to 1
Tyres: 27 × 4·4

Year: 1929
Model: 'Brooklands'.
Specification as 'Nine' but

Wheelbase: 8' 0", and *Final Drive Ratio:* 4·75 to 1

The 'Monaco' fabric-bodied sports-saloon version of the 'Nine' appeared in 1928 and sold briskly

Year: 1929
Maker's HP: 14
R.A.C. Rating: 13·53 hp
Number of Cylinders: 6
Bore and Stroke: 60·3 × 95·2 mm
Engine Capacity: 1·6 litres
Valves: overhead
Wheelbase: 10′ 0″
Forward Speeds: 4
Final Drive Ratio: 5·75 to 1
Tyres: 30 × 5

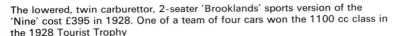

The lowered, twin carburettor, 2-seater 'Brooklands' sports version of the 'Nine' cost £395 in 1928. One of a team of four cars won the 1100 cc class in the 1928 Tourist Trophy

Rochet-Schneider France

The firm of Rochet-Schneider has no connection with the Th. Schneider Company, similarly Rolland-Pilain have no association with the Pilain Company (who made a car with transmission by cardan shaft driving to each rear wheel)—a state of affairs almost as confusing as Talbot and Darracq.

After the war Rochet-Schneider produced a series of side-valve touring cars. After 1923 the Company reverted to an overhead valve policy, until the end of the vintage period. Their only unusual features were a combustion chamber so designed that no valve could drop down in the event of a breakage; and an engine-driven tyre pump fitted beside the gearbox.

1924 ohv 4-litre saloon with coachwork by Million-Guiet. The company based at Lyons, expired in 1932

Year: 1920
Maker's HP: 12
R.A.C. Rating: 15·9 hp
Number of Cylinders: 4
Bore and Stroke: 80 × 130 mm
Engine Capacity: 2·6 litres

Valves: side
Wheelbase: 9′ 11″
Forward Speeds: 4
Final Drive Ratio: 4·4 to 1
Tyres: 820 × 120

Year: 1920
Maker's HP: 18
R.A.C. Rating: 22·4 hp
Number of Cylinders: 4
Bore and Stroke: 95 × 140 mm
Engine Capacity: 4 litres

Valves: side
Wheelbase: 11′ 10″
Forward Speeds: 4
Final Drive Ratio: 4·15 to 1
Tyres: 880 × 120

Year: 1920
Maker's HP: 30
R.A.C. Rating: 37·2 hp
Number of Cylinders: 6
Bore and Stroke: 100 × 130 mm
Engine Capacity: 6·1 litres

Valves: side
Wheelbase: 12′ 3½″
Forward Speeds: 4
Final Drive Ratio: 3·9 to 1
Tyres: 895 × 135

Rolland-Pilain   France

The Rolland-Pilain firm claim to have manufactured the first monobloc engine—in 1906. In 1918 the Company became allied with the Gnome et Rhone concern and constructed rotary aero engines, while also producing 12, 30 and 40 hp cars.

In 1922 and 1923 a team of three cars competed for the French Grand Prix races with 8-cylinder, twin overhead camshaft engines. None finished the race, although No 1 car held fifth place in the early stages. Contemporary reports spoke favourably of their clean design and excellent road-holding. In

1925 20/30 hp 4-cylinder Type CRK coupé de ville

1926 a 2-litre 8-cylinder sports model was produced that could have been based on the Grand Prix model, but very little is known about the car to confirm this supposition.

Le Mans, 1926: the 2-litre car of Stremler/Chalamal, *left*, neck-and-neck with the Bouriat/Dollfus 1·5-litre E.H.P. (see page 137). No. 21 retired but one of its team-mates, driven by Nezeloff/Lasalle, finished in 7th place overall

Year: 1920	*Valves:* side
Maker's HP: 12/16	*Wheelbase:* 9′ 6″
R.A.C. Rating: 12·1 hp	*Forward Speeds:* 4
Number of Cylinders: 4	*Final Drive Ratio:*
Bore and Stroke: 70 × 125 mm	*Tyres:* 765 × 105
Engine Capacity: 1·9 litres	

Year: 1920	*Valves:* side
Maker's HP: 20/30	*Wheelbase:* 11′ 0″
R.A.C. Rating: 22·4 hp	*Forward Speeds:* 4
Number of Cylinders: 4	*Final Drive Ratio:*
Bore and Stroke: 95 × 140 mm	*Tyres:* 880 × 120
Engine Capacity: 4 litres	

Year: 1926	*Valves:* overhead
Maker's HP and R.A.C. Rating: 17 hp	*Wheelbase:* 9′ 6″
	Forward Speeds: 4
Number of Cylinders: 8	*Final Drive Ratio:*
Bore and Stroke: 59·2 × 90 mm	*Tyres:* 765 × 105
Engine Capacity: 2 litres	

Rolls-Royce England

For vintage motoring Rolls-Royce continued their well-tried 'Silver Ghost', first introduced in 1907. In the subsequent seven years it had undergone various modifications which may briefly be summarized as follows.

The original 1907 car had a 'square' engine of 114 × 114 mm, giving 48 bhp at 1200 rpm on a 3·2 to 1 compression ratio. It had a four-speed gearbox with overdrive top.

In 1909 the overdrive was omitted as being too noisy and the stroke was increased to 121 mm at which it subsequently remained.

In 1912 rear springing was changed to cantilever and by this time the power output was probably 65 bhp.

In 1914 a fourth speed was added in the form of an emergency bottom gear, and aluminium pistons, and the compression ratio was raised to 3·8 to 1. In this form, known as the 'Alpine Eagle', the car did extremely well in the Alpine Trials of 1913–14, and it was pretty well the form in which manufacture was resumed after the war, in 1919. Compared with the new Continental luxury cars, such as the Hispano-Suiza, the 'Ghost' seemed pretty obsolete by 1919, but they could not match its refinement.

In 1924 front brakes became optional. In 1926 the 'Ghost' was finally withdrawn after being in production for almost twenty years.

In 1925 the 'New Phantom' was offered, the engine having pushrod operated overhead valves, and a smaller bore and longer stroke, giving a slightly larger total capacity than the 'Ghost'. It probably developed about 100 bhp. The chassis was unaltered.

In 1929 came the 'Phantom II', with slightly modified 'Phantom I' engine and an entirely new chassis with semi-elliptic rear springs. It had a $5\frac{1}{4}$ to 1 compression ratio and probably gave about 120 bhp. The gearbox was in unit with the engine.

In 1930 a short chassis, higher compression version of the 'Phantom II' became available, known as the 'Continental'.

Going back to 1922, in this year a small, 3·2-litre, 6-cylinder was introduced,

Late Ghost: John Hampton's 1925 Barker-bodied tourer. The 'Silver Ghost' is the model upon which the Rolls-Royce reputation was founded. The Derby factory built 6,173 chassis and Springfield, Massachusetts, 1,703

known as the 'Twenty'. It had a three-speed gearbox with central ball change.

In 1925 the 'Twenty' acquired four speeds with right-hand gate change, and front-wheel brakes.

In 1929 an increased bore of 82·5 mm produced an additional half-litre capacity, the model becoming the '20–25'.

1928 'Twenty' sedanca-de-ville. Earlier models had horizontal slats to the radiator

There can be no doubt that the 'Ghost', which richly deserved its early fame, became decreasingly attractive as it got heavier and more powerful. In its Edwardian form the combination of extreme silence, flexibility and smoothness; brisk acceleration up to the modest maximum speed of about 60 mph, sensitive steering, and excellent road-holding and cornering, was remarkable. Even in its latest forms these qualities were more notable than in the 'Phantoms' I and II, while in the 'Continental Phantom' a great deal of the traditional engine smoothness was sacrificed in the interests of a 90 mph maximum speed. Despite this, however, the Rolls-Royce contrived to remain pre-eminent in its class.

It was not until the advent of the V-12 'Phantom III', in 1935, that Rolls-Royce mastered the problem of combining really high power output with a refinement worthy of the earliest 'Ghosts'.

The vintage '20' and '20–25' were both cars of great refinement and charm despite their quite negligible performance.

Years: 1907–26	*Valves:* side
Model: 'Silver Ghost'. As for 1919	*Wheelbase:* 11' 11½"
Maker's HP: 40/50	*Forward Speeds:* 4
R.A.C. Rating: 48·6 hp	*Final Drive Ratio:* choices between
Number of Cylinders: 6	2·9 and 3·4 to 1
Bore and Stroke: 114 × 121 mm	*Tyres:* 895 × 135
Engine Capacity: 7·4 litres	

Year: 1922
Maker's HP: 20
R.A.C. Rating: 21·6 hp
Number of Cylinders: 6
Bore and Stroke: 76·2 × 114·3 mm
Engine Capacity: 3·2 litres

Valves: overhead
Wheelbase: 10′ 9″
Forward Speeds: 3
Final Drive Ratio: 4·55 to 1
Tyres: 812 × 114

Year: 1925
Model: 'Phantom I'
Maker's HP: 40/50
R.A.C. Rating: 43·3 hp
Number of Cylinders: 6
Bore and Stroke: 108 × 140 mm

Engine Capacity: 7·7 litres
Valves: overhead
Wheelbase: 12′ 0″ or 12′ 6½″
Forward Speeds: 4
Final Drive Ratio: usually 3·4 to 1
Tyres: 33 × 5

Year: 1929
Model: '20–25'. Specification as for
'20' but *Bore and Stroke:* 82·5 × 114
mm and four speeds

Year: 1929
Model: 'Phantom II'. Specification
as 'Phantom I'

Phantom I and its designer: Sir Frederick Henry Royce (right) at Le Canadel in about 1928

Rover   England

The history of the Rover Company goes back to the early days of the cycle industry. The first motor-car was produced in 1904, an 8 hp single-cylinder with tubular chassis. In 1907 Rover won the Tourist Trophy at a speed of 28·8 mph. During the later half of the Edwardian period the most popular models were the 12/16 and 18/20 4-cylinder models. 12/16 Sunbeam cars were made by Rover during the war under the name of 'Rover Sunbeam'.

After the war the Rover Company turned towards light cars, and produced the 8 hp twin-cylinder, air-cooled light car. This model continued until 1925 when people began to get tired of 'cherry red' cylinder heads, so the 4-cylinder water-cooled 9/20 was introduced, to run to the end of the vintage period.

The most interesting models produced by the Company were the 14/45 and 16/50 of 1925 and 1926 respectively. These cars were designed by P. A. Poppe, who built the engine for the first Morris car. The engine had hemispherical combustion chambers and overhead valves inclined at 45 degrees. The valves were driven by a single camshft on the inlet side of the engine, the exhaust side being operated by a system of bell cranks. The crankshaft was supported by three bearings. The car was undoubtedly an advanced design but proved expensive to produce. In 1926 the engine was increased to 16 hp and became known as the 16/50. This model survived until 1929, and was persuaded to lap Brooklands in streamlined form at 102·9 mph. The last vintage Rovers were the 'Light 6's' produced in 1928, which were developed into the more sporting 'Meteor' of 1930—both sturdy and dependable cars.

Year: 1919
Maker's HP: 12
R.A.C. Rating: 13·96 hp
Number of Cylinders: 4
Bore and Stroke: 75 × 130 mm
Engine Capacity: 2·3 litres

Valves: side
Wheelbase: 9' 2"
Forward Speeds: 3
Final Drive Ratio: 4·6 to 1
Tyres: 810 × 90

Year: 1920
Maker's HP: 8
R.A.C. Rating: 8·8 hp
Number of Cylinders: 2
Bore and Stroke: 85 × 88 mm
Engine Capacity: 1 litre

Valves: side
Wheelbase: 7' 4"
Forward Speeds: 3
Final Drive Ratio: 4·84 to 1
Tyres: 28 × 3

1922 air-cooled twin: the catalogue explains 'the horn is fitted through the dash so that it is handy to the driver's hand, and does not get wet in rainy weather and spoil one's gloves every time it is used'

Year: 1925
Maker's HP: 9/20
R.A.C. Rating: 8·9 hp
Number of Cylinders: 4
Bore and Stroke: 60 × 95 mm
Engine Capacity: 1·1 litres

Valves: overhead
Wheelbase: 7′ 10″
Forward Speeds: 3
Final Drive Ratio: 4·84 to 1
Tyres: 27 × 4·4

Year: 1928
Model: 'Light 6'
R.A.C. Rating: 15·7 hp
Number of Cylinders: 6
Bore and Stroke: 65 × 101·6 mm
Engine Capacity: 2 litres

Valves: overhead
Wheelbase: 9′ 10″
Forward Speeds: 3 or 4
Final Drive Ratio: 4·7 to 1
Tyres: 29 × 4·95

Year: 1930
Model: 'Meteor'
R.A.C. Rating: 19·3 hp
Number of Cylinders: 6
Bore and Stroke: 72 × 105 mm
Engine Capacity: 2·6 litres

Valves: overhead
Wheelbase: 9′ 10″
Forward Speeds: 4
Final Drive Ratio: 5·3 to 1
Tyres: 18 × 5·5

1930 'Light Six' Sportsman's Saloon, with Weymann body—and 70 mph for £325

Ruston-Hornsby England

Ruston and Hornsby, established in the reign of George IV, engaged in producing agricultural and general machinery and until fairly recent times it was possible to see a Ruston-Hornsby steam roller still doing service for Rutlandshire and Lincolnshire Councils. During the 1914 war the firm was engaged in the manufacture of aeroplanes and their engines, so that in 1920 the plant was readily adapted for car production.

First produced in 1920 the Ruston-Hornsby had several unconventional features. The cylinder head was detachable, but the inlet manifold was cast with the cylinder block. The gearbox and back axle were incorporated in a complete unit. The car soon built up a reputation for smoothness and reliability and gave quite a useful performance from the 3·3-litre engine, which developed 43 bhp. One example survives in the U.K., but many are known to have been exported to India where there may still be one or two used as mechanical bullock carts.

Year: 1920
Maker's HP: 16/20
R.A.C. Rating: 15·9 hp
Number of Cylinders: 4
Bore and Stroke: 80 × 130 mm
Engine Capacity: 3·3 litres
Valves: side
Wheelbase: 9′ 9″
Forward Speeds: 3
Final Drive Ratio: 4·23 to 1
Tyres: 820 × 120

1923 20/25 Model A3 'with Rigid Side Curtains in position' says the catalogue

Salmson   France

The Salmson Company was originally concerned with making aero engines, and their first venture in car manufacture was to make the G.N. in France under licence from the English company.

From this they advanced to a sporting light car of their own, retaining little of G.N. except for the quarter-elliptic rear springs. The water-cooled 4-cylinder engine was only unusual as to the operation of its overhead valves, in having but one pushrod to each cylinder. It operated the exhaust valve normally, as a pushrod. It then worked the inlet valve as a pull-rod, the push-rod being forced by a weaker spring into a recess in the camshaft. It is not known what merits were claimed for this arrangement.

The performance of the car was considerably handicapped by a wide-ratio three-speed gearbox. The standard body was a very narrow two-seater with staggered seats and a pointed tail.

Most Salmsons had solid back axles.

For racing, the Company produced a twin ohc 4-cylinder of slightly larger bore, which was later marketed in three stages of development and tune. The 'Grand Prix' had splash-feed and a three-speed gearbox. The 'Grand Prix Special' had force-feed and generally a four-speed gearbox. The 'San Sebastian' had a number of additional mechanical refinements and was available with a

Cozette supercharger. The twin-cam cars had a long run of class wins at Le Mans and in the 200-mile race at Brooklands and in 1926 one lapped Brooklands at 114½ mph.

For 1100 cc class racing the Company produced an exceedingly interesting 50 × 70·8 mm straight-eight. It had two overhead camshafts with desmodromic operation, and two Cozette superchargers, one on each side of the engine. 140 bhp at 8000 rpm was claimed, but it was not developed to the pitch of achieving any racing success.

At the end of the vintage period the original 62 × 90 mm was increased to 65 × 90 mm as the 12/24, and there was also an uninteresting six.

Year: 1922
Maker's HP: 10
R.A.C. Rating: 8·9 hp
Number of Cylinders: 4
Bore and Stroke: 62 × 90 mm
Engine Capacity: 1·1 litre
Valves: overhead
Wheelbase: 8′ 6″
Forward Speeds: 3
Final Drive Ratio: 4 to 1
Tyres: 650 × 65

Year: 1929
Model: 'Grand Prix', or San Sebastian' with supercharger
Maker's HP: 10/20
R.A.C. Rating: 9·6 hp
Number of Cylinders: 4
Bore and Stroke: 62·2 × 90 mm
Engine Capacity: 1·1 litres
Valves: overhead
Wheelbase: 8′ 6″
Forward Speeds: 3 or 4
Final Drive Ratio: 4·5 to 1
Tyres: 720 × 120

above 1922 Scottish Rally: 1,088 cc. Type AL
below 10/20 in the 1928 Great West Spring Cup

Scott Sociable   England

The Scott Sociable used the famous Scott two-stroke vertical twin engine, in a very simple offset three-wheeler chassis, intended to be one stage more comfortable than a motor-cycle and sidecar. It was current from 1921 to 1925.

Year: 1921
Maker's HP: 5/6
R.A.C. Rating: 7·2 hp
Number of Cylinders: 2
Bore and Stroke: 3″ × 3½″
Engine Capacity: 0·6 litre
Valves: none (two-stroke)
Wheelbase: 5′ 1″
Forward Speeds: 3
Final Drive Ratio: 4·5 to 1
Tyres: 700 × 80

1924 5/6 hp. The complete car
weighed only 5 cwt and it returned
70 mpg

Sheffield-Simplex   England

The Sheffield-Simplex car was developed from the Brotherhood car whose
rather curious, though logical, distinguishing feature was a horn bulb pro-
truding from the centre of the steering column.

   From their introduction in 1905 the Sheffield-Simplex had always been in
the luxury class competing with the Rolls-Royce and Napier. Under the
sponsorship of the Earl FitzWilliam, the Company produced 30 hp and 45 hp
6-cylindered models, with extremely imposing circular radiators.

   In 1912 a Sheffield-Simplex was driven from Land's End to John-o'-Groats
in top gear and then made to lap Brooklands at nearly 70 mph. Immediately
Rolls-Royce sent one of their cars to emulate this feat and succeeded in
bettering it by a faster lap speed. The Sheffield-Simplex was also one of the
first chassis to be used as tractors for drawing field guns, experiments in this
direction being carried out in 1909 by the Earl FitzWilliam.

   In 1920 a 50 hp model was introduced and remained in production as the
Company's only model until 1926. It was a curious anachronism with six,

1920 50 hp tourer. Its engine turns at marine speeds, giving 40 mph at
950 rpm

separate, L-head cylinders and all the features of a typical Edwardian design; one survives.

In 1921 the Company turned to the production of that motorized curiosity, the 'Ner-a-car'.

Year: 1920	*Valves:* side
Maker's HP: 50	*Wheelbase:* 12' 6"
R.A.C. Rating: 48·6 hp	*Forward Speeds:* 4
Number of Cylinders: 6	*Final Drive Ratio:*
Bore and Stroke: 114 × 127 mm	*Tyres:* 895 × 150
Engine Capacity: 7·5 litres	

Singer England

Bicycles were first produced in the Singer factory but cars were added to the range in 1905.

By 1914 the Singer had made a name for itself both at Brooklands, in the Alpine Trial, and in the R.A.C. Light Car Trial, where it made best performance.

After the war smaller side-valve types were made until 1923, when an overhead-valve six was produced. Rubury front-wheel brakes were added in 1924 and 1927 saw the introduction of the more famous overhead camshaft 8 hp 'Junior' model. Despite the evidence of the illustration reproduced below, all Vintage Singers have the manufacturer's name in large letters across the honeycomb radiator.

Year: 1918	*Valves:* side
Maker's HP: 10	*Wheelbase:* 7' 6"
R.A.C. Rating: 9·8 hp	*Forward Speeds:* 3
Number of Cylinders: 4	*Final Drive Ratio:* 4·5 to 1
Bore and Stroke: 63 × 88 mm	*Tyres:* 700 × 80
Engine Capacity: 1·1 litres	

1919 10 hp, with Harry Tate of music-hall fame at the wheel

Year: 1922
Maker's HP: 15
R.A.C. Rating: 15·7 hp
Number of Cylinders: 6
Bore and Stroke: 63 × 88 mm
Engine Capacity: 1·9 litres

Valves: side
Wheelbase: 9' 9"
Forward Speeds: 3
Final Drive Ratio: 5 to 1
Tyres: 815 × 105

Year: 1927
Model: 'Junior'
Maker's HP: 8
R.A.C. Rating: 7·78 hp
Number of Cylinders: 4
Bore and Stroke: 56 × 86 mm
Engine Capacity: 0·8 litre
Valves: overhead
Wheelbase: 7' 6"
Forward Speeds: 3
Final Drive Ratio: 5 to 1
Tyres: 27 × 4

1930 'Senior Six', with 7-bearing
crankshaft

Year: 1927
Model: 'Senior Six'
Maker's HP and R.A.C. Rating:
14·34 hp
Number of Cylinders: 6
Bore and Stroke: 63 × 95 mm

Engine Capacity: 1·8 litres
Valves: overhead
Wheelbase: 9' 6"
Forward Speeds: 3
Final Drive Ratio: 4·54 to 1
Tyres: 29 × 4·95

Sizaire-Berwick France

In 1912 the Sizaire Frères ended their connection with M. Naudin with whom
they had designed some very successful voiturette racing cars in the 'long
stroke' era, these cars being noted for their pioneering of independent front
suspension.

In 1913 F. W. Berwick & Co., an engineering firm, commissioned the Sizaires
to design a chassis for their 4-litre engine. This model was an immediate
success and was greatly admired at the 1914 Paris Salon. In 1916 the Sizaire-
Berwick Company was formed with its works at Park Royal. About this time
Rolls-Royce brought an action against Sizaire-Berwick for using a Rolls-
Royce type radiator. This resulted in a settlement out of court in favour of
Sizaire-Berwick for £25,000 as they had taken the precaution of registering
the design whilst Rolls-Royce had not!

After the war the car was re-introduced in 4½-litre form with a slightly 'V'-

shaped radiator. **The Company** got into difficulties and was re-formed with Sir Herbert Austin as chairman, F. W. Berwick forming the Windsor Car Co. —perhaps accounting for the Rolls-Royce type radiator on this car. The 4½-litre 25/50 model was continued but the cheaper models had either Austin 12 or 20 hp engines installed. This state of affairs continued until 1925 when the Company finally ceased production, a large number of the staff joining the Bentley Company.

There are known to be at least two vintage 25/50 Sizaire-Berwick cars in existence.

Year: 1920
Maker's HP: 25/50
R.A.C. Rating: 22·4 hp
Number of Cylinders: 4
Bore and Stroke: 95 × 160 mm
Engine Capacity: 4·6 litres
Valves: side
Wheelbase: 11' 9"
Forward Speeds: 4
Final Drive Ratio: 4·0 to 1
Tyres: 895 × 135

1921 25/50 tourer designed by Maurice Sizaire

Year: 1923
Maker's HP: 26/52
R.A.C. Rating: 26·3 hp
Number of Cylinders: 6
Bore and Stroke: 81·5 × 102 mm
Engine Capacity: 3·1 litres

Valves: side
Wheelbase: 11' 2"
Forward Speeds: 3
Final Drive Ratio: 4·6 to 1
Tyres: 820 × 120

Spyker   Holland

The Dutch Spyker Company cannot be said to have made any great impact on the vintage era, but it has the claim to fame that it is believed to have made the

30/40 tourer, designed by Fritz Koolhoven, bowling through the Amersham, Buckinghamshire, of 1922

first 6-cylinder engine, in 1903, thus narrowly anticipating Sunbeam and Napier. Its principal vintage model was, appropriately, also a 6-cylinder, of 5·7-litre capacity, said to develop 75 bhp. In 1922 S. F. Edge set up a new 24-hour record at Brooklands, using one of these cars at an average of 74·7 mph, thus beating by nearly 10 mph the record he had set up on a Napier in 1907.

The Spyker Company went out of business in 1925.

Year: 1921	*Valves:* side
Maker's HP: 30/40	*Wheelbase:* 11′ 5″
R.A.C. Rating: 33·6 hp	*Forward Speeds:* 4
Number of Cylinders: 6	*Final Drive Ratio:* 3·9 to 1
Bore and Stroke: 95 × 135 mm	*Tyres:* 895 × 135
Engine Capacity: 5·7 litres	

Standard   England

The 'All British Standard', as it was described, first appeared as a rather quaint 'Victoria style' vehicle in 1903. Soon a programme of large Edwardian side-valve cars of up to 30 hp was embarked upon but terminated in a 9·5 hp light car in 1914.

After the war the Company concentrated on light type cars all with pushrod operated overhead-valve engines and with cantilever front and rear suspension until 1924.

In 1927 the 18/42 hp 6-cylinder engine was inevitably produced. Indeed, such was the hurry to make the car in time for the 1927 Motor Show that the bonnet had to be locked for the very good reason that an engine could not be manufactured in time.

According to several who have owned this model it was the only bad Standard made during the vintage period and largely contributed to the drastic reorganization of the Company in 1929 to avert bankruptcy.

1925 13·9 hp 'Pall Mall' saloon. This 2-litre model was introduced in 1922

Year: 1920
Maker's HP: 11·9
R.A.C. Rating: 11·6 hp
Number of Cylinders: 4
Bore and Stroke: 68 × 110 mm
Engine Capacity: 1·6 litres

Valves: overhead
Wheelbase: 9′ 0″
Forward Speeds: 3
Final Drive Ratio: 3·8 to 1
Tyres: 710 × 90

Year: 1922
Maker's HP: 8
R.A.C. Rating: 9·5 hp
Number of Cylinders: 4
Bore and Stroke: 62 × 90 mm
Engine Capacity: 1·1 litres

Valves: overhead
Wheelbase: 8′ 9″
Forward Speeds: 3
Final Drive Ratio: 4·6 to 1
Tyres: 26 × 3

Year: 1927
Maker's HP: 18/36
R.A.C. Rating: 17·2 hp
Number of Cylinders: 6
Bore and Stroke: 68 × 102 mm
Engine Capacity: 2·2 litres

Valves: overhead
Wheelbase: 10′ 2″
Forward Speeds: 3
Final Drive Ratio: 4·6 to 1
Tyres: 31 × 5·25

1928 9 hp 'Fulham' saloon. The 'Nine' was the model which saved the company—it was reliable, economical and a good buy at £198 10s

Year: 1928
Maker's HP: 9
R.A.C. Rating: 8·9 hp
Number of Cylinders: 4
Bore and Stroke: 60 × 102 mm
Engine Capacity: 1·2 litres
Valves: side
Wheelbase: 7′ 8″
Forward Speeds: 3
Final Drive Ratio: 5 to 1
Tyres: 27 × 4·4

Stanley

America

The Stanley Steamer had the longest production run of any steam car. The car side of the Company existed from 1897 to 1927.

In earlier days Stanleys attained heroic speeds, even up to two miles a minute, in chassis of the most exiguous scantling. In production form, the early Edwardian 'Gentleman's Speedy Roadster' was at least theoretically capable of some 80 mph, though it would have been a brave man who actually availed himself of the full potentialities of the vehicle.

By vintage days, however, the Stanley had put on weight, and lost interest as it gained respectability.

Perhaps the main reason for its long-maintained popularity lay in its use of the pot-boiler, which had the merit of simplicity. The corresponding disadvantages are that it takes a long time to raise steam, and it is difficult to satisfy the Boiler Insurance Inspector, which is avoided by a flash boiler.

Steam still has its enthusiasts, but in the past, the theoretical simplicity, silence and speed of the steam car had not been borne out in practice.

Year: 1919
Maker's HP: 20hp
R.A.C. Rating: 16·5 hp
Number of Cylinders: 2
Bore and Stroke: 4″ × 5″
Engine Capacity: 2 litres

Valves: slide
Wheelbase: 10′ 10″
Forward Speeds: 1
Final Drive Ratio: 1·5 to 1
Tyres: 34 × 4·5

1922 Model 740 demonstrator. The conventional-looking radiator was really a condenser

Star

England

The Star Engineering Company is yet another motor-car manufacturer that started life making bicycles. The first car was made in 1898 and by 1905 Star cars were competing in the Tourist Trophy and Gordon Bennett Eliminating Trials.

Vintage Stars achieved a name for durability and excellent finish. The 20/60 of 1926, with a seven-bearing crankshaft, and duralumin connecting rods and pistons, was capable of an easy 70 mph. The 12/40 'Pegasus' model could also attain a high speed although the steering was said to be harsh at speeds over 50 mph. These models attained considerable popularity; indeed, the King of Arabia was supplied with a seatless Harem wagon and a 14/30 was driven across Africa by an adventurous authoress.

Year: 1921
Maker's HP and R.A.C. Rating:
11·9 hp
Number of Cylinders: 4
Bore and Stroke: 69 × 120 mm
Engine Capacity: 1·8 litres

Valves: side
Wheelbase: 9′ 0″
Forward Speeds: 3
Final Drive Ratio: 4·36 to 1
Tyres: 30 × 3·5

Year: 1924
Maker's HP: 12/40
R.A.C. Rating: 11·9 hp
Number of Cylinders: 4
Bore and Stroke: 69 × 130 mm
Engine Capacity: 2 litres

Valves: overhead
Wheelbase: 9′ 4″
Forward Speeds: 4
Final Drive Ratio: 4 to 1
Tyres: 765 × 105

Year: 1926
Maker's HP: 20/60
R.A.C. Rating: 20·9 hp
Number of Cylinders: 6
Bore and Stroke: 75 × 120 mm
Engine Capacity: 3·2 litres
Valves: overhead
Wheelbase: 11′ 3″
Forward Speeds: 4
Final Drive Ratio: 4·3 to 1
Tyres: 31 × 5·25

The 11·9 hp 'light car' was introduced in 1921 and became the 2-litre 12/25 in 1924. 1922 model in Richmond Park

Stellite

England

The Stellite appeared in 1913 from the Electric & Ordnance Accessories Company of Birmingham—a subsidiary of Wolseley. It started life with a 9·5 hp inlet-over-exhaust engine, a two-speed transaxle and a flitchplate frame. It was manufactured (latterly with three speeds) until 1919, but thereafter it was replaced by the ohc Wolseley Ten. The name was used again later for an economy version of that car.

Year: 1919
Maker's HP: 8/10
R.A.C. Rating: 9·5 hp
Number of Cylinders: 4
Bore and Stroke: 62 × 89 mm
Engine Capacity: 1·1 litres

Valves: ioe
Wheelbase: 8′ 3″
Forward Speeds: 3
Final Drive Ratio: 4·85 to 1
Tyres: 700 × 80

1919 9·5 hp Stellite, priced at £285

Straker-Squire   England

In 1890 an engineering firm called Brazil and Holborow established themselves at Bristol. In 1906 they amalgamated with Straker-Squire Ltd., a Blackfriars vehicle trading concern, which resulted in the firm of Brazil Straker being founded for commercial vehicle manufacture. 1907 saw a brilliant young engineer called Roy Fedden introduce himself to the firm with a design for a 2-litre ohv motor-car. This car, known as the 'Shamrock', was in production for two years, when it was succeeded by the 14/16, with an improved five-bearing crankshaft.

The 14/16 was developed until 1914 under R. S. Witchell (Experimental Department) and F. C. Clement—later of Bentley fame—as chief tester. In 1914 these two drivers were entered for the T.T. in modified production cars—Witchell finished fourth.

After the war in 1920 Fedden produced the famous 24/90 model of 3·9-litres capacity. This engine showed the marked influence of war-time aero-engine practice by having six separate cylinders with tulip-type valves driven by a single overhead camshaft. This model was available as a sports 2/3-seater, a torpedo 4-seater and a limousine. The cars were a success from their first introduction and achieved considerable racing success at Brooklands—notably in the hands of H. Kensington Moir whose fastest lap was accomplished at 103·76 mph.

In 1923 both ohv 3-litre, 4-cylinder, and 1½-litre Dorman-engined cars were introduced, the light car being notable for its engine output of 30 bhp at 3000 rpm.

It is by the 24/90 model that Straker-Squire is remembered though it is remarkable that when the Company ceased manufacture in 1926 only sixty-seven had been made—four of which at least, including H. K. Moir's Brooklands car, exist today.

Before leaving the Straker-Squire Company mention should be made of the Cosmos car designed by Fedden in 1919. It had the remarkably advanced specification of a 1000 cc, 3-cylinder radial engine with coil spring independent suspension on all four wheels and a plastic body. Although an initial success it was never produced due to financial difficulties.

Year: 1920
Maker's HP: 24/90
R.A.C. Rating: 23·8 hp
Number of Cylinders: 6
Bore and Stroke: 80 × 130 mm
Engine Capacity: 3·9 litres

Valves: overhead
Wheelbase: 10' 7½"
Forward Speeds: 4
Final Drive Ratio: 3·8 to 1
Tyres: 820 × 135

The 1921 24/90 4-seater tourer cost £1,600, and thus few were made. The company survived until 1926

Year: 1922
Maker's HP: 15/20
R.A.C. Rating: 20·1 hp
Number of Cylinders: 4
Bore and Stroke: 90 × 120 mm
Engine Capacity: 3·1 litres
Valves: overhead
Wheelbase: 9' 9"
Forward Speeds: 4
Final Drive Ratio: 4 to 1
Tyres: 815 × 105

Studebaker

America and Canada

The fortunes of the Studebaker Company started in a smithy in 1852 and by 1874 horse-drawn vehicles were being mass-produced. The first 'horseless carriage' was made in 1902 in the form of an electric runabout: a petrol-driven

'President' 8-cylinder at Brooklands, where it averaged over 70 mph in the 1929 'Double Twelve' hours race

car followed two years later. Electric vehicles were discontinued in 1912 but horse-drawn carriages, including the well-known 'Canopy-top Surrey', were produced until 1920.

During the period 1920–30 the Company relied on three models—the 'Standard Six', the 'Special Six' and the 'Big-Six'. These models were available with 4-wheel hydraulic brakes and disc wheels in 1925. In 1929–30 the 8-cylindered 'President', 'Commander' and 'Director' were introduced.

Year: 1920	*Valves:* side
Model: 'Special Six'	*Wheelbase:* 9′ 11″
R.A.C. Rating: 29·5 hp	*Forward Speeds:* 3
Number of Cylinders: 6	*Final Drive Ratio:*
Bore and Stroke: 89 × 127 mm	*Tyres:* 32 × 4
Engine Capacity: 4·7 litres	

Year: 1925	*Valves:* side
Model: 'Big-Six'	*Wheelbase:* 10′ 7″
R.A.C. Rating: 35·7 hp	*Forward Speeds:* 3
Number of Cylinders: 6	*Final Drive Ratio:* 3·69 to 1
Bore and Stroke: $3\frac{7}{8}'' \times 5''$	*Tyres:* 34 × 7·30
Engine Capacity: 5·7 litres	

Year: 1930	*Valves:* side
Model: 'Commander'	*Wheelbase:* 10′ 0″
R.A.C. Rating: 30 hp	*Forward Speeds:* 3
Number of Cylinders: 8	*Final Drive Ratio:* 4·36 to 1
Bore and Stroke: $3\frac{1}{16}'' \times 4\frac{1}{4}''$	*Tyres:* 19 × 5·50
Engine Capacity: 4·1 litres	

Stutz   America

The 'Bearcat' Stutz was one of the greatest of American Edwardian sports cars, and was the principal rival of the Mercer. Like the Mercer, it had a large 4-cylinder, T-head engine and this type of engine survived into the early twenties. In 1924 there was a rather desultory 4·7-litre 6-cylinder 'Speedway Six' with pushrod operated overhead-valves, but in all this time the Company was in somewhat failing health and it was taken over by an entirely new management in 1926. It is from this time that come the models which revived the reputation of Stutz.

The straight-eight AA was introduced in 1926, with a single overhead camshaft, but after various intermediate stages, the DV.32 arrived in 1931, with enlarged bore of 85 mm and four valves per cylinder operated by two overhead camshafts. For this extremely effective model the name 'Bearcat' was confusingly revived. It developed 155 bhp at 3900 rpm and each car was sold with a 100 mph guarantee.

In 1928 an enlarged version of the AA was introduced called the 'Black Hawk' after the Miller-engined machine which was designed for, but failed to capture, the world speed record. It was followed, a year later by a 6-cylinder version.

A team of Stutzs competed at Le Mans from 1928 to 1930, finishing second to a Bentley in 1928. In the latter years, when they also experimented with supercharging, they were not successful.

The Stutz and Duesenberg are America's most worthy representatives as vintage sports-cars. The firm survived until 1936.

Year: 1926	*Engine Capacity:* 4·6 litres
Model: AA	*Valves:* overhead
Maker's HP and R.A.C. Rating:	*Wheelbase:* 10′ 11″ or 12′ 1″
32·4 hp	*Forward Speeds:* 3
Number of Cylinders: 8	*Final Drive Ratio:* 4·3 or 5·25 to 1
Bore and Stroke: 81 × 114 mm	*Tyres:* 32 × 6·5

above 1919 T-head 'Bearcat' owned by the Long Island Automotive Museum
below 1929 Le Mans: Bouriat/Philippe's 5·3-litre 8-cylinder came fifth. Three cars were entered, all with Weymann bodies and Roots-type superchargers

Year: 1929
Model: 'Black Hawk'
Maker's HP and R.A.C. Rating:
27·3 hp
Number of Cylinders: 6
Bore and Stroke: 85 × 114 mm
Engine Capacity: 3·9 litres

Valves: overhead
Wheelbase: 10' 7"
Forward Speeds: 4
Final Drive Ratio: 4·5 to 1
Tyres: 650 × 20

Year: 1931
Model: DV.32 'Bearcat'

As AA but *Bore:* 85 mm and
Capacity: 5·2 litres

Sunbeam England

The Sunbeam Company turned from the manufacture of japanned and tin-plate products to motor engineering in 1899. The second car made was a twin-cylinder and described as 'of modified Panhard type throughout'.

The Sunbeam-Mabley was introduced in 1901 and was considered an

Henry Segrave brings the 1923 French Grand Prix winner home to the
Sunbeam showrooms in Hanover Square, London

eccentric design even in those days. T. C. Pullinger joined the firm in 1902 and imported Berliet chassis to be modified and sold in England as Sunbeams. Sunbeam have a strong claim to being amongst the first three manufacturers to market a 6-cylindered car, this model appearing in February 1904.

In 1909 Louis Coatalen joined the Company and at once began to mould the Sunbeam into one of the great names in motoring history. He had an extremely fertile mind and by 1911 was conducting experiments at Brooklands with shock absorbers and overhead camshaft engines. After considerable racing success during 1912 and 1913, Coatalen produced a team of 3·3-litre twin ohc racing cars, the engines being almost exact replicas of the 1913 G.P. Peugeot which he had studied throughout the previous winter.

After the war two models were offered—the 16/40 and 24/60 side-valve cars; both were extremely well built but neither showed any influence of pre-war racing practice. The 24/60 was modified to pushrod overhead valves in 1921 and in 1923 servo brakes on all wheels were provided. Overhead camshaft operated valves were available at extra charge and in this form with 'light sports' body the 24/60 (or 24/70 as it was known in 1924) was undoubtedly one of the most delightful cars of the period. Lady Colin Campbell's comment on the 1904, 6-cylinder car seems very applicable to this model: 'The engine is as smooth and silent as a silken thread drawn off a reel.'

The ohv 14 hp, later 14/40, was introduced in 1921, to run until 1926. The 20/60 was introduced in 1924 to succeed the 24/60, but due to its greater weight did not achieve the same popularity.

In the meantime the Sunbeam Company was occupied with an intense programme of racing. Their Grand Prix cars followed the typical Henry design with twin overhead camshafts and four valves per cylinder. Their first major success was in the 1922 T.T. where a solitary 3-litre, 8-cylinder Sunbeam finished in first position, repeating the 1914 performance. In 1923 the most famous Sunbeam success of an outright victory in French Grand Prix was achieved. It was in 1924, however, that the climax of the G.P. Sunbeam was reached. The Bertarione-designed 6-cylinder supercharged car was universally accepted to be both the fastest and most reliable G.P. car in Europe. Un-happily the magnetos were changed on the eve of the race, as a result of which the cars suffered from incurable misfiring. The final Coatalen racing car was the 1925 V-12, 4-litre. This car took the world land speed record in 1926 at 152·33 mph, and one still survives in active racing.

The 20/60 6-cylinder saloon—a refined and beautifully-made car but of somewhat sluggish performance for a capacity of 3·1 litres

Last year of the ohv 14/40s: 1926 'Doctor's Coupé' with dickey seat, and Rudge-Whitworth centre-lock splined hubs à la Rolls-Royce, priced at £725— Vintage Sunbeams were in an (expensive) class of their own

In 1925 the 3-litre supersports model was introduced, although a prototype had been running as early as 1923. This car is considered one of the classic vintage designs. The 3-litre was introduced to capture the 3-litre Bentley market. The 6-cylinder engine had twin overhead camshafts driven by a train of helical gears, operating two valves per cylinder set at 90 degrees in the head. The engine produced 93 bhp at 4000 rpm but was set in what was virtually a 20/60 touring chassis, this being the limiting factor of the car. The 3-litre continued until 1930 in various series. In 1929 a Cozette supercharger was added, increasing the bhp to 135. In 1931 a much lowered version with modified chassis was envisaged, but the Company was by then in decline so this interesting project was never carried out.

Between 1926 and 1930 a host of different models was made, mainly with the pushrod ohv engine, including the 30/90 straight-eight. The Company was reorganized in 1931 and eventually taken over by the Rootes Group in 1935.

Year: 1919
Maker's HP: 16/40
R.A.C. Rating: 15·9 hp
Number of Cylinders: 4
Bore and Stroke: 80 × 150 mm
Engine Capacity: 3 litres

Valves: side
Wheelbase: 10′ 4″
Forward Speeds: 4
Final Drive Ratio: 3·59 to 1
Tyres: 820 × 120

Year: 1919
Maker's HP: 24/60
R.A.C. Rating: 23·8 hp
Number of Cylinders: 6
Bore and Stroke: 80 × 150 mm
Engine Capacity: 4·5 litres

Valves: side
Wheelbase: 11′ 4″
Forward Speeds: 4
Final Drive Ratio: 3·59 to 1
Tyres: 820 × 120

Year: 1921
Maker's HP: 14
R.A.C. Rating: 12·8 hp
Number of Cylinders: 4
Bore and Stroke: 72 × 120 mm
Engine Capacity: 2 litres

Valves: overhead
Wheelbase: 9′ 10″
Forward Speeds: 3
Final Drive Ratio: 4·15 to 1
Tyres: 815 × 105

Year: 1924
Maker's HP: 20/60
R.A.C. Rating: 20·9 hp
Number of Cylinders: 6
Bore and Stroke: 75 × 120 mm
Engine Capacity: 3·1 litres

Valves: overhead
Wheelbase: 11′ 5″
Forward Speeds: 4
Final Drive Ratio: 4·5 to 1
Tyres: 820 × 120

Year: 1924
Maker's HP: 24/70
R.A.C. Rating: 23·8 hp
Number of Cylinders: 6
Bore and Stroke: 80 × 150 mm
Engine Capacity: 4·5 litres

Valves: overhead
Wheelbase: 12′ 0″
Forward Speeds: 4
Final Drive Ratio: 4 to 1
Tyres: 895 × 135

Year: 1926
Model: 3-litre
R.A.C. Rating: 20·9 hp
Number of Cylinders: 6
Bore and Stroke: 75 × 110 mm
Engine Capacity: 3 litres

Valves: overhead
Wheelbase: 10′ 10″
Forward Speeds: 4
Final Drive Ratio: 4·5 to 1
Tyres: 820 × 120

Year: 1926
Maker's HP: 30/90
R.A.C. Rating: 31·7 hp
Number of Cylinders: 8
Bore and Stroke: 80 × 120 mm
Engine Capacity: 4·8 litres

Valves: overhead
Wheelbase: 11′ 6″
Forward Speeds: 4
Final Drive Ratio: 4·77 to 1
Tyres: 33 × 6

1927 3-litre: these cars had excellent engines in over-long chassis. Nevertheless one of them finished second at Le Mans in 1925 despite a broken frame

Swift

England

After a very early start in making bicycles the first Swift car was made in 1900, and the Company competed with success in many English and Continental reliability trials during the Edwardian period.

During the vintage period the Company confined itself exclusively to side-valve light cars and was one of the few of its kind not to have succumbed to the 'Light Six' disease.

Year: 1919
Maker's HP: 10
R.A.C. Rating: 9·8 hp
Number of Cylinders: 4
Bore and Stroke: 63 × 90 mm
Engine Capacity: 1·1 litres

Valves: side
Wheelbase: 7′ 3″
Forward Speeds: 3
Final Drive Ratio: 4·5 to 1
Tyres: 700 × 80

Year: 1920
Maker's HP: 12
R.A.C. Rating: 11·9 hp
Number of Cylinders: 4
Bore and Stroke: 69 × 130 mm
Engine Capacity: 1·9 litres
Valves: side
Wheelbase: 9′ 0″
Forward Speeds: 4
Final Drive Ratio: 4·5 to 1
Tyres: 30 × 3·5

A 10 hp finishes the Scottish Six Days Trial of 1922

Talbot

England

The British Talbot Company, at first known as Clement-Talbot, was founded in 1903. By 1908 Talbot and Vauxhall were about the leading pioneers of the high-speed engine and in the 1908 2000-mile Trial, the Talbot was little inferior to the Vauxhall. In 1913 a 4-cylinder, side-valve 26 hp Talbot was the first car in the world to cover 100 miles in an hour, and it had a maximum of nearly 115 mph.

The first post-war range consisted of Edwardians carried on as a stop-gap. There was a 12, 16 and 20/40, of which the 12 is listed in the specifications below; but in 1922 came a new programme, concentrating on small cars of very high quality. The 8/18 had overhead valves, a rather inadequate three-speed gearbox and, surprisingly, a solid back axle. It had a very lively performance, which would have been greatly improved by a four-speed box. The whole machine was beautifully made and, with coachwork to match, was perhaps the outstanding light car of its time. It later appeared in slightly expanded form as the (not quite so pleasant) 10/23 and there was a 12/30, 6-cylinder, of similar dimensions, which must have been a fairly rare car, as none is known to survive.

In about 1927 the Company engaged George Roesch as their chief designer and, starting with the 12/30 as a basis, he immediately produced an outstanding success in the new 14/45. The pushrod ohv engine was of very clean external finish, and had an amazing capability for sustained high speeds; which was just as well, having regard to its top gear ratio of 5·87 to 1. The chassis was extremely rigid and well braked, but rather on the heavy side for its 1·7-litre engine. It was usually equipped with handsome, fabric-covered saloon coachwork.

In 1930 came a 2·2-litre engine available as the '75 Sports' and the '90' short 'Speed' chassis. These were highly successful, both in road and track racing.

In post-vintage years a 3-litre engine was produced, with cylinder dimensions 75 × 112 mm, first with a crash-type and later a pre-selector gearbox. This was known as the '105'. The final expansion was to the 80 × 112 mm, 3·4-litre model '110', of 1934. Then came the engulfing of the Company by the Rootes Group.

The numbers of the various models—45, 70, 90, 105, represent the bhp developed in each case.

Year: 1920
Maker's HP: 12
R.A.C. Rating: 15·9 hp
Number of Cylinders: 4
Bore and Stroke: 80 × 120 mm
Engine Capacity: 2·4 litres

Valves: side
Wheelbase: 11' 0"
Forward Speeds: 4
Final Drive Ratio:
Tyres: 820 × 120

Year: 1922
Maker's HP: 8 (shortly afterwards 8/18)
R.A.C. Rating: 8 hp
Number of Cylinders: 4
Bore and Stroke: 57 × 95 mm
Engine Capacity: 1 litre
Valves: overhead
Wheelbase: 8' 1"
Forward Speeds: 3
Final Drive Ratio: 4·5 to 1
Tyres: 700 × 80

12/30 tourer passing through Castle Combe, Wiltshire, in 1925

Year: 1923
Maker's HP: 10/23
R.A.C. Rating: 8·9 hp
Number of Cylinders: 4
Bore and Stroke: 60 × 95 mm
Engine Capacity: 1·1 litre
Valves: overhead
Wheelbase: 9' 0"
Forward Speeds: 3
Final Drive Ratio: 4·5 or 5·11 to 1
Tyres: 710 × 90

top W. J. Brunell, well-known photographer of Vintage and early 'thirties motoring events, at the wheel of his 1927 14/45 tourer
above Le Mans 1930: Talbot '90', no. 15, was driven into third place by Hon. Brian Lewis *(right)* and H. S. Eaton, seen here alongside the two 'Speed Six' Bentleys which were first and second

Year: 1923
Maker's HP: 12/30
R.A.C. Rating: 12 hp
Number of Cylinders: 6
Bore and Stroke: 57 × 95 mm
Engine Capacity: 1·4 litres
Valves: overhead
Wheelbase: 10' 0"
Forward Speeds: 3
Final Drive Ratio: 5·11 or 5·3 to 1
Tyres: 765 × 105

Year: 1927
Maker's HP: 14/45
R.A.C. Rating: 13·8 hp
Number of Cylinders: 6
Bore and Stroke: 61 × 95 mm
Engine Capacity: 1·7 litres
Valves: overhead
Wheelbase: 10' 0¾"
Forward Speeds: 4
Final Drive Ratio: 5·87 to 1
Tyres: 30 × 4·75

Year: 1930
Model: A/O '75' Sports
R.A.C. Rating: 17·97 hp
Number of Cylinders: 6
Bore and Stroke: 69·5 × 100 mm
Engine Capacity: 2·2 litres

Valves: overhead
Wheelbase: 10' 0⅜"
Forward Speeds: 4
Final Drive Ratio: 4·9 to 1
Tyres: 6 × 18

Year: 1930
Model: A/O '90' Speed Short. As
A/O '75' but *Wheelbase:* 9' 3⅜"

Final Drive Ratio: 4·6 to 1
Tyres: 5·25 × 19

Talbot-Darracq

France

Some of the early vintage Talbot-Darracqs are to be confused with the English Talbot equivalent, but the V-8 is to be confused with the identical French Darracq, and again in 1929–30 their range was identical. In 1926 the 17/75 model seems to have been more or less of a solo effort.

In racing, the Company was outstandingly successful with its 67 × 105·6 mm, 1½-litre, twin ohc machine, which was completely invincible in its class up to about 1925. They also made a straight-eight 1½-litre for the Grand Prix formula of 1926–27. On paper the engine should have been the equal of the successful Delage, and its chassis was definitely superior; but it was never brought to a successful stage of development.

1927 TL 20/98, with body by Grose

Year: 1920
Maker's HP: 16
R.A.C. Rating: 17·9 hp
Number of Cylinders: 4
Bore and Stroke: 85 × 130 mm
Engine Capacity: 3 litres

Valves: side
Wheelbase: 10' 9"
Forward Speeds: 4
Final Drive Ratio:
Tyres: 820 × 120

Year: 1920. V-8, 4·6-litre, identical with Darracq, q.v.

Year: 1922. 8 hp, identical with Talbot equivalent, q.v.

Year: 1926
Maker's HP: 17/75
R.A.C. Rating: 18·22 hp
Number of Cylinders: 6
Bore and Stroke: 70 × 110 mm
Engine Capacity: 2·5 litres

Valves: overhead
Wheelbase: 11' 0"
Forward Speeds: 3 or 4
Final Drive Ratio:
Tyres: 860 × 160

Years: 1929–30. Identical with Darracq models M.67 and H.78

Tamplin   England

The Tamplin had a short success and its design was slightly more interesting than most of its cycle-car contemporaries, although it was no better made.

A 1000 cc, V-twin, air-cooled J.A.P. engine transmitted its power via a Sturmey Archer, three-speed, motor-cycle gearbox, and final drive by belt. There was no reverse until 1923. The engine was set going by a kick starter in the driver's compartment. Suspension was of independent, Morgan type at the front and quarter-elliptic at the back. The chassis-cum-body was the most interesting feature, consisting of an ash frame with waterproof fibre-board panels, and some reinforcement by steel plates. The two seats were in tandem.

Miraculously, at any rate one of these ephemeral vehicles has survived.

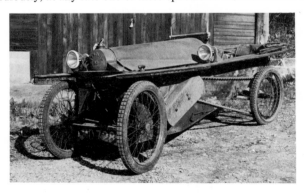

Designed by Captain Carden, who had perpetrated a pre-war cyclecar, the tandem 2-seater of 1921 became a side-by-side two-seater, with all-chain transmission, in 1922. Impecunious masochists are said to have been able to obtain one, to order, as late as 1927

Year: 1920
Maker's HP: 8
R.A.C. Rating: 8·96 hp
Number of Cylinders: 2
Bore and Stroke: 85 × 85 mm
Engine Capacity: 0·9 litre

Valves: side
Wheelbase: 7' 0"
Forward Speeds: 3
Final Drive Ratio: 4·25 to 1
Tyres: 26 × 2·25

Th. Schneider   France

The Societé Anonyme Théophile Schneider began manufacture in 1910 and almost at once embarked on an extensive racing campaign, supporting both the Grand Prix and *Coupe de l'Auto* events before the war. Until 1914 the racing cars had the already somewhat archaic feature of dashboard radiators.

In 1920 two side-valve models appeared which could also be had in more sporting form with overhead valves. The Company retained their fascination for the rear-mounted radiator, and the dashboard carried no less than four ancillary levers controlling spark, throttle, mixture, and lubrication to the valve gear. In 1925 came the better-known 'Le Mans' model with conventionally mounted, V-shaped radiator. It had a 2-litre, pushrod ohv engine, and with its light four-seater body was capable of 75 mph. The 'Le Mans' was in production until 1929 when the Company ceased manufacture.

Year: 1920
Maker's HP: 14
R.A.C. Rating: 16·9 hp
Number of Cylinders: 4
Bore and Stroke: 82·5 × 140 mm
Engine Capacity: 3 litres

Valves: side (or overhead optional)
Wheelbase: 11' 0"
Forward Speeds: 4
Final Drive Ratio: 4 to 1
Tyres: 820 × 120

1925 2-litre 13/50 10CV (unfortunately minus front wings) —an excellent French Vintage tourer with a long stride

Year: 1921
Maker's HP: 20
R.A.C. Rating: 25·3 hp
Number of Cylinders: 6
Bore and Stroke: 82·5 × 140 mm
Engine Capacity: 4·5 litres

Valves: side (or overhead optional)
Wheelbase: 11′ 6″
Forward Speeds: 4
Final Drive Ratio: 4 to 1
Tyres: 895 × 135

Year: 1925
Maker's HP: 13/50
R.A.C. Rating: 12·8 hp
Number of Cylinders: 4
Bore and Stroke: 72 × 120 mm
Engine Capacity: 2 litres

Valves: overhead
Wheelbase: 9′ 10″
Forward Speeds: 4
Final Drive Ratio: 4·25 to 1
Tyres: 765 × 105

Tracta   France

Introduced at the Paris Salon of 1927 the Tracta was an early attempt to produce a small front-wheel-drive car with a reasonable performance. Designed by M. J. A. Grégoire it was available in sports trim or as a smart little coupé; a supercharged version was also produced. The Tracta was a consistent performer at Le Mans during the latter part of the vintage period.

Year: 1930
Maker's HP: 12
R.A.C. Rating: 11·1 hp
Number of Cylinders: 4
Bore and Stroke: 67 × 105 mm
Engine Capacity: 1·5 litres
Valves: overhead
Wheelbase: 8′ 6″
Forward Speeds: 4
Final Drive Ratio: 4·75 to 1
Tyres: 29 × 5

A handsome drophead coupé on the 1500 cc fwd chassis, 1929

Triumph   England

Triumph cars were first made in 1923 when they produced a not-very-distinguished 10/20.

However in 1927–28 there appeared a 'Super Seven' of which the engine was designed by H. R. Ricardo. Despite this eminent parentage it did not gain for itself a particularly good reputation and it was certainly not a good looking car. A shorter stroke (74·5 mm) version was made available to bring it within the 750 cc class for competition, but despite the advantage of a three-bearing crankshaft it never seriously threatened the Austin '7'. A supercharged model is even said to have been made.

The Triumph 'Super Seven' suffered from the usual disadvantage of a three-speed gearbox. It was among the first production cars to be fitted with hydraulic brakes.

Year: 1923
Maker's HP: 10/20
R.A.C. Rating: 10 hp
Number of Cylinders: 4
Bore and Stroke: 63·5 × 110 mm
Engine Capacity: 1·3 litres

Valves: side
Wheelbase: 8' 6"
Forward Speeds: 4
Final Drive Ratio: 4·75 to 1
Tyres: 28 × 3·5

Beside the seaside—Donald Healey in a 'Super Seven' in 1928

Year: 1928
Maker's HP: 8
R.A.C. Rating: 7·9 hp
Number of Cylinders: 4
Bore and Stroke: 56·5 × 83 mm
(Sports version 74·5 stroke)
Engine Capacity: 0·8 litre
Valves: side
Wheelbase: 6' 9"
Forward Speeds: 3
Final Drive Ratio: 5·25 to 1
Tyres: 27 × 4

Trojan   England

All the really great designs in automobile history have been uncompromising, and no design has been more intransigently uncompromising that the Trojan. Leslie Hounsfield's aim was to produce cheap, comfortable and reliable motoring for the impoverished unmechanical and in this he succeeded completely. Appearance and performance were entirely unconsidered.

The two-stroke engine, disposed horizontally under the front seats, had two double cylinders, each pair coupled by a communal head. Induction was to the upper cylinder and exhaustion from the lower of each pair. There were only seven moving parts in the engine. It was flexibly connected to a two-speed epicyclic gearbox giving ratios of 4 and 12 to 1 respectively. Thence the final drive was by a single duplex chain to the solid rear axle. Suspension was by immensely flexible cantilever springs. The chassis was a sort of metal punt.

Three prototypes were made in 1913 of which one survives. Six more cars were made in 1921 and after these had been tested to destruction by the Leyland Company they took over the design and went into production in 1923. In 1928 the Trojan Company again took over production. Manufacture of private cars continued until 1935 after which the Company concentrated on the van. However, a few private cars were made up to 1937. In this year an interesting new model was shown but never went into production. This was the 'Mastra' with a 6-cylinder, 2·2-litre two-stroke engine.

Despite its eminently domestic design, the combination of a solid rear axle with the ability of the engine to slog at minimum rpm, gave the Trojan an ability to climb where few others could go, and it thus acquired an unexpected success in trials, which it continues to display in current vintage events.

The cantilever springing made pneumatic tyres genuinely unnecessary, but whether because the solid tyres tended to peel off, or because even Trojan owners were not entirely impervious to convention, pneumatics became optional from 1925. They were announced by the manufacturers as follows:

'The combination of solid tyres and wonder-springs makes the Trojan as comfortable to ride in as most cars with pneumatic tyres; but fitted with pneumatic tyres the Trojan is SHEER LUXURY.'

Year: 1923
Maker's HP and R.A.C. Rating: 10 hp
Number of Cylinders: 2 (double)
Bore and Stroke: $2\frac{1}{2}'' \times 4\frac{3}{4}''$
Engine Capacity: 1·5 litres
Valves: none (two stroke)
Wheelbase: 8' 0"
Forward Speeds: 2
Final Drive Ratio: 4 to 1
Tyres: solid rubber

upper right Basic motoring: 10 hp PB utility model. The body cost Trojan just £10 to make. £125 in 1925, 2d. per mile to run, and a maximum speed of under 40 mph. 15,000 of the original type were built
right Sophistication? 10 hp Saloon of 1927

Turcat-Méry
France

This Company was formed in 1896 and by 1899 a 4-cylinder five-speed car was produced. In 1902 the Turcat-Méry licence was purchased by Baron Turckheim of the de Dietrich Company. In 1905 the Turcat-Méry Company was taken over by the Societé Lorraine des Anciens Ets de Dietrich, this Company producing Lorraine-Dietrich and Turcat-Méry cars until 1914.

After the war Turcat-Méry disassociated themselves from Lorraine-Dietrich and promptly went bankrupt in 1921. The Company was re-formed, a process which happened in 1924, and finally was liquidated and was taken off the Commercial Register in 1929. The cars produced during the vintage period were mostly the 4-cylinder, pushrod type, in 1924 an ohc sports model was listed, looking like a much cleaner version of the 3-litre Bentley. In 1928 came the inevitable 6- and 8-cylinder models, causing liquidation in 1929.

Year: 1925
Maker's HP: 16/60
R.A.C. Rating: 15·7 hp
Number of Cylinders: 4
Bore and Stroke: 79·6 × 120 mm
Engine Capacity: 2·4 litres
Valves: overhead
Wheelbase: 10' 6"
Forward Speeds: 4
Final Drive Ratio: 4·9 to 1
Tyres: 820 × 120

1925 VG-type, ohc, fixed-head 2·4-litre. Introduced in 1924, the sporting model was continued until production stopped in 1928

Unic
France

The name of Unic is now chiefly memorable for the very large number of Unic taxis which operated in London in late Edwardian and early vintage days, and W. O. Bentley has told in his autobiography how he started his

16/20 hp landaulette. In 1905, Georges Richard left the company bearing his name and formed the Unic Company, thus the latter cars' radiator badges had 'Georges Richard, Puteaux' round the circumference with UNIC in the middle

motoring career by maintaining a fleet of them.

Their first vintage model was a quite high-quality 13/24, whose main feature of interest was the rear suspension by double cantilever springs, one above the other. In 1923 the 13/24 was replaced by a 12 hp model designed on considerably cheaper lines.

Year: 1920
Maker's HP: 13/24
R.A.C. Rating: 15·8 hp
Number of Cylinders: 4
Bore and Stroke: 80 × 130 mm
Engine Capacity: 2·6 litres

Valves: side
Wheelbase: 10′ 6″
Forward Speeds: 4
Final Drive Ratio: $4\frac{1}{8}$ to 1
Tyres: 820 × 120

Year: 1923
Maker's HP: 12
R.A.C. Rating: 12·1 hp
Number of Cylinders: 4
Bore and Stroke: 70 × 120 mm
Engine Capacity: 1·85 litres

Valves: side
Wheelbase: 10′ 0″
Forward Speeds: 4
Final Drive Ratio: 4·3, 4·6 or 5 to 1
Tyres: 765 × 105

Vauxhall   England

The Vauxhall Company started manufacture in 1903 with some conventionally dull models, including one of the then fashionable three-cylinders-in-line.

In 1908 the directors decided to enter for the 1908, 2000-mile Trial and in the absence through illness of the chief designer his assistant, Laurence Pomeroy, quickly ran up an innocent looking 3-litre side-valve engine which made the best performance in the Trial. It was unusual, however, in running easily at 2500 rpm and was soon increased both in size and specific output. In 1913 the original 3-litre finally appeared as a $4\frac{1}{2}$-litre which, in prototype form, took the Shelsley Walsh record and went into production in 1919 as the '30/98' or 'E' type.

1924 E-type 30/98 with mahogany rear-decked, skiff-tail 'Wensum' body, named after the Norfolk river

The validity of the '98' has been often questioned, but one of these side-valve engines has recently been brought back to original specification and mint condition when, on the brake, it exceeded 100 bhp at about 2800 rpm. The fixed, L-head monobloc engine drove through a multi-plate clutch to a wide-ratio four-speed gearbox, both engine and gearbox being mounted in a sub-frame. The chassis itself was typically Edwardian and correspondingly flexible. In standard touring trim and 4-seater body the 'Velox' would reach 80–85 mph, but with special coachwork and axle ratio, 100 mph was guaranteed.

In 1922 Pomeroy left the Company and the 'E' type was rearranged with pushrod overhead valves and a shortened stroke. Performance on the 'OE' remained about the same, but with increased smoothness. In 1923 came some rather Heath Robinson front brakes operated via a kidney-shaped box on the front cross-member.

In 1927 the 30/98 acquired notoriously temperamental hydraulic brakes and a balanced crankshaft with which the engine could attain 3500 rpm and 120 bhp; a figure greatly in excess of any unblown $4\frac{1}{2}$-litre Bentley in standard form. In special trim as much as 165 bhp was recorded; a figure which even the most highly tuned Bentleys have only recently surpassed.

A more touring version of the 'E' and 'OE' was the 23/60, of slightly smaller bore, and longer wheelbase.

There were also two Ricardo-designed models, the 14/40 and 25/70. The former looks very much like a small 30/98 and has a 2·3-litre side-valve engine with the famous Ricardo turbulence head. Even so, however, it only produced 44 bhp; a substantially lower figure per litre than the earlier and cruder 30/98. The 25/70 was a single-sleeve valve 6-cylinder with the flywheel placed in the middle of the engine. It was intended to compete with the small Rolls-Royce which it certainly rivalled in smoothness and silence and exceeded in performance; but by then the Company was already running into financial difficulties

1926 14/40 'Kimberley' saloon. On the 14 hp model, the 3-speed box was a pity but 60 mph maximum was available to patient drivers

and in 1927 it was taken over by General Motors. The final vintage model was a rather flashy 20/60, betraying a good deal of the new American influence.

The 30/98 had considerable success at Brooklands and in sprints, but it can show nothing like the Bentley racing record. For this, its Edwardian chassis was partly to blame, but lack of enterprise on the part of the manufacturers even more so. The engine is almost certainly capable of giving as much power as the Bentley. In 1953 a 30/98 covered 107 miles in an hour at Monthléry and thus shares with the 4½-litre Bentley (114 miles, also at Monthléry in 1960) the distinction of being the only vintage cars to have covered 100 miles in an hour within the last twenty-five years.

A team of 3-litre, twin ohc, 4-cylinder, 16-valve cars was designed by H. R. Ricardo and competed unsuccessfully in the 1922 T.T. race. One of these subsequently achieved great sprint successes when supercharged, as the 'Vauxhall Villiers'. Apart from the 'blower' this car has now been restored to its 1922 form.

Year: 1919	*Engine Capacity:* 4·5 litres
Model: 'E'	*Valves:* side
Maker's HP: 30/98	*Wheelbase:* 10' 0"
R.A.C. Rating: 23·8 hp	*Forward Speeds:* 4
Number of Cylinders: 4	*Final Drive Ratio:* 3 to 1
Bore and Stroke: 98 × 150 mm	*Tyres:* 820 × 120

Year: 1922	*Valves:* side
Maker's HP: 14/40	*Wheelbase:* 9' 6"
R.A.C. Rating: 13·9 hp	*Forward Speeds:* 3
Number of Cylinders: 4	*Final Drive Ratio:* 4·5 to 1
Bore and Stroke: 75 × 130 mm	*Tyres:* 815 × 105
Engine Capacity: 2·3 litres	

1926 S-type, or 25/70, single-sleeve valve: silence plus performance, with hydraulic brakes, for £1,250

Year: 1922
Model: 'OE'
Maker's HP: 30/98
R.A.C. Rating: 23·8 hp
Number of Cylinders: 4
Bore and Stroke: 98 × 140 mm

Engine Capacity: 4·3 litres
Valves: overhead
Wheelbase: 9' 10"
Forward Speeds: 4
Final Drive Ratio: 3·3 to 1
Tyres: 820 × 120

Year: 1923
Model: 'OD'
Maker's HP: 23/60
R.A.C. Rating: 22·4 hp
Number of Cylinders: 4
Bore and Stroke: 95 × 140 mm

Engine Capacity: 4 litres
Valves: overhead
Wheelbase: 10' 10"
Forward Speeds: 4
Final Drive Ratio: 3·6 to 1
Tyres: 880 × 120

Year: 1926
Maker's HP: 25/70
R.A.C. Rating: 24·7 hp
Number of Cylinders: 6
Bore and Stroke: 81·5 × 124 mm
Engine Capacity: 3·9 litres

Valves: sleeve
Wheelbase: 11' 4"
Forward Speeds: 4
Final Drive Ratio: 4·08 to 1
Tyres: 33 × 6·75

Year: 1928
Maker's HP: 20/60
R.A.C. Rating: 19·8 hp
Number of Cylinders: 6
Bore and Stroke: 73 × 110 mm
Engine Capacity: 2·7 litres

Valves: overhead
Wheelbase: 10' 3"
Forward Speeds: 4
Final Drive Ratio: 4·7 to 1
Tyres: 4 × 21

Vernon-Derby   France

Despite its English-sounding name the Vernon-Derby was entirely French.
It followed the typically sketchy proportions of such established French light
sporting makes as Amilcar and Salmson, but had, from the first, the advantage
of a four-speed gearbox. Various makes of proprietary engine could be
supplied, and in 1929 there was the inevitable small side-valve six.

Year: 1927
Maker's HP: 9
R.A.C. Rating: 8·6 hp
Number of Cylinders: 4
Bore and Stroke: 59 × 100 mm
Engine Capacity: 1·1 litres

Valves: overhead
Wheelbase: 7' 8"
Forward Speeds: 4
Final Drive Ratio: 4·2 to 1
Tyres: 27 × 4·4

Year: 1929
Maker's HP: 9
R.A.C. Rating: 8·9 hp
Number of Cylinders: 4
Bore and Stroke: 60 × 97 mm
Engine Capacity: 1·1 litres

Valves: overhead
Wheelbase: 7' 8"
Forward Speeds: 4
Final Drive Ratio: 4·2 to 1
Tyres: 27 × 4

Year: 1929
Maker's HP and R.A.C. Rating:
13·75 hp
Number of Cylinders: 6
Bore and Stroke: 60 × 88 mm
Engine Capacity: 1·5 litres

Valves: side
Wheelbase: 8' 6"
Forward Speeds: 4
Final Drive Ratio: 4·2 to 1
Tyres: 27 × 4·4

1929 9 hp. The French Derby was imported into England by Vernon Balls (of Amilcar fame) hence the prefix

Voisin

France

Gabriel Voisin the famous pioneer aeronaut, turned to motor manufacture in 1919. His cars all displayed the highest standard of craftsmanship and many of them showed considerable originality (or, as some might say, eccentricity). All had double, cast-iron sleeve valves, but despite this, the reciprocating weight was kept down to a creditably low level, and Voisin engines were capable of extremely creditable rpm and power outputs for sleeve valves.

For some time the only model was the 4-cylinder, 4-litre 22/30 whose maximum speed steadily advanced from 70 to 80 mph. In 1922 came a minute, 1·2-litre, and in 1926 the 6-cylinder 16/50 which largely succeeded the 22/30 in popularity. It was capable of running at 4000 rpm.

Last of all came the fabulous V-12, with complicated safeguards against valves falling into the sump if anything went seriously wrong.

Voisin also built a number of experimental cars including a team of stream-lined machines for the 1923 Grand Prix which rivalled the contemporary streamlined Bugattis for ugliness. In 1927 an 8-litre Voisin took the world hour record at 128 mph.

Even throughout the thirties, Voisin continued to build his extremely elegant cars, with their superbly proportioned V-radiators, and always with sleeve valves. As late as 1934 came the crowning eccentricity, described as follows in a contemporary press announcement:

'Another twelve-cylinder Voisin has the cylinders arranged in line, in two separate blocks of six. The engine is narrow and the rear portion projects into the driving compartment between the driver and passenger. A Cotal gearbox and half-elliptic springing are other features of this car. The twelve-cylinder-in-line engine is, of course, revolutionary but it is adopted, according to M. Voisin, in order to bring the centre of gravity of the power unit closer to the geometrical centre of the car.'

Year: 1919
Maker's HP: 22/30
R.A.C. Rating: 22·4 hp
Number of Cylinders: 4
Bore and Stroke: 95 × 140 mm
Engine Capacity: 4 litres

Valves: sleeve
Wheelbase: 11′ 6″
Forward Speeds: 4
Final Drive Ratio: 3·5 to 1
Tyres: 820 × 120

Year: 1922
Maker's HP: 11/14
R.A.C. Rating: 8·9 hp
Number of Cylinders: 4
Bore and Stroke: 60 × 110 mm
Engine Capacity: 1·2 litres

Valves: sleeve
Wheelbase: 9′ 4″
Forward Speeds: 3
Final Drive Ratio: 3·5 to 1
Tyres: 765 × 105

Grand Prix de Tourisme, Strasbourg 1922: Piccioni's 4-litre clearly shows the cigar-shaped bulges on its flanks which got round the regulation calling for a minimum body width of 52 inches, at the same time keeping down frontal area! Voisins came 1st, 2nd, 3rd and 5th

Year: 1926
Maker's HP: 16/50
R.A.C. Rating: 16·6 hp
Number of Cylinders: 6
Bore and Stroke: 67 × 110 mm
Engine Capacity: 2·4 litres

Valves: sleeve
Wheelbase: 10′ 6½″
Forward Speeds: 3
Final Drive Ratio: 5 to 1
Tyres: 775 × 145

Year: 1928
Maker's HP: 27/120
R.A.C. Rating: 27·5 hp
Number of Cylinders: 6
Bore and Stroke: 86 × 140 mm
Engine Capacity: 4·9 litres

Valves: sleeve
Wheelbase: 11′ 9″
Forward Speeds: 4
Final Drive Ratio:
Tyres: 905 × 165

above Rudolf Valentino poses beside his 1925 18CV Model C5, with 4-litre
4-cylinder Knight sleeve-valve engine
below 1929 Model C12, 4·9-litre, 6-cylinder fixed-head coupé, with
detachable luggage trunk shaped to the back of the Weymann fabric body

Year: 1930
Model: C.12
Maker's HP: 25/100
R.A.C. Rating: 30·4 hp
Number of Cylinders: 12(V)
Bore and Stroke: 64 × 100 mm

Engine Capacity: 3·9 litres
Valves: sleeve
Wheelbase: 11′ 9″
Forward Speeds: 4
Final Drive Ratio: 3·5 to 1
Tyres: 32 × 6·75

Vulcan

England

The late Edwardian Vulcan was a typical slogging side-valve which was carried on as the first vintage model. Its main interest lay in the friction drive electric self-starter of somewhat frightening design.

The most interesting models were 2- and 4-cylinder sleeve valves of which, unfortunately, no specimen is known to have survived. The private car side of the Company only did so until 1928.

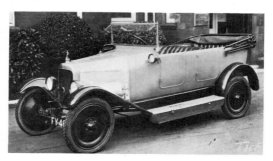

Sleeve-valve, 1·4-litre, flat-twin, 1922—note navel engagement of the starting handle

Year: 1919
Maker's HP: 16
R.A.C. Rating: 15·9 hp
Number of Cylinders: 4
Bore and Stroke: 80 × 130 mm
Engine Capacity: 2·6 litres

Valves: side
Wheelbase: 11′ 5″
Forward Speeds: 4
Final Drive Ratio: 4·5 to 1
Tyres: 815 × 105

Year: 1920
Maker's HP: 12
R.A.C. Rating: 11·8 hp
Number of Cylinders: 4
Bore and Stroke: 69 × 120 mm
Engine Capacity: 1·8 litres

Valves: overhead
Wheelbase: 9′ 0″
Forward Speeds: 4
Final Drive Ratio: 4 to 1
Tyres: 760 × 90

Year: 1922
Maker's HP: 9
R.A.C. Rating: 8·9 hp
Number of Cylinders: 2
Bore and Stroke: 85 × 90 mm
Engine Capacity: 1 litre

Valves: sleeve
Wheelbase: 9' 0"
Forward Speeds: 4
Final Drive Ratio:
Tyres: 710 × 90

Willys Knight   America

This make is interesting because it was the only American car of consequence
to use Knight sleeve valves. The 'Company', collectively and at one time and
another between 1903 and 1963 (when it became the Kaiser Jeep Corporation)
incorporated Overland (q.v.), Willys and Willys-Knight. The latter's sleeve
valve-engined cars were introduced in 1914 and departed the scene in 1932.

Year: 1921
Maker's HP and R.A.C. Rating:
21 hp
Number of Cylinders: 4
Bore and Stroke: $3\frac{5}{8}'' × 4\frac{1}{2}''$
Engine Capacity: 3 litres

Valves: sleeve
Wheelbase: 9' 10"
Forward Speeds: 3
Final Drive Ratio: 4·44 to 1
Tyres: 32 × 4·5

Year: 1926
Maker's HP: 25
R.A.C. Rating: 25·35 hp
Number of Cylinders: 6
Bore and Stroke: $3\frac{1}{4}'' × 4\frac{3}{4}''$
Engine Capacity: 3·9 litres

Valves: sleeve
Wheelbase: 10' 6"
Forward Speeds: 3
Final Drive Ratio: 5·11 to 1
Tyres: 30 × 5·77

1928/29 Model 66A sleeve-valve, 6-cylinder of 4,714 cc. Contemporary with
it was the Model 70A of similar specification but of only 2,915 cc

Wolseley

In 1896 the Wolseley Sheep Shearing Machine Company of Birmingham constructed a 2 hp motor tricycle, somewhat similar to the Léon-Bollée of the period. A four-wheeled car followed in 1899 utilizing a pressed steel frame. There has been considerable controversy as to whether Sir Herbert (then Mr) Austin designed these early Wolseley cars. He was, however, chief designer of the firm in 1900 when Vickers Sons & Maxim took over the motor-car manufacturing side of the old Sheep Shearing Machine Company.

Wolseleys were frequent contestants for places in the British 'Gordon Bennett' teams from 1902 to 1904, with their curious low-slung 'Beetle' cars. However, they achieved no notable success in this field. In 1905 the Siddeley Autocar Company was absorbed, the cars being known as Wolseley-Siddeley until 1910.

During the war Hispano-Suiza aeroplane engines were made under licence, this fact undoubtedly accounting for the introduction of 10 hp and 15 hp single overhead camshaft models. These cars had monobloc engines, a combined gearbox and back axle, and soon made a name for themselves for performance and reliability, indeed the 10 hp sports model could attain 70 mph. At Brooklands too the 10 hp, 12 hp and 15 hp Wolseley track cars with streamlined bodies were extremely successful during the 1921–23 period.

The 10 hp, ohc engine is the basis of the 'Becke Powerplus' special which made a considerable name for itself and is still occasionally seen at Prescott and Shelsley Walsh. Despite being supercharged, its two-bearing crankshaft has proved completely reliable up to very high speeds.

After introducing an eight hp water-cooled flat twin the Company very soon reverted to the smaller side-valve models, but from 1928 until 1935 all models had an overhead camshaft.

1929 Bognor Regis Trials: competing 7 hp Wolseley of earlier date

Year: 1920
Maker's HP: 20
R.A.C. Rating: 23·5 hp
Number of Cylinders: 6
Bore and Stroke: 80 × 130 mm
Engine Capacity: 3·9 litres

Valves: side
Wheelbase: 11' 5"
Forward Speeds: 3
Final Drive Ratio: 4·1 to 1
Tyres: 820 × 135

Year: 1922
Maker's HP: 7
R.A.C. Rating: 8·3 hp
Number of Cylinders: 2
Bore and Stroke: 82 × 92 mm
Engine Capacity: 0·9 litre

Valves: side
Wheelbase: 8' 1"
Forward Speeds: 3
Final Drive Ratio: 5·6 to 1
Tyres: 26 × 3

Year: 1922
Maker's HP: 10
R.A.C. Rating: 10·5 hp
Number of Cylinders: 4
Bore and Stroke: 65 × 95 mm
Engine Capacity: 1·2 litres

Valves: overhead
Wheelbase: 8' 3"
Forward Speeds: 3
Final Drive Ratio: 5·25 to 1
Tyres: 710 × 90

Year: 1928
Maker's HP: 21/60
R.A.C. Rating: 21 hp
Number of Cylinders: 8
Bore and Stroke: $2\frac{9}{16}'' \times 4''$
Engine Capacity: 2·8 litres

Valves: overhead
Wheelbase: 10' 7"
Forward Speeds: 4
Final Drive Ratio: 5·57 to 1
Tyres: 31 × 5·25

1928 21/60 hp 4-door tourer. The body, by Jarvis of Wimbledon, includes all-weather equipment and detachable rear-mounted luggage trunk

Zedel

Known as Donnet Zedel (q.v.) after 1924.

1923 10/12 hp Zedels were built at Pontarlier until the merger with Donnet, after which Donnet-Zedels came from Nanterre

Year: 1922
Maker's HP: 10/12
R.A.C. Rating: 12·1 hp
Number of Cylinders: 4
Bore and Stroke: 70 × 120 mm
Engine Capacity: 1·8 litres

Valves: side
Wheelbase: 9' 6"
Forward Speeds: 4
Final Drive Ratio: 4·5 to 1
Tyres: 760 × 90

Year: 1922
Maker's HP: 15/30
R.A.C. Rating: 17·9 hp
Number of Cylinders: 4
Bore and Stroke: 85 × 140 mm
Engine Capacity: 3·2 litres

Valves: side
Wheelbase: 11' 0"
Forward Speeds: 4
Final Drive Ratio: 4 to 1
Tyres: 880 × 120